Criminal Law

(Second Edition)

T.J. MCINTYRE, B.C.L., LL.M, B.L

University College Dublin

SINÉAD MCMULLAN, LL.B, B.C.L. (OXON), B.L.

Trinity College Dublin

Dublin

Thomson Round Hall

2005

Published in 2005 by
Thomson Round Hall
43 Fitzwilliam Place
Dublin 2
Ireland

Typeset by
Thomson Round Hall

Printed by
ColourBooks, Dublin

ISBN 1-85800-410-1

A catalogue record for this book
is available from the British Library.

7-DAY LOAN

for ref   be

Edition)

UNITED KINGDOM

Sweet & Maxwell Ltd
London

AUSTRALIA

LBC Information Services
Sydney

CANADA AND USA

Carswell
Toronto

NEW ZEALAND

Brooker's
Wellington

SINGAPORE AND MALAYSIA

Thomson Information (S.E. Asia)
Singapore

ABOUT THE AUTHORS

Sinéad McMullan, LL.B., B.C.L. (Oxon), is a practising barrister specialising in criminal law. She lectures at Trinity College Dublin and Stanhope Street Law School. She has also lectured at Dublin Institute of Technology.

T.J. McIntyre, BCL, LL.M, Barrister at Law, is a lecturer in law at University College Dublin and was formerly a Judicial Research Assistant to the High Court and Supreme Court. He is also a specialist in information technology law.

To Clodagh, with love
T.J.M.

Contents

Table of Cases

TABLE OF LEGISLATION

Bunreacht na hÉireann

Table of Statutes

EUROPEAN LEGISLATION

INTERNATIONAL LEGISLATION

1. INTRODUCTION TO FUNDAMENTAL PRINCIPLES AND CONCEPTS

1.1 Distinction between criminal and civil matters

Criminal law is the most public face of the legal system, with intense media coverage of trials, arrests and all the other aspects of the criminal justice system. As such, readers of this book will certainly have no difficulty in understanding in general terms what is meant by crime and the criminal law. However, when we try to formalise that understanding—to define precisely what we mean by the criminal law—we run into difficulties. For example, most people would describe crime as relating to serious wrongdoing—but parking offences are treated as criminal in nature. Crime is often understood as involving an identifiable victim—an understanding which breaks down when we consider the so-called victimless crimes, such as drug use. Crimes are regarded as being particularly morally reprehensible—a description that it is hard to apply to our example of parking offences. Crime is generally thought to be a matter for the police—but certain crimes are investigated and prosecuted almost exclusively by other State bodies. Crime generally requires intentional wrongdoing—but (as we shall see) some crimes can be committed without any intention or even fault on the part of the criminal.

Nor can we simply dismiss the definition of crime as being of academic interest only. In practical terms, it is important to be able to distinguish crimes from other legal wrongs. The trial of criminal offences is governed by Art.38 of the Constitution, which confers special protections on those accused of such offences. In particular, paras.1, 2 and 5 of Art.38 provide that:

> "1. No person shall be tried on any criminal charge save in due course of law."
> "2. Minor offences may be tried by courts of summary jurisdiction."
> "5. Save in the case of trial of offences under section 2, no person shall be tried on any criminal charge without a jury."

In addition, Art.38 must be read in conjunction with Art.37.1, which allows for limited powers and functions of a judicial nature to be carried out by persons who are not judges appointed under the

Constitution, or bodies which are not courts established under the Constitution (*e.g.* the Employment Appeals Tribunal, or the Labour Court). However, Art.37.1 is limited to "matters other than criminal matters".

The net effect of these two articles is, therefore, that once we determine that a matter is criminal, it must be tried before courts established under the Constitution, with a jury unless the matter is minor and in due course of law. We will see that this last phrase encompasses certain rules of law, such as the right to silence and the presumption of innocence, which are not applicable to civil trials. How, then, do we determine when a matter is criminal?

From a theoretical point of view, the criminal law is a branch of public law, and concerns itself with public wrongs. It is thus distinct from branches of private law, such as contract or tort. If a person commits a tort, or a breach of contract, this is a matter solely for the person injured. Only that person may sue, and he may settle or discontinue those proceedings freely. The criminal law, by contrast, deals with conduct which is felt to be injurious to the community as a whole. For that reason, enforcement is not left to the victim of a crime but is carried out by public bodies. (However, it is possible for prosecutions to be brought by ordinary members of the public in some circumstances.) For the same reason, if the prosecution succeeds, the victim cannot pardon the offender; this power is reserved to the State. In short, the offence is not merely the concern of the victim.

Another general characteristic of the criminal law is that it deals with moral wrongs, although this fact is not particularly helpful in defining what is or is not a crime. Many crimes bear little moral stigma, while many immoral acts are perfectly legal. Moreover, the perceived moral quality of crimes varies from time to time. For example, drink driving was for a long time regarded as a trivial offence and not a real crime and only recently have attitudes begun to harden against it.

A third identifying feature of the criminal law is that the sanctions imposed are punitive rather than compensatory. In the law of contract or tort, damages are measured by reference to the position of the injured party, to compensate the victim for the loss suffered. In the criminal law, however, the sanction is primarily measured having regard to the blameworthiness of the offender, and if a monetary fine is imposed it does not go to the victim. This reflects the wider scope of the criminal law; while the civil law confines itself to the position of the wrongdoer and the injured party, the criminal law also seeks to deter others by punishing the wrongdoer.

The main Irish case applying these criteria is *Melling v O Mathghamhna* (1962). In this case, the conduct penalised was the smuggling of butter, which was made subject to a penalty of £100 or treble the value of the goods. This was held by the Supreme Court to amount to a criminal charge for the purposes of Art.38, with each of the judgments taking a slightly different approach to determining whether a matter was criminal. Lavery J. looked primarily to the practical effect of the proceedings:

> "It seems to me clear that a proceeding, the course of which permits the detention of the person concerned, the bringing of him in custody to a Garda station, the entry of a charge in all respects appropriate to the charge of a criminal offence, the searching of the person detained and the examination of papers and other things found upon him, the bringing of him before a District Justice in custody, the admission to bail to stand his trial and the detention in custody if bail be not granted or is not forthcoming, the imposition of a pecuniary penalty with the liability to imprisonment if the penalty is not paid has all the *indicia* of a criminal charge." (At p.9.)

Kingsmill Moore J. took a more abstract approach, holding that a criminal charge was distinguished by three elements: its nature as an offence against the community at large, the punitive nature of the sanction, and the requirement of *mens rea*. Ó Dálaigh J. took a similar approach to Lavery J., looking primarily to the practical effect of the proceedings.

The tests set out in *Melling* have since been applied by the Supreme Court in *McLoughlin v Tuite* (1989). This case also involved a revenue matter, concerning various sections of the Income Tax Act 1967, imposing a fixed penalty on any person failing to comply with a notice to make income tax returns and allowing the penalty to be recovered by civil proceedings. The taxpayer claimed that this section was invalid as it imposed a criminal penalty other than in accordance with Art.38. The Supreme Court, however, rejected this argument, holding that although the penalty payment was punitive in effect, the proceedings did not otherwise have the indicia of a criminal offence. In particular: *mens rea* was not required, no question of detention or arrest arose and imprisonment could not be imposed in default of payment. In addition, the sum could be recovered from the estate of a deceased taxpayer, in a way which was characteristic of a civil debt but entirely inconsistent with a criminal penalty.

Another case which applied the *Melling* principles is *Goodman v Hamilton (No 1)* (1992). This case involved the Beef Tribunal, set up to investigate allegations of misconduct, including criminal activity, in the beef industry. The plaintiff, who controlled companies accounting for a large part of the industry, alleged that this would amount to the trial of a criminal charge. This argument was, however, rejected by the Supreme Court, which held that although the Tribunal was investigating allegations of criminal misconduct, it was not conducting a criminal trial. In particular, Finlay C.J. stated:

> "The essential ingredient of a trial of a criminal offence in our law, which is indivisible from any other ingredient, is that it is had before a court or judge which has got the power to punish in the event of a verdict of guilty. It is of the essence of a trial on a criminal charge or a trial on a criminal offence that the proceedings are accusatorial, involving a prosecutor and an accused, and that the sole purpose and object of the verdict, be it one of acquittal or of conviction, is to form the basis for either a discharge of the accused from the jeopardy in which he stood, in the case of an acquittal, or for his punishment for the crime which he has committed, in the case of a conviction.
>
> The proceedings of the inquiry to be held by this Tribunal have none of those features. The Tribunal has no jurisdiction or authority of any description to impose a penalty or punishment on any person. Its finding, whether rejecting an allegation of criminal activity or accepting the proof of an allegation of criminal activity, can form no basis for either the conviction nor acquittal of the party concerned on a criminal charge if one were subsequently brought, nor can it form any basis for the punishment by any other authority of that person." (At p.588.)

The effect of this judgment is that if a proceeding deals with criminal matters, this will not necessarily make it a criminal trial. For example, if A hits B, causing injury, this may amount to a criminal act. Prosecution of A for this act by the DPP would clearly be a trial of a criminal charge within the meaning of Art.38.1, and all the relevant constitutional safeguards would apply. If, however, B sues A seeking compensation for the injury suffered, then this is not the trial of a criminal charge. A may be liable to pay compensation; he is not, however, liable to be punished. *Mens rea* is not an issue, nor is there any question of detention or arrest.

1.1.1. Proceeds of crime legislation

The civil/criminal distinction also arises in the context of the Proceeds of Crime Act 1996. This Act provides for the confiscation of property alleged to be the proceeds of crime on a civil standard of proof, and as such expressly sets out to use the civil law in order to deal with criminal problems. The first case to deal with this Act was *Gilligan v Criminal Assets Bureau* (1998). Here, the plaintiff claimed that the scheme of the Act, which provides for the forfeiture of property that constitutes the proceeds of crime, violated his Art.38.1 right to a trial on any criminal charge in due course of law, since the proceedings were in essence criminal rather than civil yet lacked the constitutional safeguards applicable to a criminal trial. It was argued by the defendants that forfeiture proceedings under the Act were civil and not criminal in nature, although they necessarily involved the determination of some matters which may constitute elements of criminal offences.

In resolving this issue, McGuinness J. looked to the earlier case law setting out the indicia of a criminal offence. Applying that case law, she first noted that the procedure under the Act was *in rem* rather than *in personam* (meaning that the action dealt with the status of property rather than the status of an individual). There was no question of the detention of a party to proceedings under the Act, nor the infliction of any specific penalty, whether imprisonment or fine. Although money or property could be taken from a party to the proceedings, if shown to be the proceeds of crime, "its removal could well be viewed in the light of reparation rather than punishment or penalty." As for the determination of whether a crime had been committed, McGuinness J. accepted that civil actions could validly make determinations in respect of matters which may also constitute the elements of a crime.

This decision was appealed, along with a similar matter, in *Murphy v GM and others* (2001). Before the Supreme Court, the appellants expanded on the arguments made before the High Court, submitting that the Proceeds of Crime Act involved all the indicia of the criminal law. In particular, they pointed to the following features of the Act:

- it was general in application;
- it did not provide for compensation of victims of the alleged crimes;
- its clear policy was the deterrence of crime;
- it was enforced in each case by senior garda officers;
- it effectively punished persons for alleged wrongdoing; and
- powers exclusively associated with the criminal law, such as search warrants, were used in its enforcement.

The Supreme Court, however, held that the forfeiture provisions of the Act could not be considered criminal. Applying *Melling*, it noted that the elements which were decisive in that case (arrest, detention, admission to bail, imposition of a fine and imprisonment in default of payment) were absent in this case. In addition, there was no requirement of *mens rea* for forfeiture to take place, while as a historical matter the forfeiture of the proceeds of crime had always been considered to be civil in nature. The court therefore held that the matter was civil in nature, and the civil standard of proof and civil procedures were constitutionally acceptable.

Shortly afterwards, a very similar issue arose in *Gilligan v Special Criminal Court* (2002). In that case, the plaintiff had been convicted in the Special Criminal Court of the importation of cannabis. Under s.4 of the Criminal Justice Act 1994, the court, on convicting a person of a drug trafficking offence, could make a confiscation order covering the proceeds of the drug trafficking. This confiscation order jurisdiction applied a civil standard of proof, created a number of presumptions which would apply against the person convicted and provided for imprisonment where a person failed to comply with the confiscation order. In this case, the confiscation order assessed that the defendant had benefited to the tune of £17 million, and required him to pay over that sum within 12 months.

The plaintiff argued that this s.4 procedure amounted to a criminal procedure contrary to Art.38.1 of the Constitution. McCracken J., however, applied *Murphy v GM* to hold that this forfeiture system did not amount to the trial of a criminal charge. McCracken J. emphasised in particular that the s.4 procedure did not operate as a punishment:

> "[P]enalties by way of punishment [are] an essential element of a criminal charge. However, what the 1994 Act deals with is not penalising the person for having committed drug trafficking offences, but rather it is seeking to recover from that person the value of the benefits which accrued through drug trafficking ... This is unlike financial penalties imposed for criminal offences, which are absolute, irrespective of the defendant's means."

Another application of this principle can be seen in *England v DPP* (2003). In that case, the applicant, while travelling through Dublin Airport in 1998, was found to be carrying approximately £80,000 in cash, despite having no visible source of income. The DPP applied for forfeiture of that sum under s.39 of the Criminal Justice Act 1994, on the basis that the money was either the proceeds of drug trafficking or was intended for use in drug trafficking. The trial judge adjourned the application to allow the DPP to put in additional evidence, and the defendant objected on the basis that as this was a criminal matter the evidence was closed and he was entitled to a ruling. On application to the High Court, Kearns J. held that while this could be described as a "hybrid" jurisdiction, it was essentially civil in nature, since:

> "Section 39 provides for a forfeiture proceeding which is *in rem*. It is the monies or the proceeds which are proceeded against, whereas in a criminal prosecution it is the wrongdoer in person who is proceeded against, convicted and punished."

1.1.2 *Criminal v. civil – summary*

Criminal Law	Civil Law
Harm caused to public	Harm restricted to individual
Action brought by State	Action brought by individual
Deals with moral wrongs	Does not concern itself with moral guilt
Proof beyond reasonable doubt	Proof on the balance of probabilities
Presumption of innocence, right to silence	n/a
Procedure includes arrest, search, admission to bail	n/a
Tried before judge and jury (except in the case of minor offences)	Tried before judge alone (except in some cases - for example defamation)
Outcome is punishment of offender	Outcome is compensation of plaintiff or forfeiture of property

Further reading:

Kelly, *The Irish Constitution* (4th ed., Hogan and Whyte (eds.), Butterworths, 2003), pp.1138–1143.

1.2 Presumption of innocence

The presumption of innocence is not explicitly stated in the Constitution, but is implicit in the requirement of Art.38.1 that "no person shall be tried on any criminal charge save in due course of law". It is fundamental to the Irish legal system and is internationally recognised as an essential safeguard. For example, the European Convention on Human Rights, to which Ireland is a party, requires in Art.6(2) that "everyone charged with a criminal offence shall be presumed innocent until proved guilty according to law".

The application of the presumption of innocence can be seen in *Woolmington v DPP* (1935). This case is the authoritative statement of the presumption in the UK and in a number of Commonwealth countries; while there is a distinct constitutional foundation for the presumption in this jurisdiction, *Woolmington v DPP* (1935) remains an oft-cited and persuasive authority. In that case the charge was murder. The accused admitted killing the deceased but claimed that the gun went off accidentally. The trial judge directed the jury that once the prosecution proved that the deceased was killed by the accused, the burden then shifted to the accused to prove the facts alleged to constitute a defence. This direction was held by the House of Lords to be incorrect, and a definitive statement of the law was given: the burden at all times remains on the prosecution, and once a defence is raised, the accused is entitled to be acquitted unless the prosecution disproves that defence. Viscount Sankey emphasised, at p.481, that:

> "... it is not for the prisoner to establish his innocence but for the prosecution to establish his guilt ... while the prosecution must prove the guilt of the prisoner there is no such burden placed on the prisoner to prove his innocence and it is sufficient for him to raise a doubt as to his guilt; he is not bound to satisfy the jury of his innocence ... Throughout the web of the English criminal law one golden thread is always to be seen, that it is the duty of the prosecution to prove the prisoner's guilt ... the principle ... is part of the common law of England and no attempt to whittle it down can be entertained."

1.2.1 The Presumption of innocence and shifting the burden of proof

There is some uncertainty as to whether rules which shift the burden of proof to a defendant on a particular point are compatible with the presumption of innocence. The Supreme Court has recently considered this issue in two cases. The first is *Hardy v Ireland* (1994). This case concerned s.4(1) of the Explosive Substances Act 1883, which criminalises possession of explosives under circumstances giving rise to "a reasonable suspicion that [the defendant] does not have it in his possession ... for a lawful object", unless the defendant "can show that he ... had it in his possession ... for a lawful object". The defendant claimed that the effect of this was to impermissibly undermine the presumption of innocence. This was rejected by the Supreme Court, but in a way which showed that it was divided as to what the presumption of innocence required. All the members of the court accepted that the presumption of innocence was a necessary component of a trial in due course of law pursuant to Art.38.1. However, the judges differed on whether the burden of proof can be shifted in a way which is compatible with the presumption of innocence.

The majority judgment, delivered by Hederman J., solved the problem by reading the section narrowly, so that it required the prosecution to prove beyond reasonable doubt that the accused did not have the items in his possession for a lawful purpose. He stated, at p.564, that:

> "... the prosecution has to prove beyond reasonable doubt ... (1) that the accused knowingly had in his possession a substance which it proves is an explosive substance; (2) that he had it under such circumstances as to give rise to a reasonable suspicion that he did not have it in his possession for a lawful object and that, in turn, means that there is an onus on the prosecution to prove that the accused could not show that he had it in his possession for a lawful object. Once those ingredients are in place, it is still open to the accused to demonstrate in any one of a number of ways, such as by cross-examination, submissions or by giving evidence, that a prima facie situation pointing to his guilt should not be allowed to prevail ... this analysis ... protects the presumption of innocence; it requires that the prosecution should prove its case beyond all reasonable doubt; but it does not prohibit that, in the course of the case, once certain facts are established, inferences may not be drawn from those facts ..."

This reading essentially side-stepped the issue of whether a statute may require an accused to prove a particular defence on the balance of probabilities, from which it may be inferred that this issue presented some difficulties for the majority.

By contrast, the minority judgments of Murphy and Egan JJ. accepted that the section imposed an onus on the accused to prove on the balance of probabilities that he had the explosives in his possession for a lawful purpose, but held that such a shifting of the burden of proof with regard to a defence did not violate Art.38.1. Egan J. remarked, at p.566, that "There is nothing in the Constitution to prohibit absolutely the shifting of an onus in a criminal prosecution or to suggest that such would inevitably offend the requirements of due process." Murphy J. reasoned as follows, at p.568:

> "... the second limb of the section deals not with the charge but with a statutory exoneration or exculpation from a charge already made and sustained beyond reasonable doubt. I am convinced that the burden which the accused must discharge if he is to avail of that procedure is a duty to satisfy the jury of the statutory condition, that is to say, the existence of a lawful object on the balance of probabilities ... I do not see that there is any inconsistency between a trial in due course of law as provided for by Article 38(1) of the Constitution and a statutory provision such as is contained in s.4 of the Explosive Substances Act, 1883, which affords to an accused a particular defence of which he can avail if, but only if, he proves the material facts on the balance of probabilities."

The second case is *O'Leary v Attorney General* (1995). Here, the plaintiff challenged the constitutionality of two sections of the Offences Against the State Act 1939, which provided that the possession of an "incriminating document" (in this case, a poster saying "IRA calls the shots") would be evidence of membership of an unlawful organisation, as would the belief of a chief superintendent to this effect. The plaintiff claimed that the effect of these sections was to reverse the presumption of innocence, requiring him to prove that he was not a member of an unlawful organisation.

The Supreme Court rejected this argument, however, holding that these sections provided for *evidence* of membership, but not *proof* of membership; the onus always remained on the prosecution to prove the accused's membership, and possession of an incriminating document or the belief of a chief superintendent would not necessarily constitute proof of membership. The section did not pass a legal burden of proof onto the accused to prove that he was not guilty of the offence, but an evidential burden only. The probative value of the evidence might be shaken in many ways, for example by cross-examination, by pointing to the mental capacity of the accused or the circumstances by which he came to be in possession of the document.

1.2.2 *Jury directions on the presumption of innocence*

In *People (DPP) v D. O'T.* (2003), the Court of Criminal Appeal recently reaffirmed the importance of the presumption of innocence and the necessity for the jury to be directed as to the presumption. In that case, the defendant was charged with various sexual offences. The trial judge directed the jury as to the burden of proof but failed to deal adequately with the presumption of innocence. The Court of Criminal Appeal held that it was not enough to explain that the burden of proof rested on the prosecution; the presumption of innocence had also to be explained. *Per* Hardiman J.:

> "It may thus be seen that the presumption of innocence is a vital, constitutionally guaranteed, right of a person accused in a criminal trial and that the right has been expressly recognised in all of the major international human rights instruments currently in force.
>
> [...]
>
> The presumption of innocence, thus so securely entrenched nationally and internationally, is not only a right in itself: it is the basis of other aspects of a trial in due course of law at common law. The rule that, generally speaking, the prosecution bears the burden of proving all the elements of the offence necessary to establish guilt is a corollary of the presumption. To state the incidence of the burden of proof without indicating its basis in the presumption is to risk understating its importance and perhaps relegating it to the status of a mere technical rule. The presumption is the basis of the rule as to the burden of proof and not merely an alternative way of stating it
>
> [...]
>
> It is therefore important that the presumption itself should be explained as an essential feature of the criminal trial.

The prosecution's burden of proof, the corollary of the presumption, should be itself separately explained. There must then be a treatment of the standard of proof, which is proof beyond reasonable doubt, and which itself entails the corollary that the defendant is entitled to the benefit of any reasonable doubt."

1.3 Burden of proof

We have seen from *Hardy* and *O'Leary* that a necessary consequence of the presumption of innocence is the placing of the burden of proof on the prosecution. It is, therefore, the responsibility of the prosecution to establish the guilt of the accused. An important consequence flows from this: if a defence is raised by the accused, then it is the responsibility of the prosecution to disprove the defence, not the responsibility of the accused to prove the defence.

1.3.1 Exceptions

There are, however, two exceptions to this principle. First, there is the special case of the defence of insanity, which will be dealt with later. This defence must be proved by the accused on the balance of probabilities. Second, we have seen that the minority judgments in *Hardy v Ireland* (1994) accept that a statute may place similar requirements on an accused when raising a *statutory defence*. An example of this is the decision of the Court of Criminal Appeal in *People (DPP) v Byrne* (1998). Section 29(2) of the Misuse of Drugs Act 1977 provides that:

> "[Where] it is proved that the defendant had in his possession a controlled drug ... it shall be a defence to prove that —
> (i) he did not know and had no reasonable grounds for suspecting that —
> (ii) that what he had in his possession was a controlled drug ... or
>
> that he was in possession of a controlled drug ...".

In this case, the defendants were arrested in possession of packages containing drugs but claimed not to be aware of their contents. It was held, however, that once *possession* of the packages was proved, the onus shifted to the defendants to prove lack of knowledge of the contents of the packages. The prosecution was obliged to prove that an accused had, and knew that he had, a package in his control and that the package contained something. The prosecution must also prove that the package contained the controlled substance alleged. The burden of proof then rested on the defendants to bring themselves within the defence in s.29(2)(a).

1.4 Right to silence and privilege against self-incrimination

We now turn to the principles of law which are usually described as the right to silence and the privilege against self-incrimination. These are closely related to the presumption of innocence; if it is the role of the prosecution to prove that an offence has been committed, then it should not be incumbent on the suspect or accused person to facilitate the prosecution by being compelled to speak.

What specific issues are covered under this heading? One Australian study gave the following list:

> "the right of a suspect to refuse to answer questions put to him or her by criminal investigators; and
> the right of an accused person to choose whether or not to testify at his or her trial; and the consequences for the accused of exercising either or both of these rights; in particular, the question of whether adverse inferences can be drawn from, or adverse comments made about, the exercise of the right to refuse to answer questions and/or the right to not testify." (*The Right to Silence: An Examination of the Issues* (Parliament of Victoria, 1998), Ch. 1).

To this we can add the right not to have compelled answers used in evidence in a criminal matter (the privilege against self-incrimination). We will look at each of these rights in turn.

1.4.1 Pre-trial right to silence

First we will look at the right to silence at the pre-trial stage, that is, while a crime is being investigated, but before a person has been charged with that crime. At common law, it was clear that suspects enjoyed a right to refuse to answer police questions. However, recent legislation has increasingly tended to require answers to be given in specific circumstances, or to allow a court to draw an adverse inference from the failure to give answers. Consequently, we must ask whether there is a constitutional right to silence which could be asserted against such legislation.

This issue came before the Supreme Court in *Heaney v Ireland* (1996). This case dealt with s.52 of the Offences Against the State Act 1939, which requires suspects to give accounts of their movements around the time at which a crime is alleged to have taken place. Failure to give such an account is an offence. The two defendants challenged the constitutionality of this provision, claiming that it infringed their constitutional right to silence.

The Supreme Court accepted that there is a constitutional right to silence at the pre-trial stage, stating that such a right exists as a corollary of the right to freedom of expression under Art.40 of the Constitution. However, the court went on to hold that this right was not absolute and that the State was entitled to encroach on it in the interests of maintaining public peace and order, provided that the limitation of the right was proportionate to the purpose of the legislation. In this case, the court took the view that s.52 struck an acceptable balance between "any infringement of the citizen's rights with the entitlement of the State to defend itself", so that the section was constitutional.

A similar conclusion was reached by the Supreme Court in the next case to come before it on this issue, *Rock v Ireland* (1997). In that case, the validity of ss.18 and 19 of the Criminal Justice Act 1984 was challenged. These sections apply where a person is arrested without a warrant, and permit a court to draw adverse inferences from a failure by that person to account for their possession of any object, or the presence on their person of any mark, or their presence at a particular place, which a Garda believes may be related to the offence for which they have been arrested. These inferences may amount to corroboration of other evidence—however, a person may not be convicted solely on the basis of such an inference. In short, therefore, under ss.18 and 19 a person's silence when arrested may be used in evidence against that person at trial.

Here, the applicant was arrested while in possession of a quantity of banknotes, which proved to be forged US dollars. After his arrest, he was invited to account for his possession of these, which he declined to do, so that ss.18 and 19 came into play. He sought a declaration that ss.18 and 19 were repugnant to the Constitution.

This was, however, refused by the Supreme Court, which reiterated that the constitutional right to silence was not absolute. The court went on to apply a test of proportionality in deciding whether this limitation of the right was constitutional. It pointed out that the restriction on the right to silence was limited, and in particular emphasised that: an adverse inference could not form the basis for a conviction without other evidence being present; an adverse inference could only be drawn where the court deemed it proper to do so; and the weight or value of any such adverse inference could be challenged by the accused. Consequently, the court found that the restriction of the right to silence was justified, and upheld ss.18 and 19.

It is clear from these two decisions that legislation can validly restrict the right to silence at the pre-trial stage. Recent examples of such legislation include s.7 of the Criminal Justice (Drug Trafficking) Act 1996 and ss.2 and 5 of the Offences Against the State (Amendment) Act 1998, which in each case allow adverse inferences to be drawn against a defendant who remains silent when questioned. The effect of these provisions is that an accused person will have to decide what facts he will be relying on during his trial and to decide whether to bring such facts to the attention of the Gardaí at an early stage.

However, it is important to note that, where no such legislation has been enacted, then the right to silence remains available. An example of this can be seen in *People (DPP) v Finnerty* (1999). In this case, the defendant was accused of rape and put forward an alternative account of the events on the night in question. In response, the prosecution sought to put it to the defendant that he had not given any such account when arrested and questioned. The implication of this would, of course, be that the defendant's account was a recent fabrication.

The trial judge allowed the prosecution to question the defendant on his silence when arrested, and the defendant was thereafter convicted. On appeal, the Court of Criminal Appeal upheld this decision, stating that it did not impinge on the defendant's right to silence, inasmuch as it was limited to the credibility of the defendant's account of events and was not in itself evidence of guilt. On further appeal, however, the Supreme Court disagreed and quashed the conviction, stating that, while legislation might validly allow adverse inferences to be drawn from silence, in this case no such legislation existed. Consequently, since there was no statutory provision allowing adverse inferences to be drawn, the defendant's constitutional right to silence applied, and that right could not be undermined by informing the jury that the defendant had remained silent when questioned.

Another example of a violation of the right to silence under the principles in *Finnerty* is the decision in *People (DPP) v Cummins* (2003). In that case the defendant was accused of a bank robbery. When arrested and questioned by police, he failed to account for his movements on the day. The prosecution was allowed to cross examine him on that fact at trial, and the trial judge ultimately directed the jury that it was "incredible" that the accused had not explained his movements to the guards. The Court of Criminal Appeal accepted that, since there was no relevant legislation allowing an adverse inference to be drawn, both the cross-examination and direction to the jury were in "clear breach" of the principles set out in *Finnerty*, and the defendant's conviction was quashed.

1.4.2 At-trial right to silence

Moving to the trial itself, it is clear that there is a constitutional right of an accused person, arising from Art.38.1, to refuse to testify (see the decision of Costello J., in the High Court, in *Heaney v Ireland* (1994)). However, where an accused person does choose to testify, he then waives that right. He must answer questions put to him or her by the prosecution, and cannot decline to do so on the basis that the answers would incriminate him: Criminal Justice (Evidence) Act 1924, s.1(e).

1.4.3 Privilege against self-incrimination

We have seen that legislation may validly require a person to answer questions connected with a criminal investigation. However, the fact that a person may be compelled to answer does not necessarily mean that any information which they give can be used in evidence against them at trial, and the question must be asked as to whether the privilege against self-incrimination will prevent such use.

This issue came before the Supreme Court in *Re National Irish Bank* (1999). This case concerned s.10 of the Companies Act 1990, which imposes an obligation on company officers and agents to co-operate with inspectors investigating a company by, amongst other things, answering questions posed by the inspectors. Here, National Irish Bank was being investigated in connection with a number of criminal offences, including tax evasion and fraudulent charging of customers. Employees of the bank refused to answer questions put to them by the inspectors, stating that they constituted an infringement of their right to silence and potentially required them to incriminate themselves.

On the matter coming before the Supreme Court, the court (Barrington J.) accepted that the employees enjoyed a right to silence under *Heaney v Ireland* (1996). However, the powers given to the inspectors were proportional and no greater than required by the public interest, and therefore the right to silence had been validly restricted. The employees could, therefore, be required to answer questions put by the inspectors, notwithstanding their right to silence.

Could the answers to such questions be used in evidence against the employees? In considering this point, Barrington J. looked to case law dealing with the privilege against self-incrimination and in particular whether involuntary confessions could be admitted against an accused person, and came to the conclusion that:

> "It appears to me that the better opinion is that a trial in due course of law requires that any confession admitted against an accused person in a criminal trial should be a voluntary confession and that any trial at which an alleged confession other than a voluntary confession was admitted in evidence against the accused person would not be a trial in due course of law within the meaning of Article 38 of the Constitution and that it is immaterial whether the compulsion or inducement used to extract the confession came from the executive or from the legislature." (At p.359.)

It follows, therefore, that while legislation may validly restrict the pre-trial right to silence, it may not limit the privilege against self-incrimination. In other words, while a criminal suspect may in some circumstances be required to answer questions before trial, the answers to such questions may not, under the Constitution, be used in evidence against him or her at trial.

This principle has since been applied in *Dunnes Stores v Ryan* (2002). Under s.19 of the Companies Act 1990, an authorised officer could compel persons to make statements in respect of the affairs of a company. Failure to make a statement was an offence under subs.(5), while under subs.(6) a statement was admissible in evidence in criminal proceedings against the person who made it. In the High Court, Kearns J. held that subs.(5) was a proportionate limitation of the right to silence, which was justified by the public interest in good corporate governance. Subsection (6), however, was more problematic, as it purported to allow compelled statements to be introduced in evidence at a criminal trial. As such, it violated the privilege against self-incrimination, as set out by the Supreme Court in *Re National Irish Bank* (1999), and was unconstitutional.

1.4.4 Offences of withholding information and silence as a crime

Irish law features a great deal of legislation which makes it an offence to withhold information. For example, s.9 of the Offences Against the State (Amendment) Act 1998 introduces a new offence of withholding information which a person knows or believes might be of material assistance in "(a) preventing the commission by any other person of a serious offence, or (b) securing the apprehension, prosecution or conviction of any other person for a serious offence". Where a person is aware of such information, they come under a duty to report it to a member of the Garda Síochána; failure to do so, without reasonable excuse, is a criminal offence.

It will be clear that this represents a substantial inroad on the right to silence, and this provision has yet to be considered by the courts. What is particularly unusual about s.9 is that it does not merely impose a duty to answer police questions—instead, it creates a duty to *volunteer* information. However, the effect of s.9 is limited by the fact that it refers to the apprehension, prosecution, etc. of *any other person*. As such, it may be insulated from the constitutional problems associated with the privilege against *self*-incrimination.

Another example is s.19 of the Criminal Justice (Theft and Fraud Offences) Act 2001, which introduces an offence of withholding information in relation to stolen property. This section is less invasive, however, in that a person is only obliged to answer questions once asked; they are not obliged to volunteer information. In addition, the person must be warned in advance that failure to give information is a crime. Finally, information given by a person under this section is not admissible in evidence against the person. Section 19 provides:

"19.—(1) Where a member of the Garda Síochána—

(a) has reasonable grounds for believing that an offence consisting of stealing property or of handling stolen property has been committed,

(b) finds any person in possession of any property,

(c) has reasonable grounds for believing that the property referred to in paragraph (b) includes, or may include, property referred to in paragraph (a) or part of it, or the whole or any part of the proceeds of that property or part, and

(d) informs the person of his or her belief, the member may require the person to give an account of how he or she came by the property.

(2) If the person fails or refuses, without reasonable excuse, to give such account or gives information that the person knows to be false or misleading, he or she is guilty of an offence and is liable on summary conviction to a fine not exceeding £1,500 or imprisonment for a term not exceeding 12 months or both.

(3) Subsection (2) shall not have effect unless the person when required to give the account was told in ordinary language by the member of the Garda Síochána what the effect of the failure or refusal might be.

(4) Any information given by a person in compliance with a requirement under subs.(1) shall not be admissible in evidence against that person or his or her spouse in any criminal proceedings, other than proceedings for an offence under subs.(2)."

1.4.5 *Influence of the European Convention on Human Rights*

Article 6 of the European Convention on Human Rights guarantees the right to a fair trial, and the question must be asked as to whether limitations on the right to silence or the privilege against self-incrimination infringe this right. This question becomes particularly important in the wake of the European Convention on Human Rights Act 2003, which now requires the courts to interpret Irish law (so far as possible) in a manner which is compatible with the Convention.

Saunders v United Kingdom (1996) is the leading case on the privilege against self-incrimination. In that case the applicant was the chief executive of Guinness and was responsible for a controversial takeover of another company. The Department of Trade and Industry appointed inspectors to investigate the takeover; failure to cooperate with the inspectors and to answer their questions was an offence. The inspectors interviewed the applicant on a number of occasions, and it was eventually decided to bring criminal charges against him. The transcripts of his interviews formed a large part of the prosecution case at trial, and were held by the English courts to be admissible notwithstanding that they had been obtained by compulsion.

The European Court of Human Rights, however, held that this use of compelled answers at trial amounted to a breach of the Art.6 right to a fair trial, holding that:

> "although not specifically mentioned in Article 6 of the Convention, the right to silence and the right not to incriminate oneself are generally recognised international standards which lie at the heart of the notion of a fair procedure under Article 6 (art. 6). Their rationale lies, inter alia, in the protection of the accused against improper compulsion by the authorities thereby contributing to the avoidance of miscarriages of justice and to the fulfilment of the aims of Article 6 ... The right not to incriminate oneself, in particular, presupposes that the prosecution in a criminal case seek to prove their case against the accused without resort to evidence obtained through methods of coercion or oppression in defiance of the will of the accused. In this sense the right is closely linked to the presumption of innocence contained in Article 6 para.2 of the Convention."

As regards drawing adverse inferences from pre-trial silence, the most important decision is *Averill v United Kingdom* (2000). Here it was held that the drawing of an adverse inference could infringe Art.6, depending on all the circumstances of a particular case. Relevant factors included the situations where inferences may be drawn, the weight to be attached to them by national courts, the degree of compulsion inherent in the situation (for example, whether a person could be penalised for failure to answer), and whether an accused person had access to a lawyer during questioning.

In this case, the defendant was arrested and questioned in

connection with a murder in Northern Ireland. He was initially refused access to a solicitor but was later allowed to consult with one. He was warned by police that an adverse inference could be drawn from silence, but refused to answer any questions relating to the offence. At trial, he put forward an alibi for the date of the murder. The trial judge drew what he stated to be "a very strong adverse inference" from the defendant's silence when arrested, and the defendant was convicted. The defendant then applied to the European Court of Human Rights, alleging that this adverse inference amounted to an interference with his right to a fair trial under Art.6.

However, the court rejected this application, stating that the drawing of an adverse inference was not, in itself, a breach of Art.6. In this case there was no obligation on the trial judge to draw an adverse inference, and the trial judge was free to consider if there was an excuse or a justification for the failure to speak. In deciding to draw an adverse inference, the trial judge provided detailed reasons for his decision, which were subject to review on appeal. In addition, the inferences had not been the sole reason for the conviction, which was supported by other evidence. In light of all these factors and safeguards, the court found that the drawing of an adverse inference did not interfere with the accused's right to a fair trial.

Turning to the question of compelled answers to police questioning, this issue came before the European Court of Human Rights in *Heaney and McGuinness v Ireland* (2000). This case arose from the facts of *Heaney v Ireland* (1996), discussed above, and was brought by the two applicants following the dismissal of their Supreme Court appeal. Here they alleged that their conviction for failure to answer questions under s.52 was a breach of their right to a fair trial under Art.6, in that it amounted to punishment for invoking their rights to silence and against self-incrimination. The court upheld this argument, finding that:

> "the 'degree of compulsion', imposed on the applicants by the application of s. 52 of the 1939 Act with a view to compelling them to provide information relating to charges against them under that Act, in effect, destroyed the very essence of their privilege against self-incrimination and their right to remain silent." (Para.55.)

Applying a test of proportionality, it went on to find that the national security concerns expressed by the Irish Government did not amount to a sufficient justification for this measure, so that there had been a violation of the applicants' rights to silence and against self-incrimination under Art.6. (An identical conclusion was reached in the companion case of *Quinn v Ireland* (2000), which also concerned s.52.) It would appear, therefore, that s.52 may have to be amended or repealed in order for the State to comply with the decision of the court, and there may now be a question mark over any other legislative provisions which require criminal suspects to answer questions put to them by the police.

1.5 Standard of proof

Having dealt with the burden of proof, we turn to the standard of proof the prosecution must meet to secure a conviction. In civil law matters, the standard of proof is on the balance of probabilities. That is, the plaintiff will succeed if he can establish that his version of events is more likely than not. However, a higher standard applies in the criminal law, where guilt must be proven beyond a reasonable doubt. This standard requires that the accused be acquitted, even if the jury think it possible or even likely that he committed the crime charged, so long as they have a reasonable doubt as to his guilt. It has been explained by Denning J. in *Miller v Minister of Pensions* (1947), as follows:

> "Proof beyond reasonable doubt does not mean proof beyond the shadow of doubt. The law would fail to protect the community if it admitted fanciful possibilities to deflect the course of justice. If the evidence is so strong against a man as to leave only a remote possibility in his favour which can be dismissed with the sentence 'of course it is possible but not in the least probable' the case is proved beyond reasonable doubt, but nothing short of that will suffice." (At p.373.)

The standard is constitutionally required in this jurisdiction, and has been authoritatively defined by Kenny J. in the Court of Criminal Appeal in *People (AG) v Byrne* (1974):

> "The correct charge to a jury is that they must be satisfied beyond reasonable doubt of the guilt of the accused, and it is helpful if that degree of proof is contrasted with that in a civil case. It is also essential, however, that the jury should

be told that the accused is entitled to the benefit of the
doubt, and that when two views on any part of the case are
possible on the evidence, they should adopt that which is
favourable to the accused unless the State has established
the other beyond reasonable doubt." (At p.9.)

Applying that standard, the Court of Criminal Appeal held that a
charge to the jury was defective in that it told the jury they could
convict if "satisfied" of the guilt of the accused, without making it
clear that they must be satisfied beyond a reasonable doubt.

Further reading:

Ní Raifeartaigh, "Reversing the Burden of Proof in a Criminal Trial"
(1995) 5 I.C.L.J. 135; Law Reform Commission, *Report on the
Confiscation of the Proceeds of Crime* (LRC 35-1991), pp. 52–
55; Dillon-Malone, "Voluntariness, the Whole Truth and Self-
Incrimination after In *Re NIB*" (1998/99) 4 Bar Review 237;
McCutcheon & Walsh, "Seizure of Criminal Assets: An Overview"
(1999) I.C.L.J. 127; Ní Raifeartaigh, "The Criminal Justice System
and Drug Related Offending: Some Thoughts on Procedural
Reforms" (1998/99) 4 Bar Review 15; Editorial, "Offences Against
the State (Amendment) Act, 1998—Two Views" (1998/99) 4 Bar
Review 5; Hogan, "The Right to Silence after *National Irish Banks
and Finnerty*" (1999) 21 D.U.L.J. 176; McDermott, "Evidence and
Procedure Update" (2000) I.C.L.J. 18.

1.6 Classification of crimes

1.6.1 Felony v. misdemeanour

Until 1997, crimes were primarily classified as being either felonies
or misdemeanours, and depending on this classification, different
rules applied in a number of areas, the most important of which
were powers of arrest and the liability of accomplices. The Criminal
Law Act 1997 abolished this distinction (s.3) and provided detailed
rules governing powers of arrest (ss.4, 5 and 6) and the liability of
accomplices (ss.7 and 8) which do not depend on this classification.

1.6.2 Minor v. non-minor

However, other distinctions between crimes remain significant. The
most important is the distinction between minor and non-minor

offences. This is of significance having regard to Art.38.2, which provides that minor offences may be tried without a jury. It follows that whether an offence is minor determines whether an accused has a right to trial by jury.

How do we determine if an offence is minor? The main case on this point is the case of *Melling v O Mathghamhna* (1962), which we have already looked at in connection with determining whether a particular matter is a criminal matter. The issue also arose in that case as to whether the offence of smuggling butter was a minor offence, and the Supreme Court held that in making that decision, one must look primarily to the severity of the penalty involved and to the moral quality of the offence. As a rule of thumb, it is generally taken that an offence is minor if the maximum penalty possible is a fine of £1500 and/or 12 months' imprisonment.

An interesting issue arises in looking at the severity of the penalty. Suppose that conviction for an offence carries with it consequences other than a fine or imprisonment, such as disqualification from driving, the loss of some licence or forfeiture of property. Should these consequences be considered in deciding whether the offence is a minor one?

This issue arose in *Conroy v AG* (1965), in relation to disqualification from driving where a person was convicted of driving under the influence. The Supreme Court in that case held that the disqualification could not be considered to be part of the punishment for the offence; although it might have a deterrent effect, it was not a "primary punishment", nor was it intended to be punitive in its effect, but instead was the regulation of a statutory right in the interests of public safety.

1.6.3 Indictable v. summary

Another distinction is that between indictable and summary offences. This distinction is related to the distinction between minor and non-minor offences, and again hinges on mode of trial. An indictable offence is one which may or must be tried before a jury, while a summary offence is one which can only be tried before a judge sitting without a jury.

1.6.4 Serious v. non-serious

A new distinction has been created by the Bail Act 1997 between serious and non-serious offences. The 1997 Act allows bail to be refused where an accused is charged with a serious offence and it is established that if released on bail he is likely to commit further serious offences. The Act defines a serious offence as one of a number of specified offences for which a person, if convicted, could face five or more years' imprisonment. The Bail Act will be considered further in Chapter 2, Criminal Procedure.

1.6.5 Arrestable v. non-arrestable

Another new distinction is created by the Criminal Law Act 1997, which establishes a category of arrestable offences. Since that Act abolished the felony/misdemeanour distinction on which powers of arrest hinged, it was necessary to specify when Gardaí would enjoy powers of arrest without warrant. The Act does so by providing (in s.4) that a Garda may arrest without warrant any person he believes to be guilty of an arrestable offence. The Act goes on to define an arrestable offence as an offence for which a person could be punished by imprisonment for five or more years, which is essentially the same definition as that of a serious offence.

2. CRIMINAL PROCEDURE

2.1 Arrest and detention

The following is a very brief synopsis of the law in this area. For a greater understanding, the student should consult a specialist publication such as *Criminal Procedure* by Dermot Walsh.

2.1.1 Arrest

The original purpose of arrest was to enable a suspect to be charged with a criminal offence. The traditional objective of detention was to ensure the attendance of an accused in court. Indeed, the Garda Síochána was expected to have completed the investigation of an alleged offence before arresting a suspect. This approach has been broadened in recent times, and arrest and detention are increasingly being used to question suspects and investigate crimes.

There are numerous powers of arrest both under common law and set out in various statutes. Powers of arrest are not necessarily limited to those that may be exercised by gardaí, as powers of citizen's arrest also exist.

Prior to 1997, a police officer had a common law power to arrest without warrant where he reasonably suspected that a felony had been committed. In contrast, arrest warrants were necessary in the case of misdemeanours. The Criminal Law Act 1997 abolished the distinction between felonies and misdemeanours and a new category of offence, an arrestable offence, was created. This is defined as an offence punishable by imprisonment for five years or more. Section 4 permits an arrest to be effected without warrant by any person who, with reasonable cause, suspects another to be committing or to have committed an arrestable offence.

Section 30 of the Offences Against the State Act 1939 contains a power of arrest in respect of any offence under the Offences Against the State Acts 1939–1998 and any scheduled offence. The power of arrest also extends to any person suspected of being in possession of information relating to the commission or intended commission of an offence under the Acts or a scheduled offence.

2.1.2 Detention

Sections 4 to 10 of the Criminal Justice Act 1984 contain powers of detention. A person must be taken to a garda station without undue delay after arrest, as a suspect's rights will not be set in motion until his arrival in the garda station. A suspect may only be detained for an initial six hours. He must only be detained where there are reasonable grounds for believing that the detention is necessary for the proper investigation of the offence. This opinion must be formed at the time the suspect is brought to the station by the member in charge, who should not be one of the arresting gardaí. If a garda not below the rank of superintendent believes that it is necessary for the proper investigation of the offence to detain the suspect for a *further* six-hour period, this may be directed under s.4. Alternatively, at the end of the first six-hour period the suspect must either be released or charged and brought before a court as soon as possible.

Powers of detention are also to be found in s.2 of the Criminal Justice (Drug Trafficking) Act 1996. These powers are very extensive, allowing a suspect to be detained for up to a maximum of seven days. However, after two days of detention an application must be made to a district judge for an extension of up to 72 hours. The suspect must be brought before the court for the application. After this period has expired, a further extension of up to 48 hours may be applied for.

The Offences Against the State (Amendment) Act 1998 increases the powers of detention, in relation to persons arrested under s.30 of the Offences Against the State Act 1939, from 48 hours to 72 hours. The extension from 48 to 72 hours may only be granted by a district judge and the suspect must be brought before the court when the application is being made.

The Criminal Justice Bill 2004 also provides for an increase in powers of detention pursuant to s.4 of the Criminal Justice Act 1984 from 12 hours (the final six authorised by at least a superintendent) to 18 hours (the final 12 authorised by a garda not below the rank of chief superintendent).

Further reading:

Ryan, "Arrest and Detention: A Review of the Law" (2000) 10 I.C.L.J. 2.

2.2 Bail

Bail can be defined as the setting at liberty of an accused pending trial and is granted by way of a recognisance: an undertaking that the accused will appear for trial and that a certain sum of money will be forfeited if he does not. (Bail is also available while an appeal is pending, but this situation raises different considerations and will not be dealt with). An accused can be released on his personal recognisance but in serious cases independent sureties will be required.

Before 1996, the law concerning bail was largely contained in successive Supreme Court decisions which laid down when it was or was not constitutionally permissible to refuse bail. Broadly speaking, bail could be refused only where an accused was likely to fail to appear for trial, or likely to interfere with the conduct of the trial. Dissatisfaction with this regime led to the Bail Referendum in 1996, which inserted into the Constitution what is now Art.40.4.7°. This Article was implemented by the Bail Act 1997.

2.2.1 Common Law

Our starting point is the decision of the Supreme Court in *People (AG) v O'Callaghan* (1966). In this case, the grant of bail was opposed on the grounds that the accused would interfere with witnesses, and that, if released, the accused would commit further offences while on bail. The first ground was largely unsupported by evidence, and the Supreme Court unanimously held that the second ground could not be taken into account in deciding whether to grant bail. *Per* Ó Dálaigh C.J.:

> "[The second ground is] a denial of the whole basis of our system of law. It transcends respect for the requirement that a man shall be considered innocent until he is found guilty and seeks to punish him in respect of offences neither completed nor attempted." (At pp.508–509.)

And, *per* Walsh J.:

> "[I]t would be quite contrary to the concept of personal liberty enshrined in the Constitution that any person should be punished in respect of any matter upon which he has not been convicted or that in any circumstances he should be deprived of his liberty upon only the belief that he will commit offences if left at liberty." (At pp.516–517.)

The Supreme Court instead stated that the only test in deciding whether to allow bail was the probability of the accused attempting to evade justice, whether by failing to appear for trial, or by interfering with the trial (by interfering with witnesses, destroying evidence, and so on). In applying this test, the Supreme Court stated that regard could be had to the following factors:

1. The seriousness of the charge.
2. The nature of the evidence in support of the charge.
3. The likely sentence to be imposed on conviction.
4. The possibility of disposal of illegally acquired property.
5. The possibility of interference with prospective witnesses and jurors.
6. The accused's failure to answer to bail on a previous occasion.
7. The fact that the accused was caught red-handed.
8. The objections of the Attorney General or of the police authorities.
9. The substance and reliability of the sureties offered.
10. The possibility of a speedy trial.

Some comments on each of these factors must be made. Numbers 1, 2, 3, 6 and 7 each go to the likelihood that an accused will fail to appear for trial; clearly, an accused is less likely to appear where he faces a solid prosecution case and a substantial sentence if convicted. It should be noted that 7 is really just an aspect of 2, the nature and strength of the evidence against the accused. Number 4 (disposal of illegally acquired property) is only relevant insofar as this amounts to interference with evidence. Equally, number 8 (prosecution objections) is only relevant insofar as the objections relate to the accused attempting to evade justice. Finally, number 10 (prospect of a speedy trial) was stated by the Supreme Court to be a factor in favour of refusing bail where otherwise it might be granted (if extensive delays were likely before the charge was heard). However, it was stressed that the availability of a speedy trial could not justify the refusal of bail where otherwise it would be granted.

In *Ryan v DPP* (1989), the Supreme Court was invited to reconsider its decision in *People (AG) v O'Callaghan*, on the basis that the right to liberty of the accused must be balanced against the rights of other citizens who might be the victims of further crimes. This argument was, however, rejected in pithy terms:

> "The criminalising of mere intention has usually been a badge of an oppressive or unjust legal system. The proper methods

of preventing crime are the long-established combination
of police surveillance, speedy trial and deterrent sentences."
(*Per* Finlay C.J. at page 407.)

The court made clear that there was no discretion at common law to
refuse bail for the purpose of preventative detention, as this would
be an invasion of the presumption of innocence. The criminalising of
mere intentions to commit crimes would be an attempt by the judiciary
to legislate.

The net result of *Ryan v DPP* and *People (AG) v O'Callaghan*
was, therefore, that bail could not be refused on the ground of likelihood
to commit further crimes. However, a serious problem did exist with
regard to offences being committed while the accused was free on
bail, and s.11 of the Criminal Justice Act 1984 attempted to deter the
commission of such offences by providing for mandatory consecutive
sentences for offences committed while on bail.

2.2.2 Bail Act 1997

However, as already noted, dissatisfaction with the bail regime
continued, culminating in the insertion of Art.40.4.7° into the
Constitution:

"Provision may be made by law for the refusal of bail by a
court to a person charged with a serious offence where it
is reasonably considered necessary to prevent the
commission of a serious offence by that person."

This Article is permissive only— "Provision *may be made*"—and
does not in itself allow a court to refuse bail. It was given effect by
the Bail Act 1997.

The primary condition of the 1997 Act is contained in s.2(1),
which allows a court to refuse a bail application made by a person
charged with a serious offence if reasonably considered necessary
to prevent the commission of a serious offence by that person.
"Serious offence" is then defined by s.1(2) as any crime specified in
the Schedule to the Act for which a person of full capacity not
previously convicted could be punished by five or more years
imprisonment. The list of crimes specified in the Schedule is quite
extensive, and includes for example all offences under the Larceny
Acts, 1916 to 1990 as well as the more obviously serious crimes
such as murder, manslaughter and rape.

Section 2(2) then requires the court to take into account factors similar to those contained in *People (AG) v O'Callaghan* in deciding whether to refuse bail on this ground:

a. The nature and degree of seriousness of the offence charged and the likely sentence.

b. The nature and degree of seriousness of the offence apprehended as likely to be committed, and the sentence which would be likely to be imposed for that offence.

c. The strength of the evidence in support of the charge.

d. Any conviction of the accused for an offence committed while on bail.

e. Any other convictions of the accused.

f. Any other offence charged for which the accused is awaiting trial.

The court may also take into account the fact that the accused is addicted to a controlled drug. This is very important in practice. Under s.2(3) it is not necessary for the prosecution to point to the likely commission of any particular serious offence.

Bail having been refused on the ground that the accused is likely to commit a serious offence, s.3 then allows the application for bail to be renewed four months after the initial refusal, on the grounds of delay by the prosecutor, and the court may then grant bail "if the interests of justice so require".

Section 6 specifies conditions which a court may or must impose on the grant of bail. (The significance of these conditions being that failure to comply will result in rearrest, and forfeiture of any recognisances.) A recognisance must contain a condition that the accused will not commit any offence, and the court may impose further conditions which it considers appropriate, for example, requiring the accused to reside in a particular place, to report to a specified Garda station, to surrender his passport, to refrain from going to a particular place or to refrain from having contact with a particular person.

Finally, s.10 of the 1997 Act makes a significant change to the Criminal Justice Act 1984. While the 1984 Act required consecutive sentences to be imposed for crimes committed on bail, s.10 also requires that a greater sentence should be imposed for offences committed while on bail.

2.2.3 *Hearsay evidence and Bail applications*

Distinct from the question of what grounds justify the refusal of bail is the question of what evidence is required to be given to establish those grounds. From a practical point of view it is vitally important to know what form of evidence is required in opposing the grant of bail: is hearsay evidence admissible, must evidence be given *viva voce* or will affidavits suffice, and so on. In *McKeon v DPP* (1995), the Supreme Court upheld the admissibility of hearsay evidence in circumstances where a garda had given evidence that the applicant was preparing to flee the jurisdiction with the aid of an illegal organisation. The Supreme Court again addressed the issue in *People (AG) v McGinley* (1998). In that case, the accused was refused bail in the High Court on the basis of the hearsay evidence of a garda to the effect that the victim's family had been threatened by members of the accused's family. On appeal to the Supreme Court, it was held that as a rule an applicant for bail was entitled, as part of his right to fair procedures, to have any evidence against him given under oath and subject to cross-examination, unless there were any special factors present (such as confidential police sources) which would justify the admission of hearsay evidence. The court made it clear that it was not ruling that hearsay evidence could never be admitted, but the judge must weigh up the constitutional right to liberty with the public interest in the administration of justice in reaching a decision.

2.2.4 *Bail for the purposes of appeal*

The Court of Criminal Appeal made it clear in *DPP v Sweetman* (1997) that different factors come into play when a bail application is made for the purposes of appealing a conviction. The applicant in this case was convicted of murder and sought bail pending appeal. The court held that the strength of the case as it appeared on the materials before the court was the proper matter to be brought into reckoning in the first instance, and that the State case was so strong that, in the proper exercise of the court's discretion, bail could not be given to the applicant. The court emphasised that the position of a convicted person seeking bail was very different to the usual bail applicant because the applicant no longer enjoyed the presumption of innocence. The criteria relevant pre-trial were not, therefore, the same as those that operated post-conviction.

The issue of post-conviction bail was again addressed in *DPP v Corbally* (2000), where the applicant had been convicted of possession of firearms and unlawful and malicious wounding. It was held that bail should be granted post-conviction where the interests of justice demanded that it should because, for example, of the strength of the grounds. The Court of Criminal Appeal should exercise its discretion to grant bail post-conviction sparingly. Bail should be granted where the court considered there was a strong chance of the appeal succeeding. The applicant was, however, refused bail and the Supreme Court upheld this determination.

DPP v Quinn (2001) concerned an appeal on the severity of sentence only. The applicant had been sentenced to nine months for larceny and the appeal hearing was unlikely to be before the sentence expired, thereby rendering it moot. The court held that the fact that a sentence under appeal would expire before the appeal hearing took place was not a ground upon which bail should be granted. It reiterated that the discretion to admit to bail should be used sparingly as the applicant was a convicted person. The court in these circumstances was bound to consider whether there was a reasonable chance that the sentence would be reduced on appeal. The court in the instant case refused to grant bail but recommended that an early date for the appeal hearing should be arranged.

Further reading:

Bacik, "The Bail Act 1997" (June 1997) Practice and Procedure 7; O'Higgins, "Bail—A Privilege or a Right?" (1998) Bar Review 318; Law Reform Commission, *An Examination of the Law on Bail* (1995).

2.3 Appeals

This section will be limited to the case of appeals against verdicts on indictment. Where a person is convicted after a summary trial (*i.e.* in the District Court) there is a statutory right of appeal to the Circuit Court and that appeal takes the form of a re-hearing of the matter. The remedy of judicial review is also available where the procedure adopted by the District Court is defective in some way. However, we will confine ourselves to the case of appeals from conviction on indictment, that is, in the case of trials taking place before the Circuit Court, Central Criminal Court, or Special Criminal Court.

2.4 The Court of Criminal Appeal

The Court of Criminal Appeal is not a court mentioned in Art.34 of the Constitution, and is therefore entirely a statutory creation, first established by the Courts of Justice Act 1924. It is composed of one Supreme Court and two High Court judges, with the Supreme Court judge presiding, and delivers a single judgment. It operates (in theory) a two-stage procedure, where, first, one applies for *leave to appeal* (unless this has already been granted by the court of trial); having obtained leave to appeal, one proceeds to the *substantive appeal*. In practice, the court almost invariably combines the two stages, treating the application for leave to appeal as the appeal itself.

2.4.1 The "basic powers" of the Court of Criminal Appeal

What might be called its basic powers, in relation to ordinary appeals, are now set out in s.3 of the Criminal Procedure Act 1993. On the hearing of an *appeal against conviction*, the court may:

1. *affirm* the conviction;
2. *quash* the conviction, making no further order;
3. *quash* the conviction, ordering that the applicant be *re-tried for that offence*; or
4. *quash* the conviction, and *substitute a verdict of guilty for some other offence.*

Some points on each option must be made. As regards option 1, a conviction can be affirmed under s.3, even where the court would decide a point raised in the appeal in favour of the applicant, where the court considers that no miscarriage of justice has actually taken place. This is designed to deal with the situation where a trial judge makes a technical or otherwise minor mistake, which does not result in any prejudice to the accused.

As regards options 2 and 3, it will be clear that a successful appeal is not a "get out of jail free" card. The court may direct that a retrial take place, at which point the process starts over. However, the court has a discretion not to do so, and will decline to order a retrial where, for example:

- A conviction is quashed because of the weakness of the evidence against the applicant;
- The applicant has already spent such a period of time

in prison that no court on a retrial would impose a
further sentence; or
• No reasonable jury, properly directed, could convict
the applicant on the evidence presented.

Having said that, the normal practice is that a retrial will follow the
quashing of a conviction unless there are special circumstances
leaning in the other direction.

Option 4, quashing the conviction and substituting a conviction
for another offence, requires close scrutiny. The text of the relevant
subsection states:

> "the Court may ... quash the conviction and, if it appears to
> the Court that the appellant could have been found guilty of
> some other offence and that the jury must have been
> satisfied of facts which proved him guilty of the other
> offence — (i) substitute for the verdict a verdict of guilty
> of the other offence, and [sentence the appellant
> accordingly so long as the sentence is not more severe
> than the original]."

The problems with this power will be obvious. In allowing the court
to find a person guilty of an offence, in circumstances where he has
not been convicted by a jury of that offence, this section appears to
fall foul of Art.38.5 of the Constitution that "no person shall be tried
on any criminal charge without a jury, save in the case of minor
offences, special courts and military tribunals." The constitutionality
of this power must therefore be suspect, and it seems that it has
never been exercised.

On the hearing of an *appeal against sentence*, the court may
let the original sentence stand, or quash the sentence and impose
such sentence as it considers appropriate. This includes the power
to vary the sentence upwards; an appeal against sentence may,
therefore, be a risky option.

It should be noted that these two forms of appeal, against
conviction and sentence, can be brought only by a convicted person;
appeals by the prosecution are dealt with below.

2.4.2 Prosecution appeal against sentence

The "basic powers" of the Court of Criminal Appeal are in essence
the same powers as it enjoyed until 1993. In that year, however, two
fundamental changes were made to the jurisdiction of the court.

The first was contained in the Criminal Justice Act 1993, s.2 of which allows the DPP to apply to the court to review a sentence imposed by a court on conviction of a person on indictment, where he considers that sentence to be unduly lenient. It will then be open to the court to let the sentence stand, or to quash it and substitute a higher (or lower) sentence.

This change was prompted largely by the public outcry over two controversially lenient sentences. The first was the Lavinia Kerwick case, in which a rape victim went public over her disgust that her rapist had escaped a custodial sentence. The second was the Kilkenny incest case, where again the sentence imposed was publicly felt to be inadequate in relation to the gravity of the crime (both of these cases are discussed in the Annotation to the 1993 Act by Bird, cited below).

While it was possible for the DPP to appeal against sentence in a small class of cases before the passing of this Act, this power was useless in practical terms. By convention, it was seldom exercised. In addition, it rested on the happenstance of certain offences being tried before the Central Criminal Court; if the Circuit Court or Special Criminal Court were to impose an unduly lenient sentence, then the DPP was powerless. It was necessary, therefore, to create a comprehensive power capable of practical use, which the 1993 Act did.

Soon after the creation of the power, the case of *DPP v B* (1994) came before the court. (The following is a summary taken from the detailed analysis in O'Malley's article, cited below.) This was the first prosecution application under the new section, and the court therefore took the opportunity to outline how the new power would be operated. The facts were particularly horrific, which was no doubt a reason why the case had been chosen by the DPP as a test case. The applicant had been convicted on three charges of rape, against two different victims. The two offences had been committed shortly after each other. In each case the applicant had broken into the victim's home. The first victim was a woman who was asleep in bed with her husband: she was abducted, taken to another part of the house, and raped. The second victim was an elderly widow who was assaulted, raped and buggered by the applicant at knifepoint. He confessed when arrested soon after, and pleaded guilty at preliminary examination. He had a previous conviction for indecent assault.

The applicant came to be sentenced before Hamilton P. in the Central Criminal Court, who stated that a 14-year sentence would have been appropriate but for the early guilty plea; taking the plea into account, however, he would impose concurrent sentences of 10 years each.

On appeal, the court during argument indicated that counsel should address whether the sentencing judge had failed to take into account relevant factors, or had taken into account irrelevant factors. In reply, counsel for the DPP argued that a ten-year sentence for each offence was not of itself inappropriate; but it was inappropriate to make each sentence concurrent, since there was no element of additional punishment for an additional offence, particularly where the two offences were completely separate.

The court (O'Flaherty J.), in giving judgment, first set out four guidelines to be used in determining whether a sentence was "unduly lenient":

1. The Director of Public Prosecutions bears the onus of proof.
2. The decision of the trial judge should not be upset without good reason, since he or she is in the best position to assess sentence, having heard all the facts first-hand. His decision, if it balances the offence with the position of the offender, should not be disturbed.
3. The court should not ask if a more severe sentence would have been upheld on appeal; the test is not whether the trial judge could have imposed a higher sentence, but whether the sentence he or she did in fact impose was "unduly lenient".
4. Having regard to these guidelines, the ultimate question is whether the particular sentence is a "substantial departure from what would be regarded as the appropriate sentence". If not, the court will not intervene.

The court went on to apply those guidelines to hold that the sentence imposed by Hamilton P. would not be disturbed.

It should be noted that the existence of a prosecution appeal against sentence creates an anomaly. As a matter of practice, which is codified in para.9.20 of the Bar Code of Conduct, it is not considered appropriate for a prosecutor to make any submissions on the sentence which should be imposed on an accused. A prosecutor may play on gruesome facts during the trial; but after conviction, he or she is limited to a bare recital of whether the accused has any previous convictions. The defence lawyer, by contrast, is free to make submissions as to the appropriate sentence. It follows that the prosecutor is unable to guide the trial judge as to the factors to be taken into account, but if dissatisfied with the sentence imposed, is able to go before the Court of Criminal Appeal and argue that the trial judge failed to take all relevant factors into account. If the prosecutor can make these arguments at this later stage, it is hard to see why he cannot do so at the earlier stage, particularly where doing so might avoid the need for a prosecution appeal.

2.4.3 Miscarriages of justice

The next major change to the jurisdiction of the Court of Criminal Appeal was brought about by the Criminal Procedure Act 1993, which dealt with the position of "miscarriages of justice"—cases such as those of the Birmingham Six, where it seemed that the ordinary appeals system was inadequate to deal with lingering doubts over guilt, particularly once the normal appeals procedure has been exhausted.

Although there was a tendency to look down on the English legal system, which seemed to produce miscarriages of justice with monotonous regularity, these cases were not unknown in Ireland, with the most notorious example being the conviction of Nicky Kelly in 1978 on evidence which, he alleged, was fabricated by the Gardai following violent interrogation. After an unsuccessful appeal to the Court of Criminal Appeal, he was ultimately granted a presidential pardon in 1992, some 14 years after the event.

A commission was therefore set up in 1989 under the chairmanship of Judge Frank Martin of the Circuit Court to examine whether there was a need for a procedure over and above the normal appeals procedure, and whether there should be restrictions on the use of confession evidence. The Commission ultimately recommended that there should be a special procedure set up to review alleged miscarriages of justice, but felt that this should not be court-based, primarily on the basis that the restrictive nature of the rules of evidence would hinder attempts by a convicted person to clear his name. Instead, the Commission recommended that there should be an independent body, with statutory powers to call witnesses, demand documents, and so forth, which would investigate these matters.

This recommendation was not accepted by the 1993 Act which adopts a twin-track approach instead. Those wishing to challenge an alleged miscarriage of justice have two options open to them. First, they can petition the Minister for Justice, who has the power to set up an *ad hoc* committee to inquire into that alleged miscarriage of justice. This committee will then recommend to the Government whether a pardon should be granted. Secondly, they can proceed down the court route, launching a fresh appeal to the Court of Criminal Appeal on the basis of new or newly obtained evidence. In either event, if the applicant is successful in his or her petition or appeal, and the Minister or the court is of the opinion that there has been a miscarriage of justice, then the applicant is entitled to compensation.

2.5 The Role of the Court of Criminal Appeal

The court route is provided for in s.2, which imposes a number of preconditions before an application under this section can be brought. First, the applicant must have already appealed to the Court of Criminal Appeal. Second, the proceedings in relation to the appeal must be complete: there can be no further proceedings pending. (This does not, however, seem to preclude concurrent claims before, for example, the European Court of Human Rights.) Third, and crucially, the applicant must allege that:

"new or newly discovered facts [show] that there has been a miscarriage of justice in relation to the conviction or that the sentence imposed is excessive." (s. 2(1)(b).)

What is a newly discovered fact? Before the 1993 Act, for an appeal to be brought on the basis of new evidence, it had to be shown that the evidence was not available at the trial. Although there was no authority on the point in this jurisdiction, it had been held elsewhere that this rule excluded evidence which with reasonable diligence could have been available to the defence at trial. The 1993 Act adopts a broader definition, by stating that:

"a newly discovered fact is ... a fact discovered by or coming to the attention of the convicted person after the relevant appeal proceedings have been finally determined *or a fact the significance of which was not appreciated* by the convicted person or his advisers during the trial or appeal proceedings." (s.2(4)); and

"[a] new fact ... is a fact known to the convicted person at the time of the trial or appeal proceedings the significance of which was appreciated by him, where he alleges that there is *a reasonable explanation for his failure to adduce evidence* of that fact." (s.2(3))

It will be clear from the portions in italics that the definition of new or newly discovered facts is quite wide. In particular, s.2(3) allows an appeal to be brought where there is a reasonable explanation why evidence was not tendered, which would cover, for example, the situation where an accused is threatened if he should implicate another in a crime alleged to have been committed by him.

Once these preconditions for the jurisdiction of the court are met, and once the court has determined that a miscarriage of justice within the meaning of s.2 has occurred, it is then open to the court to certify under s.9 that a miscarriage of justice has taken place, so as to entitle the applicant to compensation. However, despite the fact that the same terminology is used in both sections, it is now clear that the two are distinct, and the quashing of a conviction under s.2 does not in itself entitle an applicant to compensation under s.9. This is the net result of two cases to come before the Court of Criminal Appeal, each of which has elaborated on the distinction between the two sections.

The first of these was *People (DPP) v Pringle* (1997), in which the Supreme Court laid down certain applicable principles. In that case, the Court of Criminal Appeal had quashed the conviction of an applicant on the basis of a newly discovered fact showing a miscarriage of justice within the meaning of s.2. Evidence had come to light querying the credibility of one of the gardaí who had taken an inculpatory statement from Pringle while he was being interrogated. The court refused, however, to certify that a miscarriage of justice had taken place within the meaning of s.9. On appeal to the Supreme Court, it was held that the mere fact of the quashing of a conviction under s.2 does not give rise to a right to compensation. Instead, before a s.9 certificate could be granted, it was for the applicant to establish, on the balance of probabilities, that he is innocent of the alleged offence. The fact that his conviction has been quashed as being unsafe and unsatisfactory could not *per se* raise an entitlement to a certificate that there had been a miscarriage of justice.

The second case was *People (DPP) v Meleady and Grogan* (1997), which dealt with the so-called "Tallaght Two". The convictions of the applicants had been quashed by the Court of Criminal Appeal, but in that case the court had felt that compensation could not be granted unless there had been a retrial at which the applicants had been found not guilty. This decision was reversed by the Supreme Court, which held that the inquiry under s.9 as to whether a miscarriage of justice had taken place did not depend on a subsequent jury acquittal: compensation could be awarded without the need for a fresh trial to take place. The case was remitted back to the Court of Criminal Appeal, and it ultimately concluded that a certificate under s.9 should issue. Meleady and Grogan had relied on newly discovered facts to ground their appeal. The newly discovered facts were, first, a thumb print belonging to a third party and, second, the existence of an internal prosecution memo stating that the chief prosecution witness had been shown a booklet of 50 photographs before taking part in an identification parade.

In *People (DPP) v Shortt* (2002), the Court of Criminal Appeal appeared to relax its attitude to the granting of certificates under s.9. In this case, the applicant had been convicted of permitting and being aware of drug dealing on his commercial premises. He lodged an appeal under s.2 on the basis of newly discovered facts. The conviction was quashed and a certificate under s.9 issued in due course. A number of documents, tending not to support the chief prosecution witness, had been deliberately concealed by two gardaí. The Court of Criminal Appeal emphasised that it was concerned with whether a miscarriage of justice had taken place—it was not confined to the question of the defendant's actual innocence but concerned the administration of justice itself. The court made it clear that it was not finding the applicant innocent of actual involvement in the events. However, a certificate could be granted even if there had been involvement.

The meaning of the term "fact" under the Criminal Procedure Act was discussed in *People (DPP) v Callan* (2002). The applicant had been convicted of capital murder and sought to rely on s.2 to allow him to adduce evidence of new or newly discovered facts. He argued that he had not adduced a fact central to his defence at the trial or subsequent appeal because he was under pressure. He also admitted to committing perjury in the original trial. However, the Court of Criminal Appeal did not entertain the application pursuant to s.2. The applicant had decided to give evidence himself at the original trial and to put a perjured account of the incident before the court. There was no reasonable explanation of failure to adduce evidence of the fact at the time of the trial.

Further reading:

Bird, "Annotations to the Criminal Justice Act 1993 (1993)" I.C.L.S.A. 6–01 *et seq.*; Hutchinson, "Annotations to the Criminal Procedure Act 1993" (1993) I.C.L.S.A. 40-01 *et seq.*; O'Malley, "The First Prosecution Appeal Against Sentence" (1994) 4 I.C. L.J. 192.

3. Mental Element of Crimes

3.1 *Mens rea*

Mens rea is the Latin term for the mental element of a criminal offence, and loosely translates as "guilty mind". As a general rule, in order for a crime to be committed a person must have a culpable state of mind: a principle summed up in the maxim *actus non facit reum nisi mens sit rea*—an act does not make a person guilty unless the mind is also guilty.

The concept of *mens rea* is closely related to moral fault, and reflects a social judgment that a person should not be convicted of a crime unless he is morally blameworthy or otherwise at fault, and should not therefore be convicted unless he was culpable in bringing about the *actus reus* of the crime charged. If, for example, A inadvertently takes B's umbrella, believing it to be his own, then it cannot be said that A is at fault, and A should not be convicted of theft. It also reflects the deterrent purpose of the criminal law: if a person does not realise that they might be punished, convicting that person can have no deterrent effect.

However, different crimes have different *mens rea*; the law does not always require the same degree of moral culpability before a person can be convicted of a crime. Depending on the crime, the *mens rea* may be intentionally bringing about a result, being reckless whether a certain result occurs or negligently bringing about a certain result. Indeed, in some cases a person can be convicted of a crime where they cause a certain result irrespective of whether they were at fault. Consequently, we can identify five separate categories of *mens rea*. In descending order of moral culpability they are:

1. Intention
2. Recklessness
3. Criminal Negligence
4. Negligence
5. Strict or Absolute Liability

We will consider each type of *mens rea* separately.

3.1.1 Mens rea *required for each element of offence*

However, before we turn to the types of *mens rea*, it is important to note that we must show *mens rea* for each element of a criminal offence, although the type of *mens rea* required may vary as between the elements.

Consider the offence of capital murder, as discussed in *People (DPP) v Murray* (1977). The *actus reus* of that offence consisted of two parts: (i) the murder, (ii) of a garda acting in the course of his duty. Accordingly, the *mens rea* required for the offence also had two parts: (i) the necessary *mens rea* for murder (*i.e.* an intention to kill or cause serious injury), and (ii) either knowledge that the victim was a garda acting in the course of his duty or recklessness as to that fact. This case also illustrates that the *mens rea* may differ as between each element of the offence. In this case, while it was necessary that there was an *intention* to kill or cause serious injury, it was sufficient that the defendant was *reckless* as to the identity of the victim.

Similarly, if we consider the offence of damaging property with intent to endanger life (contrary to s.2(2) of the Criminal Damage Act, 1991), we again see that there must be *mens rea* as regards both elements of the offence: the damage must be intentional or reckless, and the endangerment must also be either intentional or reckless. If a person deliberately damages property in a way which does in fact endanger life, but they fail to appreciate that risk, then they must be acquitted of this offence, as they lack *mens rea* as regards the endangerment element.

3.2 Intention

3.2.1 Introduction

The concept of intention is important for the criminal law as it is the most culpable state of mind: an intentional killing is (usually) regarded with more severity than one which is merely reckless or accidental, and carries a higher penalty. Consequently, intention is the *mens rea* for some of the most serious criminal offences, including the crime of murder. However, despite the importance of this concept, it is nowhere defined in statute and the courts have struggled to find an acceptable definition.

The core meaning of intention is reasonably clear—a person intends particular results where they are his conscious aim, object or purpose; where he has "sought to bring them about, by making it the purpose of his acts that they should occur". (Law Commission of England and Wales, *Legislating the Criminal Code:Offences against the Person and General Principles* (Law Com. No. 218, 1993), para.7.5)

This core meaning can be considered in a different way. We can say that a person intends a result if he would regard himself as having failed if that result is not achieved. Suppose that A sets fire to a building knowing that B is inside. A clearly intends to kill B if he would consider his actions a failure if B survived. (Duff, *Intention, Agency and Criminal Liability* (1990)).

Defining intention becomes more difficult as we move away from this core meaning and towards more borderline cases. Before discussing these, it may be helpful to contrast intention with other concepts.

Intention does not necessarily mean to *desire* a result. If A is strapped for cash and decides to kill B and collect on the life insurance policy, then A intends to kill B, notwithstanding that A is genuinely fond of B and will miss B. We might not say that A desires B's death, except as a means to an end. Nevertheless, in most cases the intended result will also be the desired result.

Nor does intention require that the result is *likely to be achieved*. If A shoots at B intending to kill B, then if the bullet does in fact kill B the crime of murder is committed. This is so notwithstanding that A knows that he is a poor shot, was shooting from a great distance, and was exceptionally lucky to hit B.

Nor is intention the same as *motive*. Suppose that A murders B for no apparent reason. The absence of motive might make it more difficult to link the crime to A, but it remains a crime nevertheless. The position is summarised in the following quote of Dickson J. in *R. v Lewis* (1979):

> "Motive is no part of the crime and is legally irrelevant to criminal responsibility. It is not an essential element of the prosecution's case as a matter of law ... Proved absence of motive is always an important fact in favour of the accused ... Conversely, proved presence of motive may be an important factual ingredient in the [prosecution] case."

Finally, intention should not be confused with *premeditation*. Planning, forethought and preparation are all aspects which prove intention but they are not necessary for intention to exist. A spontaneous act or even an instinctive reaction is equally capable of being intentional.

3.2.2 The problem of indirect/oblique intention

Problems arise in cases of *indirect* or *oblique intention*: cases where an accused foresees that they might or will cause an outcome but does not have as their aim or purpose that outcome. For example, suppose that A has cargo on board an airplane and puts a bomb on board, intending to destroy the cargo in order to collect on an insurance policy. A knows that it is very likely that the bomb will kill all those on board. However, A does not wish them dead, and would be happy in the very unlikely event that they survived. Does A *intend* to kill the passengers and crew? Or is A merely *reckless* as to their deaths? Can we equate foresight of consequences with an intention to bring about those consequences?

(1) English law

The courts have had great difficulty with this issue and a series of cases before the English courts illustrate the problems caused.

In *Hyam v DPP* (1975) the defendant was a woman whose relationship with a man (Jones) had broken down, with Jones subsequently becoming engaged to another woman (Booth). The defendant went to Mrs. Booth's house late at night, poured petrol through the letterbox, stuffed newspaper through, and lit it. She had previously made sure that Jones was not there. The resulting fire caused the death of two of Mrs. Booth's children. Her defence was that she had set the fire only in order to frighten Mrs. Booth, and did not intend to cause death or grievous bodily harm. The jury were directed that the intention for murder was present if the defendant foresaw death or grievous bodily harm as a "highly probable" result of her actions, even if she did not aim at that result. On appeal, the House of Lords approved of this direction, effectively equating foresight of high probability with intention.

In *R. v Moloney* (1985), however, a very different result was reached. Here a man was killed by his stepson. After heavy drinking at a wedding anniversary, they played a drunken game with loaded shotguns to see who was quicker on the draw. The victim then taunted his stepson to pull the trigger, which he did, killing the victim. The stepson was charged with murder, but claimed that the game was "just a lark" and that he had no idea that firing the gun would injure his stepfather.

The jury were directed that the stepson had the necessary intention for murder if either (a) he desired to kill the victim whether or not he had foreseen that it would probably happen, or (b) he foresaw that his conduct was likely to kill or cause serious bodily harm, regardless of whether he desired to do so. However, the House of Lords held that such a direction was incorrect. Departing from *Hyam*, it held that foresight that a result was probable was not the same as intending that result. Instead, the question of foresight belonged not to the substantive law, but rather to the law of evidence. Consequently, the jury should be told that if a defendant foresaw that a result was "a natural consequence" of his actions then that was evidence from which the jury could properly *infer* that he intended that result.

Shortly afterwards, in *R. v Hancock and Shankland,* the House of Lords adopted yet another position. The events in this case took place during the bitter miners' strike in England. Two miners on strike attempted to intimidate "scab" workers by pushing concrete blocks from a bridge over the road along which the workers were driving with a police escort. One block hit the windscreen of a car, killing the driver. The defendants were charged with murder, and raised the defence that they did not intend to kill or cause serious injury, but to block the road and frighten the workers. The jury was directed in accordance with *R. v Moloney* that intent could be inferred if the defendants foresaw that death or serious injury was "a natural consequence" of their actions. However, this direction was found by the House of Lords to be inadequate, which held that the jury should also be referred to the issue of *probability,* and told that they can infer intention where a result is "a natural and *probable* consequence" of the defendant's actions. In addition, the jury should be told that the more probable the result, the more likely that it was intended by the defendant.

In *R. v Nedrick,* the Court of Appeal attempted to reconcile the effects of the previous decisions. The facts in this case were very similar to those in *Hyam v DPP* (1975). The defendant had poured paraffin through the letter box of a woman against whom he had a grudge and set it alight. The woman's child died in the fire. The jury was directed that the defendant had the necessary intention if he knew that it was "highly probable" that what he did would cause serious injury to somebody in the house. This direction was clearly incorrect in light of *Moloney*, which made it clear that foresight was *evidence* from which intention could be inferred, but was not sufficient intention in itself. Accordingly, his conviction was quashed by the Court of Appeal, which went on (*per* Lord Lane C.J.) to set out guidelines for dealing with these cases:

> "It may be advisable to explain first to the jury that a man may intend to achieve a certain result whilst at the same time not desiring it to come about.
>
> > 'A man who, at London Airport, boards a plane which he knows to be bound for Manchester, clearly intends to travel to Manchester, even though Manchester is the last place he wants to be and his motive for boarding the plane is simply to escape pursuit.' (quoting from the judgment of Lord Bridge in *R. v Moloney* (1985) at p.926.)
>
> When determining whether the defendant had the necessary intent, it may therefore be helpful for the jury to ask themselves two questions: (1) How probable was the consequence which resulted from the defendant's voluntary act? (2) Did he foresee that consequence?
>
> If he did not appreciate that death or serious harm was likely to result from his act, he cannot have intended to bring it about. If he did, but thought that the risk to which he was exposing the person killed was only slight, then it may be easy for the jury to conclude that he did not intend to bring about that result. On the other hand, if the jury are satisfied that at the material time the defendant recognised that death or serious harm would be virtually certain (barring some unforeseen intervention) to result from his voluntary act, then that is a fact from which they may find it easy to infer that he intended to kill or do serious bodily harm, even though he may not have had any desire to achieve that result:
>
> Where a man realises that it is for all practical purposes

> inevitable that his actions will result in death or serious harm,
> the inference may be irresistible that he intended that result,
> however little he may have desired or wished it to happen."
> (At p.3)

As a result of *Nedrick,* therefore, a formula was adopted whereby the jury were instructed that they could infer intention from foresight only where the defendant realised that the outcome was "virtually certain".

The House of Lords approved of the *Nedrick* formula soon afterwards in *R. v Woollin* (1999). In this case, the accused was charged with murdering his three-month-old son by throwing him on the ground and thereby fracturing his skull. It was agreed that he did not *desire* to cause serious bodily harm to the infant and so the issue was whether he nevertheless had an *intention* to cause serious bodily harm. The trial judge directed the jury that they could infer the necessary intention if they were satisfied that the defendant appreciated that by throwing his son he was creating a *substantial risk* of serious injury. The House of Lords, however, held that this direction was incorrect—the reference to "substantial risk" was broader than the *Nedrick* "virtual certainty" formula, and tended to blur the distinction between recklessness and murder.

Finally, the facts of *R. v Matthews* (2003) illustrate the application of the *Nedrick/Woollin* formula. Here the defendants attacked and robbed a young student, stealing his bank card. They were unable to take any money from his account, and they returned to him, forced him into a car, and drove him to a bridge. There they threw him into the river, despite his saying that he couldn't swim. He fell about 25 feet into the river and drowned. The defendants were charged with murder, and the trial judge directed the jury that they *must* find the necessary intention if they were satisfied that the defendants appreciated that it was virtually certain that the student would die as a result of their actions. On appeal, this direction was held to be incorrect: according to the Court of Appeal, under *Nedrick* and *Woollin*, a jury is *entitled* to find intention where there is foresight of virtual certainty, but is not *bound* to do so. Consequently, the trial judge had mistakenly presented a rule of evidence by which the jury *could* find intent as a rule of law by which the jury *must* find intent.

If we step back and attempt to summarise these (rather confusing) cases, we see that the English position has evolved substantially since *Hyam*. In that case, the House of Lords equated foresight of a highly probable result with intention. In *Moloney*, however, this approach was rejected and foresight became evidence from which the jury could *infer* intention. In addition, *Moloney* refined the standard of probability, by referring to a "natural consequence", rather than a "highly probable" result. *Hancock and Shankland* refined the standard of probability further, by requiring that the jury find a "natural *and probable* consequence" before they could infer intention. *Nedrick* and *Woollin* both seem to raise the standard of probability required still further, to require that a defendant realised that an outcome was "virtually certain" before the jury can find that they intended that outcome. However, as *Matthews* illustrates, this is a rule of evidence, not of law, and the jury are not bound to find intention even if they find that a defendant foresaw a consequence as virtually certain.

It is worth noting that this limitation of oblique intent to cases of "virtual certainty" results in quite a narrow test, and will result in many borderline cases being regarded as manslaughter rather than murder. Suppose, for example, that A plants a bomb in a building hoping to destroy it. He telephones a warning, resulting in the building being evacuated. However, a member of the bomb disposal squad is killed while trying to defuse the bomb. In this case, it is not A's purpose to kill, and it would be difficult to say that he foresaw the death as a "virtuallly certain" outcome. Consequently, it would seem that A lacks the necessary intention for murder, and Lord Steyn in *Woollin* has acknowledged that such a case would be likely one of manslaughter, not murder.

(2) Irish law

Surprisingly, perhaps, the Irish courts have not yet had to grapple with the question of oblique or indirect intention in any detail. While some Irish cases do mention this issue, they generally do so only tangentially. For example, in *People (DPP) v Murray*, Walsh J. took quite a restrictive view of intention, drawing a sharp distinction between a desired outcome, on the one hand, and foresight of consequences, on the other. If followed, this distinction would seem to rule out oblique intention:

> "To intend to murder, or to cause serious injury ... is to have in mind a fixed purpose to reach that desired objective.

> Therefore, the state of mind of the accused person must have been not only that he foresaw but also willed the possible consequences of his conduct."

The most important Irish case in this area is the decision of the Court of Criminal Appeal in *People (DPP) v Douglas & Hayes* (1985). In that case, the defendants in the course of a robbery opened fire on a Garda car, hitting it with three bullets. They were charged with shooting with intent to commit murder, and were convicted by the Special Criminal Court on the basis that:

> "[I]t must have been apparent that the natural consequence of the shooting would be to cause death or serious personal injury to one or more of the guards in the car and secondly, the person who fired the shots did so with reckless disregard of the risk of killing a guard and in the legal sense, he had the intent to commit murder. It is not necessary to constitute the intent to kill that that should be the desired outcome of what was done. It is sufficient if it is a likely outcome and that the act is done with reckless disregard of that outcome."

This approach of the Special Criminal Court echoed the judgment of the House of Lords in *Hyam*, inasmuch as it held that foresight of a "likely" outcome was sufficient intention. On appeal, however, the Court of Criminal Appeal quashed the convictions. The court held that foresight and recklessness could not be equated with intention, but went on to say that foresight of consequences could constitute evidence from which an inference of intention could be drawn. *Per* McWilliam J.:

> "[E]vidence of the fact that a reasonable man would have foreseen that the natural and probable consequence of the acts of an accused was to cause death and evidence of the fact that the accused was reckless as to whether his acts would cause death or not is evidence from which an inference of intent to cause death may or should be drawn, but the court must consider whether either or both of these facts do establish beyond a reasonable doubt an actual intention to cause death.

[…]

Although it may be accepted that it is not necessary to constitute an intent to kill that that should be the desired outcome of what was done, a reckless disregard of the likely outcome of the acts performed is not of itself proof of intent to kill but is only one of the facts to be considered in deciding whether the correct inference is that the accused had an actual intent to kill."

(3) Irish Law and the presumption of intention

Irish law recognises a presumption of intention: it is presumed that a person intends the natural and probable consequences of their actions. This presumption applies to all offences and, as regards murder, has also been put in statutory form by s.4(2) of the Criminal Justice Act 1964. However, this presumption is rebuttable, and it does not affect the burden of proof, which remains with the prosecution at all times. The Court of Criminal Appeal, in *People (DPP) v McBride* (1996), has explained (*per* Blayney J.) the way in which the presumption operates as follows:

"The jury ought to have been told that while there was a presumption that the applicant intended the natural and probable consequences of his act, this was only a presumption and could be rebutted, [and] one of the things that they had to consider was whether the State had satisfied them beyond reasonable doubt that the presumption had not been rebutted."

People (DPP) v Hull (1996) gives an example of the use of the presumption. In that case the defendant was a middle-aged married man who was infatuated with a young co-worker. She repelled his advances and subsequently found a boyfriend in Galway. The defendant went to Galway and knocked on the door of the boyfriend. After an argument, the boyfriend returned inside, at which point the defendant fired a shotgun through the door, killing the boyfriend. The defendant was charged with murder, but argued that the firing was accidental, and as such he lacked an intention to kill or cause serious injury. The trial judge directed the jury that under s.4 their task was:

> "Firstly, to decide whether the natural and probable consequence of the applicant firing at the door was to cause death or serious injury, and secondly, if they decided this in the affirmative, to go on to consider whether the firing had been deliberate or accidental."

The defendant was convicted of murder and, on appeal, argued that the trial judge had not correctly directed the jury on the presumption of intention. This argument was, however, rejected by the Court of Criminal Appeal. *Per* Blayney J.:

> "The Court considers that this was a reasonable way to put the matter to the jury. If they decided that the natural and probable consequences of firing at the door was to cause death or serious injury, then the presumption arose that this was the applicant's intention, but the question remained as to whether that presumption had been rebutted and this had to be decided by considering whether the firing had been deliberate or accidental. So, in instructing the jury to acquit the applicant if the firing was accidental, the learned trial judge was in effect correctly telling them that, if they took this view, it meant that the presumption that the applicant intended to cause death or serious injury had been rebutted and so he was entitled to be acquitted."

3.2.3 Reform of intention as the mens rea for murder?

We have seen above that "intention" as a form of *mens rea* has presented a number of difficulties, almost always in the context of murder trials. Consequently, it can be argued that the problems associated with intention could be resolved by widening the *mens rea* of murder to specifically include cases of oblique intention or reckless killings.

The Law Reform Commission has recently put forward such a proposal in its *Consultation Paper on Homicide: The Mental Element in Murder* (L.R.C. 17 2001). The key argument behind the Consultation Paper is that the *mens rea* in respect of murder is too narrow, so that murder is an under-inclusive offence with many particularly serious killings falling outside its ambit. This point is made at p.44:

> "Confining the *mens rea* of murder to intention runs the risk of excluding from the definition of murder many killings which ought to be properly punishable as murder. A defendant who, while not intending to kill, is prepared to act with reckless disregard for the loss of human life, and consciously ignores even a high probability that death will result, would not be guilty of murder if death did in fact result under the current English rule. To take the much quoted example, a terrorist who plants a bomb in a public building, not intending to kill but merely to damage property, but who is nonetheless aware of a high probability of death resulting, would not be guilty of murder if death resulted on a *Woollin*-type definition of intention. Such a result seems unsatisfactory. As McAuley and McCutcheon point out: 'the presence or absence of intention in the English sense should not be allowed to trump the underlying moral issue of whether the defendant deserves to be branded as a murderer ...'."

The Law Reform Commission has, therefore, proposed that statute widen the *mens rea* for murder to include not just intentional killings, but also those carried out recklessly in circumstances which "manifest an extreme indifference to human life", a widening which would encompass most if not all cases of oblique intention, and which would mitigate judicial difficulty in directing juries as to the meaning of intention.

This proposal has, however, been criticised. Bacik ("'If It Ain't Broke'—A Critical View of the Law Reform Commission Consultation Paper on Homicide: The Mental Element in Murder" (2002) 12 I.C.L.J. 6) argues, *inter alia*, that it improperly assumes that English authorities on intention would be followed in this jurisdiction, fails to consider whether cases of oblique intention could be dealt with under the s. 4(2) presumption, would blur the distinction between murder and manslaughter, and would make the category of murder unduly broad. Instead, she suggests that many of the concerns raised by the Law Reform Commission would be better addressed either by abolition of the mandatory life sentence for murder, or by merger of murder and manslaughter into a single offence of homicide. In relation to these last two points, see further the chapter on homicide, where mandatory sentencing and the murder/manslaughter distinction are discussed in more detail.

3.3 Recklessness

3.3.1 Introduction

Recklessness exists where a person does not intend to bring about a particular result, but runs an unjustifiable risk of bringing that result about. By unjustifiable we mean a risk without good cause, having regard to the gravity of the risk, the state of mind of the defendant, and the social utility of the activity involved.

For example, a surgeon who carries out an essential operation involving a risk of the patient dying as a result is taking a substantial risk, but one which is justifiable in the circumstances. By way of contrast, in *Chief Constable of Avon and Somerset Constabulary v Shimmen* (1987), the defendant accidentally broke a shop window while showing off his martial arts skills to his friends. In this situation, the desire to show off clearly did not justify even a slight risk that he might misjudge matters and hit the window.

This form of *mens rea* is common in Irish law and applies to a wide range of crimes, including the offences of assault, assault causing harm, causing serious harm and endangerment under the Non-Fatal Offences Against the Person Act 1997, and the offence of damaging property under the Criminal Damage Act 1991.

3.3.2 Is recklessness subjective or objective in nature?

Suppose that a person creates an unjustifiable risk in circumstances where it is not clear whether he is aware of that risk. If he is aware, then he is clearly reckless. But suppose that, despite the risk being obvious, he fails to recognise it, and is blissfully unaware of the risk his conduct poses. Is that person reckless? In other words, do we describe somebody as reckless only if they are aware of a risk (a subjective approach), or will failure to recognise an obvious risk suffice (an objective approach)?

(1) Irish law

Irish law has generally taken the subjective approach: for an accused to be found to be reckless as to a particular risk, he must have foreseen the risk but proceeded with his conduct regardless. The leading Irish case is *People (DPP) v Murray* (1977). In this case, the two accused were husband and wife, and jointly held up a bank at gunpoint. They fled, but were pursued by an off-duty garda, who was out of uniform. The wife shot and killed him. Both were charged with capital murder, which was, so far as relevant, committed where a person murdered a garda acting in the course of his duty. Their defence was that the necessary *mens rea* was not present for all the elements of the offence: although there may have been an intention to kill or cause serious injury, they did not know that their pursuer was a garda and they therefore lacked *mens rea* as to an essential part of the crime.

The Supreme Court, in dealing with this argument, accepted the general principle that *mens rea* must be shown in respect of each component of an offence. In particular, it noted that the offence was meant to have a deterrent effect, which was lacking where a person was not aware that his intended victim was a garda. Equally, it pointed out that a much more severe penalty was attached to capital murder, and it was unfair and arbitrary to impose that higher penalty on the basis of a circumstance which the defendant knew nothing about.

It was argued for the prosecution that the necessary *mens rea* was present if the wife *was or should have been aware* that the pursuer might be a garda—that is, that objective recklessness would suffice. The Supreme Court, however, rejected objective recklessness. It held that Irish criminal law had, at its core, the determination of moral blameworthiness, which could only be decided based on the subjective state of mind of the person charged. *Per* Walsh J. at p.386:

> "In this context objective recklessness is really constructive knowledge: and constructive knowledge has no place in our criminal system in establishing intent."

The Supreme Court, therefore, required that a defendant be subjectively reckless as to the identity of their victim before they could be convicted of capital murder. As to what was meant by subjective recklessness, Henchy J. adopted the following definition from the American Law Institute Model Penal Code (s 2.02(2)(c)):

> "A person acts recklessly with respect to a material element

of an offence when he consciously disregards a substantial and unjustifiable risk that the material element exists or will result from his conduct. The risk must be of such a nature and degree that, considering the nature and purpose of the actor's conduct and the circumstances known to him, its disregard involves culpability of high degree."

This result was widely accepted in the Irish legal system, on the grounds of fairness:

"All modern common law systems reject a criminal law which imposes blame on the basis of what a reasonable man would have known, intended or suspected in the situation under analysis.". (Charleton, *Criminal Law - Cases and Materials* (Butterworths, 1992))

In addition, we will see that this preference for subjective tests over objective tests is a motif which repeats itself throughout Irish criminal law, particularly in the field of defences.

(2) The English experience

English law has had rather more difficulty with the concept of recklessness. For many years it was considered that recklessness could only exist where a defendant perceived a risk. The leading authority was *R. v Cunningham* (1957). In this case, the defendant stole money from a gas meter, fracturing the gas pipes and causing gas to leak into a neighbouring house, where it asphyxiated a person asleep in bed. The defendant was charged with unlawfully and maliciously causing the victim to take a noxious thing, thereby endangering her life, contrary to s.23 of the Offences Against the Person Act 1863. The trial judge, directing the jury, stated that it was enough that the defendant acted "wickedly" without requiring that he should be aware of the danger he was creating. The Court of Appeal, quashing the conviction, held that this direction was incorrect. Malice could not be equated with a vague concept of "wickedness", but rather referred to either intention or recklessness, and the court went on to describe the latter as meaning that the defendant foresaw that a particular kind of harm might be done and yet went on to take that risk.

This so-called *Cunningham* recklessness was, however, departed from in two House of Lords decisions in 1981. The first of these was *R. v Caldwell*. In that case, the defendant set fire to a hotel, avenging a supposed grievance against the proprietor. He was charged with arson, for which the *mens rea* was intention to endanger the life of another or recklessness as to whether the life of another would be endangered. His defence was that he was so drunk at the time that he did not appreciate the risk he was creating.

In dealing with this defence, it was necessary for the House of Lords to decide whether a person could be said to be reckless where he fails to recognise a risk. The House of Lords held that a person in those circumstances was reckless. *Per* Lord Diplock (at p.353):

> "Reckless ... is an ordinary English word. It had not by [the date of the legislation] become a term of legal art with some more limited esoteric meaning than that which it bore in ordinary speech, - a meaning which surely includes not only deciding to ignore a risk of harmful consequences resulting from one's acts that one has recognised as existing, but also failing to give any thought to whether or not there is any such risk in circumstances where, if any thought was given to the matter, it would be obvious that there was."

In reaching this conclusion, Lord Diplock was influenced by a moral judgment that a person who failed to appreciate an "obvious risk" should not be allowed to escape liability, by concern over practical difficulties of proving the defendant's state of mind, and by some disapproval of the use of drunkenness as a defence in this way. He stated (at p.352):

> "Neither state of mind [i.e. appreciating or failing to appreciate a risk] seems to me to be less blameworthy than the other; but if the difference between the two constituted the distinction between what does and what does not in legal theory amount to a guilty state of mind ... it would not be a practicable distinction for use in a trial by jury. The only person who knows what the accused's mental processes were is the accused himself ... If the accused gives evidence that because of his rage, excitement or drunkenness the risk of particular harmful consequences of his acts simply did not occur to him, a jury would find it hard to be satisfied beyond reasonable doubt that his true mental process was [that he recognised a risk]."

Accordingly, *R. v Caldwell* adopted a standard of objective recklessness, at least in respect of obvious risks. Immediately after this decision, the House of Lords decision in *R. v Lawrence* (1981) confirmed the application of this standard of recklessness to the crime of reckless driving.

These decisions were almost immediately heavily criticised as a substantial departure from the law as it had previously stood in both England and numerous other common law countries, as being difficult to apply in practice, and as having the possibility of leading to substantial unfairness. One obvious risk of injustice arose where a risk might be obvious to a reasonable person, but was not obvious to the particular accused by reason of age, disability, lack of experience or understanding.

For example, in *Elliott v C. (a minor)* (1983), a 14-year-old girl set fire to a shed by pouring white spirit onto the floor and throwing a lighted match onto the spirit. She had given no thought to any possibility of the shed being destroyed as a result and, as she suffered from a slight mental handicap, would not have appreciated the risk even it she had considered the matter. She was, nonetheless, convicted, the Court of Appeal taking the view that whether a risk was obvious was to be judged by the standards of a "reasonably prudent person", not whether it was obvious to this particular accused.

These criticisms were eventually heeded by the House of Lords in *R. v G. and R.* (2004), which departed from *R. v Caldwell* and returned to a test of subjective recklessness. In this case, two young boys (aged 11 and 12) entered the back yard of a shop in the early hours of the morning. Finding bundles of newspapers, they set fire to some newspapers and threw them under a plastic dustbin. After leaving the yard, the fire spread to the dustbin and thence to the shop itself and adjoining buildings, causing approximately £1m worth of damage. They were charged with arson in respect of the damage to the shop, and convicted on the basis that their conduct created a risk which would have been obvious to an adult, notwithstanding that neither of them appreciated that there was any risk of the fire spreading.

On appeal, the House of Lords considered that *Caldwell* recklessness was wrong in principle. *Per* Lord Bingham:

"First ... conviction of serious crime should depend on proof not simply that the defendant caused (by act or omission) an injurious result to another but that his state of mind when so acting was culpable ... It is clearly blameworthy to take an obvious and significant risk of causing injury to another. But it is not clearly blameworthy to do something involving a risk of injury to another if ... one genuinely does not perceive the risk. Such a person may fairly be accused of stupidity or lack of imagination, but neither of those failings should expose him to conviction of serious crime or the risk of punishment. Secondly, the present case shows, more clearly than any other reported case since *R v Caldwell*, that [*Caldwell* recklessness] is capable of leading to obvious unfairness ... It is neither moral nor just to convict a defendant (least of all a child) on the strength of what someone else would have apprehended if the defendant himself had no such apprehension." (At paras.32–33)

Instead, the House of Lords held that a person acts recklessly when he is aware of a risk and it is in the circumstances (as known to him) unreasonable to take the risk. The House of Lords also rejected the argument, central to *Caldwell*, that a subjective test of recklessness would lead to difficulties in proving a defendant's state of mind and thus to unjustified acquittals. *Per* Lord Bingham:

"There is no reason to doubt the common sense which tribunals of fact bring to their task. In a contested case based on intention, the defendant rarely admits intending the injurious result in question, but the tribunal of fact will readily infer such an intention, in a proper case, from all the circumstances and probabilities and evidence of what the defendant did and said at the time. Similarly with recklessness: it is not to be supposed that the tribunal of fact will accept a defendant's assertion that he never thought of a certain risk when all the circumstances and probabilities and evidence of what he did and said at the time show that he did or must have done." (At para.39)

3.4 Criminal negligence

This particular class of *mens rea* is confined to the offence of manslaughter. Essentially, this class of *mens rea* is objective recklessness as defined in *People (DPP) v Murray* (1977), that is, a very high class of negligence. This form of *mens rea* is discussed in detail under the topic of manslaughter.

3.5 Negligence

This type of *men rea* corresponds to the civil standard of negligence in the law of tort, and refers to conduct which falls below the standard of a reasonable and prudent man. An example of a crime which has this *mens rea* is driving without due care and attention contrary to s.52 of the Road Traffic Act 1961. While negligence overlaps somewhat with recklessness, it is important to remember that the test of negligence is entirely objective: it is not necessary to show that the defendant was aware that his conduct fell below the necessary standard.

3.6 Strict or absolute liability

3.6.1 Introduction

Strict liability (sometimes described as absolute liability) exists where there is an absolute prohibition on the doing of a particular act, and where a person who voluntarily does that act is subject to punishment regardless of any further intention, negligence or other fault on their part. Liability is described as "strict" or "absolute" because the prosecution does not have to prove *mens rea* as to one or more of the elements of the *actus reus*.

For example, in *Pharmaceutical Society of Great Britain v Storkwain Ltd.* (1986), the defendant firm of pharmacists supplied drugs in good faith under a prescription which turned out to be a forgery. They were convicted of the offence of supplying drugs without a prescription, notwithstanding that they reasonably believed the prescription to be valid.

Strict liability offences raise obvious concerns about the fairness of punishing a person who is not morally blameworthy. In particular, it can be said that it is unjust to punish a person for an outcome where they have taken all reasonable steps to prevent that outcome. Strict liability offences are also criticised on the basis that they improperly impose the stigma of a criminal conviction on a person who may be blameless.

As against that, however, arguments can be made in favour of strict liability. One of the most common is that strict liability is necessary for the protection of the public. Many strict liability offences apply to areas (such as transport, or the supply of food or drugs) which have innate risks. Strict liability, so the argument goes, will encourage persons in those areas to take every possible step to avoid those risks. A related point is sometimes made that a person who chooses to engage in activities which they know to be risky must be prepared to take the consequences should those risks become reality.

Another commonly made argument is that offences of strict liability are not "truly criminal". Such offences are sometimes described as "quasi-criminal" or "public welfare offences" and are distinguished from "true crimes" on the basis that they carry minor punishments and little or no social stigma.

Finally, one pragmatic argument in favour of strict liability is that it is sometimes necessary in order to make a particular law enforceable, by easing what would otherwise be insurmountable difficulties of proof. An example given by one author is that speeding cases would be almost impossible to prove if the prosecution had to prove that the motorist knew that he was speeding. (Michaels, "Constitutional Innocence", (1999) 112 *Harvard Law Review* 828.)

3.6.2 Strict liability v absolute liability

There is a tendency for the terms "strict liability" and "absolute liability" to be used interchangeably in this jurisdiction, particularly in older cases. However, it is important to note that elsewhere, Canada in particular, the two terms have distinct meanings. In *R. v City of Sault St Marie* (1978), the Canadian Supreme Court held that the law should distinguish between offences of absolute liability, where it is not open to the accused to exculpate himself by showing that he was not at fault, and offences of strict liability, where there is no necessity for the prosecution to prove *mens rea*, but where it will be open to the accused to establish a defence by proving that he took all reasonable care. This approach effectively mitigates the harsh effects of the doctrine by allowing a defendant to establish a defence of reasonable diligence, while at the same time easing enforceability by relieving the prosecution of the need to establish *mens rea*, and shifting the burden of proof to the person in the best position to prove that due care was taken.

3.6.3 Determining whether an offence is one of strict liability

Almost all offences of strict liability are statutory offences, the only common law examples being the anomalous crimes of public nuisance and criminal libel. Consequently, in deciding whether an offence is one of strict liability, our starting point must be to look at the language of the statute itself. If the statute itself deals with the matter by specifying what *mens rea*, if any, is required, then there is no difficulty. Unfortunately, it is common for legislation to be silent on the question, which requires the courts to consider whether to interpret the offence as one of strict liability or to read in a *mens rea* requirement.

Our starting point is that there is a strong presumption in favour of *mens rea*. *Per* Lord Reid in *Sweet v Parsley* (1970) (at p.148–149):

> "[T]here has for centuries been a presumption that Parliament did not intend to make criminals of persons who were in no way blameworthy in what they did. That means that, whenever a section is silent as to *mens rea*, there is a presumption that, in order to give effect to the will of Parliament, we must read in words appropriate to require *mens rea* ... *mens rea* is an essential element of every offence unless some reason can be found for holding that that is not necessary."

This presumption can, however, be rebutted. Lord Scarman, in the leading case of *Gammon Ltd v A-G of Hong Kong* (1985), sets out five principles to be considered in deciding whether it has been rebutted:

1. There is a presumption of law that *mens rea* is required before a person can be held guilty of a criminal offence;

2. The presumption is particularly strong where the offence is "truly criminal" in character;

3. The presumption applies to statutory offences, and can be displaced only if this is clearly, or by necessary implication, the effect of the statute;

4. The only situation in which the presumption can be displaced is where the statute is concerned with an issue of social concern, and public safety is such an issue; and

5. Even where a statute is concerned with such an issue, the presumption of *mens rea* stands unless it can also be shown that the creation of strict liability will be

> effective to promote the objects of the statute by encouraging greater vigilance to prevent the commission of the prohibited act.

From these principles, it can be seen that the factors to be taken into account include whether the offence is "truly criminal", whether the statute involves a matter of "public concern" such as public safety, and whether strict liability is necessary to "promote the objects of the statute". Later cases, discussed below, have also added other factors such as the severity of the punishment and whether a social stigma attaches to the crime.

The Irish case of *McAdam v Dublin United Tramways Co. Ltd* (1929) adopts similar reasoning. Here the defendant company was charged with overloading a tram. The defendant claimed that it had done all that it possibly could to prevent its conductors from allowing overloading to take place. Could the defendant rely on this absence of fault or *mens rea* ? No. *Per* Sullivan P., (at p.333):

> "... the prohibitions contained in that regulation are absolute. The object of the regulation is to protect the public against the danger that may result from the overloading of an omnibus, and that object could be achieved only by absolutely prohibiting the carriage in any omnibus of more than a limited number of passengers, and by penalising the owner for any breach of such [a] prohibition, irrespective of his knowledge of such breach.

> The acts in this case are not in any real sense criminal, but in the public interest they are prohibited under a penalty. Having regard to that fact, and to the terms of the regulation and the object it had in view, I am of opinion that *mens rea* is not an essential ingredient in the offences charged against the defendants."

Another well-known example is *R. v Prince* (1875–1877). The accused was charged with abducting an unmarried girl under the age of 16 out of the possession of her father. The girl was 14, but the accused honestly and reasonably believed her to be 18. This was held to be irrelevant: the crime was created for the protection of young girls, and, the court held, this statutory purpose would be frustrated if the absence of intention was accepted as a defence.

More recently, the Irish courts have been confronted with several cases in respect of strict liability. The first is *Maguire v Shannon Regional Fisheries Board* (1994). This concerned the Fisheries (Consolidation) Act 1959, which provides that any person who causes to fall into any waters any deleterious matter shall be guilty of an offence. The defendant operated a piggery near a river; a pipe fractured, resulting in the pollution of the river. The defendant was found to have taken all reasonable steps to prevent any accident of this sort, and to prevent pollution of the river once the accident had taken place (by using temporary dams, sandbags, *etc.*). The question presented was whether the offence was one of strict liability.

In deciding that it was, Lynch J. approved of *Gammon Ltd v A-G of Hong Kong* (1985) and held as follows: (1) As a rule, *mens rea* is required for every offence. (2) However, this presumption could be rebutted where, as here, the offence created was regulatory rather than truly criminal. (3) In such situations, creating strict liability would promote the policy of the underlying legislation, while if *mens rea* was required, the policy of the legislation would be undermined, since it would be very difficult to establish that an offence had been committed. Consequently, the offence was one of strict liability. (4) Despite the absence of any fault on the part of the accused, he had caused the pollution by virtue of the running of his piggery, and the accused was therefore guilty of the offence.

The later case of *Shannon Regional Fisheries Board v Cavan County Council* (1996) is on the same point. Here the Supreme Court had to deal with a situation where Cavan County Council had caused sewage to enter the water. Despite a statutory duty to provide sewage treatment, the County Council had not been provided with sufficient funds from central government to carry out that duty and was therefore unable to process the sewage, which it discharged in its untreated form. The County Council was charged under the Fisheries Acts. In the High Court, the decision in *Maguire v Shannon Regional Fisheries Board* (1994) was followed, and the offence found to be one of strict liability. (Although Murphy J. did point out that the degree of fault which was found to be present would determine what penalty, if any, was appropriate.) This was accepted by the majority in the Supreme Court, which also found on the facts that the County Council was in fact acting with *mens rea* in that it was deliberately discharging untreated sewage.

However, the dissenting judgment of Keane J. is particularly interesting. He outlined the historical development of offences of strict liability in "public welfare" or "regulatory" areas of the law, and went on to question whether it is appropriate that this particular fisheries offence, which carries a maximum penalty of £25,000 or five years' imprisonment, or both, should be held to be one of strict liability. In particular, he questioned whether to make such a serious crime into one of strict liability would be compatible with the constitutional guarantee of trial in due course of law. He accepted that not all crimes need have some moral culpability attached to them, but rejected the argument that there was no need for moral culpability in the present case as this sort of crime carries no real stigma. Instead, he argued, such an offence would in fact carry a social stigma, making it unjust for a person to be convicted without any blame on their part.

Keane J. also pointed out that to allow a defence of taking all reasonable care would encourage greater vigilance on the part of potential offenders. To deny such a defence would in effect force the accused to act at his peril and would be a disincentive to maintaining standards. Since the expenditure of time and money on improving standards would not be acknowledged by the courts then some people in the position of the accused might not bother to take adequate precautions.

Keane J. referred to the position taken in Canadian law as set out in *R. v City of Sault Ste. Marie* (1978), and proposed that the middle-ground established in that case should be adopted in Irish law, holding (at p.291) that:

> "the law should recognise that there is an intermediate range of offences, of which this is one, in which, while full proof of *mens rea* is not required and the proof of the prohibited act *prima facie* imports the commission of the offence, the accused may escape liability by proving that he took reasonable care."

He went on to argue that the County Council did in fact take all reasonable care to prevent the discharge of sewage and should not, therefore, be found guilty of the crime.

In *Director of Corporate Enforcement v Gannon* (2002), the High Court held that the offence of acting as an auditor to a company while disqualified is one of strict liability. In reaching this conclusion, O'Caoimh J. relied on the fact that the penalties involved were "relatively limited", and as such the offence could not be described as "truly criminal". He also ruled that the issue was one of social concern, in respect of which strict liability would encourage greater vigilance.

In *DPP v Behan* (2003), the High Court had to consider whether the offence of refusal or failure to give a specimen of breath (under s.13 of the Road Traffic Act 1994) should be interpreted as one of strict liability. In this case, s.13 created a requirement to give two specimens of breath, but s.23 went on to provide a defence whereby a defendant could avoid liability by satisfying the court that there was a special or substantial reason for the refusal or failure to give specimens. In holding that the offence was one of strict liability, the court was particularly influenced by two factors. First, the offence was one of "failing" or "refusing" to give a specimen, and while the word "refuse" might involve an element of intention, a "failure" could take place without any intention. Second, the court was influenced by the fact that s.23 created a limited right of defence, which it took to indicate a legislative decision to rule out other defences such as the lack of *mens rea*.

3.6.4 The constitutional status of strict liability offences

We have already noted that in *Shannon Regional Fisheries Board v Cavan County Council* (1996) Keane J., in his dissenting judgment, raised a query as to the constitutionality of strict liability offences, particularly where an offence does not permit a defence of reasonable care to be established. That analysis drew on Canadian jurisprudence, where it has been held that absolute liability crimes may be invalid where there is the possibility of imprisonment.

The leading Canadian case is *Reference re Section 94(2) of the Motor Vehicle Act* (1985). That case concerned an offence of driving without a valid driver's license, which carried a minimum sentence of imprisonment, and which was an offence of absolute liability, irrespective of any knowledge on the part of the driver, and with no defence of reasonable diligence. It was held by the Canadian Supreme Court that a law with the potential of convicting a person who was in no way at fault offends the principles of fundamental fairness and violates a person's right to liberty under s.7 of the

Canadian Charter of Rights and Freedoms if imprisonment is available as a penalty.

In this jurisdiction, there has, until recently, been no comparable constitutional challenge to the principle of strict liability. However, in *Coleman, Molloy and Grace v Ireland (2004/2005)* such a challenge is currently being made. That case concerns a number of applicants charged with sexual offences against an underage girl. The particular offences charged were sexual assault contrary to s.2 of the Criminal Law (Rape) Amendment Act 1990 (as amended by s.37 of the Sex Offenders Act 2001), and unlawful carnal knowledge of a girl under the age of 15 contrary to s.1(1) of the Criminal Law (Amendment) Act 1935. In interpreting these offences, the Supreme Court held that *mens rea* is required in respect of sexual assault, but not in respect of unlawful carnal knowledge, where the legislation made it clear that even a bona fide mistake as to age was not a good defence. In this case, however, it is also alleged that the 1935 Act, by making the offence one of strict liability, is inconsistent with the Constitution. At the time of writing, the Supreme Court has not yet heard argument on the constitutionality point, but this is expected to take place shortly.

3.7 The doctrine of transferred malice

Suppose A intends to shoot and kill B, but misses and hits and kills C. Has murder been committed? A did not intend to kill C, but the so-called doctrine of transferred malice will apply. This doctrine provides that where A has the *mens rea* required for a particular crime, and carries out the *actus reus* of that crime, then he will be found to have committed that crime, notwithstanding that the final result is in fact unintended, particularly with regard to the identity of the victim. An example is the case of *R. v Latimer* (1886–1887). In this case, A hit B with his belt; the belt glanced off B and hit C, cutting her severely. This ricochet was held by the jury to be accidental and unforeseeable; nevertheless, the accused was found guilty of unlawfully wounding C.

However, the doctrine is limited. It applies only where the *actus reus* and the *mens rea* are of the same crime. If A shoots at a window, misses, and kills a person who unknown to him is standing close by, then he has not committed murder: the *actus reus* of murder and the *mens rea* of a crime against property do not together add up to the crime of murder. Similarly, in *R. v Pembliton* (1874) the defendant was acquitted of intentional damage to property in a situation where he threw a stone intending to hit a person, but missed and broke a pub window instead.

It should be pointed out that the doctrine has been put on a statutory footing, in respect of murder, by virtue of s.4(1) of the Criminal Justice Act 1964: "Where a person kills another unlawfully the killing shall not be murder unless the accused person intended to kill, or cause serious injury to, some person, *whether the person actually killed or not.*" (emphasis added)

Further reading:

McAleese, "Just What is Recklessness?" (1981) D.U.L.J. 29; Newman, "Reforming the Mental Element of Murder" (1995) 5 I.C.L.J. 194; Law Reform Commission, *Consultation Paper on Homicide: The Mental Element of Murder* (L.R.C. CP17–2001); Bacik, "'If It Ain't Broke'— A Critical View of the Law Reform Commission Consultation Paper on Homicide: The Mental Element in Murder" (2002) 12 I.C.L.J. 6; Kaveny, "Inferring Intention from Foresight" (2004) 120 *Law Quarterly Review* 81; Stannard, "Murder, Intention and the Interference of Intention" (1999) 34 *Irish Jurist (ns)* 202.

4. ACTION ELEMENT OF CRIMES

4.1 Introduction

The *actus reus* is the action element of a crime. It may be contrasted with the *mens rea*, the mental element. For example, a person cannot be convicted of murder unless he has the required mental state (intention to kill or cause serious personal injury) and has caused the death of his victim (the *actus reus*) A person who intends to kill or cause serious personal injury, yet does nothing but daydream about it, will not be guilty of any crime.

There must be an *actus reus* before any crime can be committed. With crimes of strict liability a defendant may be convicted on the basis of *actus reus* alone but the converse is never true: a person can never be convicted on the basis of *mens rea* alone. In *R. v Deller* (1952), the accused was charged with obtaining a car by false pretences. He represented that he owned the vehicle he had traded in for the car but, in fact, he believed that a hire purchase company owned it. This turned out to be untrue as, due to an error in registering the hire purchase agreement, the accused was legally the owner of the vehicle. Deller was acquitted as, although he had the necessary *mens rea*, he was actually telling the truth when he claimed that the car was free from any encumbrances. There was no *actus reus* even though he had believed he was committing a crime.

4.2 *Actus reus* as a state of affairs

The *actus reus* does not always amount to an action. In certain circumstances it may be defined as a state of affairs not including an act at all. This is illustrated by the case of *Larsonneur* (1933) in which the accused was convicted of "being found" in a particular situation. An alien who had been refused leave to land, she was convicted under the Aliens Order 1920 of being found in the United Kingdom even though the police had brought her from Ireland against her will. Larsonneur had initially been required to leave the United Kingdom by a certain date and had travelled to the Irish Free State. She was deported from Ireland and brought to Holyhead in the custody of the Irish police. It was held that the woman had "in circumstances which are perfectly immaterial as far as this appeal is concerned, come back to Holyhead."

A similar result was reached in *Winzar v Chief Constable of Kent* (1983). Winzar was taken to hospital but was found to be intoxicated and asked to leave. Eventually the police were called and he was removed from the hospital to the public highway outside. Once there, he was charged by the police of being found drunk in the highway and was subsequently convicted. The court rationalised as follows: "Suppose a person was found as being drunk in a restaurant ... and was asked to leave ... he would walk out the door of the restaurant and would be in a public place ... of his own volition ... because he had responded to a request ... if [he] refused to leave ... he would not be there of his own volition ... It would be nonsense if one were to say that the man who responded to the plea to leave could be found drunk in a public place or in a highway, whereas the man who had been compelled to leave could not."

Larsonneur and *Winzar* have been criticised as being contrary to the general principle that the action element of a crime must be voluntary. For example, a conviction for assault cannot be sustained if the accused's hand was forcibly grabbed by another and used to strike a third party. Voluntariness is an essential attribute of the *actus reus*. If the act is done without any control by the mind, such as a spasm or reflex action, then the accused may be able to rely on the defence of automatism. *Larsonneur* has been rejected by the Supreme Court of New Zealand in *Kilbride v Lake* (1962). In that case, a driver was charged with failing to display a current warrant of fitness on his motor car. It was accepted that the warrant had disappeared from his vehicle while he was absent from it. In finding the accused not guilty of the offence, Woodhouse J. remarked (at p.593):

"... it is a cardinal principle that ... a person cannot be made criminally responsible for an act or omission unless it was done or omitted in circumstances where there was some other course open to him. If this condition is absent, any act or omission must be involuntary or unconscious, or unrelated to the forbidden event in any causal sense regarded by the law as involving responsibility."

4.3 *Actus reus* and *mens rea* must coincide

In looking at the *actus reus*, it is important to note that a crime is committed only when the *actus reus* and the *mens rea* exist at the same time. Suppose a husband decides to kill his wife by poisoning her at dinner that evening. However, that afternoon his careless driving causes a crash in which his wife, a passenger in the car, is killed. We have the *actus reus* of murder: he caused the death of his wife. We have the *mens rea* of murder: he intended to kill her. However, this is clearly not a case of murder, since the two did not coincide.

This can be seen from the case of *R. v Scott* (1967), an Australian case in which the defendant escaped from jail after suffering a blow to the head. He claimed that he did not know what he was doing until two days after he left the jail, at which point he decided not to give himself up. Charged with escape from lawful custody, his defence was that he was incapable of forming the necessary *mens rea* at the time of the escape, although he later formed the intent to remain at large. This defence was accepted by the Supreme Court of Victoria, which held (*per* Gillard J.) that "[t]he two elements necessary to constitute the crime were never brought together. An unlawful action and an evil intention never concurred".

However, where the *actus reus* is an ongoing act, then it is sufficient if the *mens rea* coincides with part of the *actus reus*: it need not coincide with the whole. This principle was illustrated by *R. v Thabo Meli* (1954). A group of men decided to commit a murder and make it appear to be an accident. They struck the victim on the head and, presuming he was dead, then threw him off a cliff. The victim was not dead when thrown off the cliff but died of exposure some time later. The accused argued that there had been no coincidence of *actus reus* and *mens rea*—they had *mens rea* when they struck him but there had been no *actus reus* as he had merely been stunned. However, when the *actus reus* occurred there had been no *mens rea* as they had believed him to be already dead. This argument was rejected as the events amounted to one single transaction and could not be divided up in the manner argued by the defendants.

A further example is the case of *Fagan v Metropolitan Police Commissioner* (1969). In that case, the defendant accidentally drove his car onto the foot of a policeman, and then deliberately left it there. Charged with assault, his defence was that his conduct was complete before he formed any intention However, this argument was rejected. His conduct was treated by the court as continuous, and the crime was committed when he decided to *leave* the car on the policeman's foot. *R. v Kaitamaki* (1985) applied similar reasoning in the case of rape. The defendant became aware that the woman was not consenting after intercourse had begun. It was held that sexual intercourse is a continuing act and, if the defendant became aware of lack of consent at any stage during intercourse and did not withdraw, he would be guilty of the offence of rape.

4.4 The *actus reus* may be an omission

Under most circumstances, the criminal law does not punish failure to act. Suppose A is on a beach and sees B struggling in the sea. A stands by and watches B drown, despite the fact that A is a strong swimmer and could easily rescue B without any danger to himself. A is not guilty of a crime, however morally reprehensible his conduct is. As Hawkins J. put it in *R. v Paine* (1880):

> "If I see a man, who is not under my charge, taking up a tumbler of poison, I should not become guilty of any crime by not stopping him. I am under no legal obligation to protect a stranger."

However, there are many situations where the law recognises a positive duty to act.

4.4.1 Duty of parents towards their children

The most obvious example is the duty of parents towards their children. If a parent deliberately fails to feed a child, intending to cause death or serious injury, then the crime of murder is committed if the child dies. In the case of *R. v Bubb* (1851), the defendant was an aunt of a child and was *in loco parentis*. She was charged with causing the child's death by deliberate neglect. It was held that the aunt, on those facts, had a duty to care for the child.

4.4.2 Duty voluntarily assumed

The law has recognised several further categories where such a duty arises. One is where a duty has been voluntarily assumed. In *R. v Stone & Dobinson* (1977), a man of low intelligence and his cohabiting girlfriend kept his elderly sister as a lodger. She refused to eat and lived in her room in appalling conditions of her own making. The girlfriend attempted to wash her when she became bedridden and made inadequate efforts to summon medical help. The defendants had decided to contact the deceased's doctor but she had refused to tell them his name. The defendants walked a considerable distance in their search for the doctor but it transpired that they had walked to the wrong village. Efforts were made to contact a local doctor but the neighbour who volunteered to do the telephoning (as the defendants were incapable of managing the instrument themselves) was unsuccessful. The deceased's clothes had to be cut off in an effort to wash her and her back was covered with sores. Her bedclothes and mattress were soiled and sodden. When the sister died soon afterwards it was discovered that her body was ulcerated and there were maggots in the ulcers. Evidence was given that she could have been saved had she received the appropriate medical attention three weeks before her death. The defendants were convicted of manslaughter by criminal negligence because they had accepted responsibility for the deceased and owed a duty to help her, even though her death had been largely caused by her own behaviour. The court also emphasised that the deceased was a blood relative of Stone's.

R. v Instan (1893) was an earlier case decided along similar lines. The defendant lived with her elderly aunt who developed gangrene in her leg as she was nearing death. She was unable to fend for herself and the only person aware of her predicament was the defendant. The defendant failed to provide her with any food for 12 days and she was charged with her aunt's manslaughter. The court held that the defendant had a duty to feed her aunt as "it was only through the instrumentality of the prisoner that the deceased could get the food."

R. v Gibbins and Proctor (1918) is an example of voluntary assumption of a duty and also of parental responsibility. The wife of Gibbins had left him and he began to live with Proctor. The couple allowed Gibbins's seven-year-old daughter to starve to death while ensuring that his other children and those of Proctor were well provided for. Both defendants were convicted of manslaughter. Gibbins argued that he had given money to Proctor to feed the children and therefore bore no responsibility for his daughter's death. However, the court held that he had lived in the same household as the deceased and could not have failed to notice her plight. Proctor argued that she had no duty towards the child, but this argument failed as she was deemed to have assumed responsibility for her welfare and had in fact excluded the real mother from her life.

In the Australian case of *R. v Taktak* (1988), the principle of voluntary assumption of risk was applied to find the defendant guilty of manslaughter. He had hired a prostitute for a party but left her for a while. On his return he became aware that the prostitute was unconscious as a result of an overdose. The defendant took her away from the party and attempted to revive her. By the time he decided to summon medical help, however, she was already dead. It was held that he had assumed responsibility for her by removing her from the party, thereby preventing others from potentially coming to her aid.

4.4.3 Creation of a danger

If a person creates a danger there may be a duty to act to minimise the dangerous situation. In *R. v Miller* (1983), a tramp set fire accidentally to a mattress by dropping a cigarette. He failed to take steps to put out the fire and was found to have been under a duty to do so and was convicted of arson.

A recent English decision illustrates that an omission can amount to the *actus reus* of an assault. In *DPP v Santana-Bermudez* (2004), the defendant injured a police officer by allowing her to search him, knowing that he had hypodermic needles in his pockets. The police officer asked him if he had removed all the items from his pocket himself and he replied "Yes". She then asked him if he was sure he did not have any needles or sharps on him and he said he did not. The police officer was stuck by a needle. She noticed that the defendant had a smirk on his face when this occurred. It was held that when someone, by act or word or a combination of the two, created a danger and thereby exposed another to a reasonably foreseeable risk of injury which materialized, there was an evidential basis for the *actus reus* of an assault. However, the prosecution still had to prove an intention to assault or appropriate recklessness. In this case the defendant had given the police officer a dishonest answer when questioned about his pockets and had thereby exposed her to a reasonably foreseeable risk of injury.

4.4.4 Duty under contract

A positive duty to act can also be created under contract or by virtue of one's status as a public official. In *R. v Pittwood* (1902), a gatekeeper who failed to close the gate at a level-crossing, resulting in a death, was found guilty of manslaughter on the basis of his obligations under contract. *R. v Dytham* (1979) was a case where a policeman failed to intervene in a brawl to come to the aid of the deceased. The deceased had been ejected from a nightclub and violently kicked to death in the vicinity of the policeman. The defendant observed what was taking place and, when the assault was over, merely adjusted his helmet, said he was going off duty and drove away. He was found guilty of misconduct of an officer of justice in that he willfully omitted to take any steps to preserve the peace.

4.4.5 Statutory duties to act

Certain statutory offences also create a positive duty to act. Section 49 of the Road Traffic Act 1961 provides that a motorist who has been brought to a Garda station and who fails to provide a specimen of breath when properly requested to do so is guilty of an offence. Section 13 of the Criminal Justice Act 1984 places an obligation on a person who has been released on bail in criminal proceedings to appear before a court in accordance with his recognisance. A further example is s.9 of the Offences Against the State (Amendment) Act 1998, which creates the offence of withholding information which might be of material assistance in preventing the commission by any other person of a serious offence.

4.5 *Actus reus* and causation

Before a defendant can be found to be criminally liable, it must be shown that his conduct caused the prohibited outcome (for example, death in the case of homicide). This can be tested by asking whether the outcome would have happened "but for" what the defendant did. An alternative, narrower test is whether the defendant's action was an "operating and substantial" cause of the consequence. In *R. v White* (1910), the defendant was charged with the murder of his mother, by putting cyanide into her drink. However, medical evidence established that she died of heart failure after drinking the drink, but before the poison could have had any effect. Consequently, the defendant could not be said to have caused her death. He was, however, convicted of her attempted murder.

It should be noted that the "eggshell skull rule" applies in the criminal law as well as the law of torts. This holds that an accused must take his victim as he finds him. If the victim has a particular weakness (such as a very thin skull) which makes him far more susceptible to injury than the average person, this cannot be used to reduce the liability of the accused. For example, if a victim dies from an assault that would not have killed the average person, the victim's vulnerability is legally irrelevant.

4.5.1 Break in the chain of causation? / Novus actus interveniens

Suppose that A is stabbed by B with a knife. A is rushed to hospital where she is advised that a blood transfusion is necessary to save her life. She refuses the transfusion on religious grounds and dies. Is A guilty of murder? These were the facts of *R. v Blaue* (1975), and in that case it was held that B was guilty of murder. B was not entitled to argue that the religious beliefs of A were unreasonable; those who use violence on other people must take their victims as they find them. If the stab wound was still an operating and substantial cause of death, then death was still a consequence of the wound. Only if another cause was so overwhelming as to make the wound merely part of the history would it be possible to say that death had not been caused by the original action.

Compare *R. v Jordan* (1956). That case involved a stabbing, from which the victim was making a good recovery. However, the victim died from pneumonia as a result of being given an antibiotic to which he was intolerant, in circumstances where it was grossly negligent for him to be given this treatment. The conviction of the accused for murder was quashed; the Court of Appeal accepted that the direct and immediate cause of death was the treatment the victim received. The medical treatment had caused the death at a time when the original wound had almost completely healed.

However, *Jordan* was distinguished in *R. v Smith* (1959). A soldier stabbed another soldier during a barrack-room fight. While being carried to a doctor the injured man was dropped twice. He was subsequently given incorrect medical treatment and died. Evidence was given that had the correct medical treatment been given there was a 75 per cent chance that he would have survived. The conviction for murder was upheld despite arguments that there had been no less than three breaks in the chain of causation. The court held that the test was whether the original wound was still an operating and substantial cause at the time of death, notwithstanding that some other cause also operated.

The same issue was later addressed in *R. v Malcherek and Steel* (1981). The victim's injuries required treatment on a life support machine, but a decision was made by doctors to switch the machine off when it became apparent that recovery was impossible. The accused argued that disconnecting the life support machine had caused death and that this had broken the chain of causation. Again the "operating and substantial cause at the time of death" test was applied by the court and the accused's argument failed.

In *R. v Cheshire* (1991), the victim of a shooting developed respiratory problems following surgery. His medical team failed to diagnose the cause of the problem and he died in hospital two months after the shooting. The court accepted that medical negligence was the immediate cause of death but held that the defendant's acts could be regarded as causing the death, even though they were not the sole or main cause, if they contributed significantly to it. The medical negligence would only relieve the defendant of responsibility for death if it was so independent of his acts and so potent in causing death that the defendant's actions could be regarded as insignificant.

Can a victim of crime break the chain of causation by his or her own actions? This was the issue in *R. v Roberts* (1972). A young girl took a lift in the defendant's car and injured herself by jumping out of the moving vehicle. She claimed she had been escaping the defendant's sexual advances. The question was whether he was responsible for the injuries sustained. The court set out the test to be applied as follows: whether the injuries were the natural result of what the alleged assailant said and did, in the sense that they were something that could reasonably have been foreseen as a consequence of what he was doing or saying: "If the victim does something so daft ... or so unexpected ... not that this particular assailant did not actually foresee it but that no reasonable man could be expected to foresee it, then it is only in a very remote and unreal sense a consequence of his assault ... [it] breaks the chain of causation between the assault and the harm or injury."

This precedent was followed in *R. v Corbett* (1996). The defendant was convicted of the manslaughter of a mentally handicapped man who was also an alcoholic. Both men had spent the day drinking, and during an argument later in the evening the defendant began to head-butt the deceased. The deceased ran away and fell into a gutter where he was struck by a car and killed. The court applied *Roberts* to hold that only a daft reaction on the part of a victim, which would be beyond the foreseeable range of consequences of what the defendant had done, would suffice to break the chain of causation.

5. HOMICIDE

5.1 Homicide

The term homicide is a general description for crimes which result in death. There are a number of such crimes in Irish law; however, for the purposes of this discussion, the primary ones which will be dealt with are murder, manslaughter, infanticide and suicide.

5.1.1 Year and a day rule

One element that was common to all the homicide crimes was the year and a day rule. Until recently, for murder, manslaughter, infanticide or even suicide to be committed, the victim had to die within a year and a day from the infliction of the injury.

This rule had a complicated origin, but served at least two purposes. First, it was adopted at a time when medical science was rudimentary, so that it was difficult or impossible to tell if deaths after longer intervals were in fact caused by the original injury. Second, it protected defendants by ensuring that if they injured someone, they would not be at risk of prosecution for murder indefinitely into the future. (This was particularly important if the defendant had already been convicted in respect of the original injury, raising the issue of double jeopardy—that is, being punished twice in respect of the same crime.)

The rule, however, became increasingly outdated. The advance of medical science meant that causation could be determined more accurately. In addition, the rule failed to recognise that modern medicine might well keep a victim alive in a coma or with severe brain damage for a number of years before death finally occurs, or before life support is finally removed. Similarly, after a syringe or needle attack, a victim may be healthy for years before developing AIDS. Should a defendant responsible for the death of such a victim escape conviction for murder due to an arbitrary time limit?

These considerations led to the repeal of the rule by s.38 of the Criminal Justice Act 1999, and there is now no requirement that the victim die within a year and a day—a prosecution can be brought no matter what the interval between the injury and the death, so long as it can be shown that one caused the other.

However, s.38 has itself been criticised. Carey points out that in England, the equivalent Law Reform (Year and a Day Rule) Act

1996 abolished the rule but substituted some procedural safeguards for a defendant. These safeguards require the special consent of the Attorney General before a prosecution is brought where the victim dies more than three years after the injury, or where the defendant has already been convicted of an offence arising out of the same facts. The Irish reform includes no such safeguards, leading Carey to argue that there is a risk of unfairness to defendants, who might be exposed to trial in cases where causation is unclear, or who might be exposed to a risk of double jeopardy.

Further Reading:

Carey, "The Year and a Day Rule in Homicide" (2001) 11 I.C.L.J. 5

5.2 Murder

The crime of murder has never been put on a purely statutory basis. Instead, it is a hybrid crime, with some parts deriving from common law and other parts governed by statute. Consequently, we must first examine the common law definition of murder before going on to consider the statutory modifications.

The elements of murder at common law were defined in a famous passage from Coke's *Institutes of the Law of England (1640)*:

> "Murder is when a man of sound memory, and of the age of discretion, unlawfully killeth within any county of the realm, any reasonable creature in *rerum natura*, under the King's Peace, with malice aforethought either expressed by the party or implied by law, so as the party wounded or hurt, etc. die of the wound or hurt, etc. within a year and a day after the same."

We will look at each element of this definition separately.

(a) "of sound memory, and of the age of discretion"

This simply means that the defendant must be unable to raise either the defence of insanity or the defence of infancy.

(b) "unlawfully killeth"

The killing must be unlawful to constitute murder. Examples of lawful killing would include a reasonable and proportionate killing in self-defence (considered further in Chapter 10) and, until recently, the infliction of the death penalty.

(c) "within any county of the realm"

In order for a court to try a person for murder, that court must have jurisdiction. At common law, this meant that the crime must have taken place within the geographic boundaries of the state; a crime which took place abroad was not the concern of the Irish courts. While this generally remains true today, Art.29.8 of the Constitution allows the Oireachtas to legislate with extra-territorial effect, and in the case of some particularly serious crimes the Irish courts can try a defendant regardless of where the crime is alleged to have taken place. Murder is one such crime, and s.9 of the Offences Against the Person Act 1861 allows an Irish court to try an Irish citizen for murder or manslaughter irrespective of where the murder is alleged to have been committed.

(d) "any reasonable creature in rerum natura*"*

For a murder charge to be brought, the victim must be a live human being. Suppose, for example, that A shoots B as B lies in bed. Unknown to A, B has already died in his sleep. In that case A could not be guilty of murder.

There are some difficulties in the case of unborn children. At common law, the view was taken that life begins at birth, so murder could not be committed until the child was born alive and completely outside the mother (though the umbilical cord need not be cut). Until the child had an existence which was separate from and independent of the mother, it was not regarded as an independent life. (*Hutty* (1953)). Consequently, killings of unborn children did not amount to murder.

It is not clear, though, whether this common law approach has survived the Eighth Amendment to the Constitution, which acknowledges (in Article 40.3.3°) the right to life of the unborn. Charleton, McDermott and Bolger argue (*Criminal Law* (1999), p.517) that the Eighth Amendment guarantees "[e]qual treatment of unborn and born life" so that the crime of murder would now extend to unborn children also.

Whether or not this argument is correct, there are other possible charges available in this situation. Abortion is a crime in Ireland, prohibited by ss.58 and 59 of the Offences Against the Person Act

1861, unless it is necessary to avoid a risk to the life of the mother (*X v Attorney General* (1992). Abortion carries a possible life sentence.

In addition, it may be possible to prosecute in respect of injuries inflicted *prior to birth*. Suppose that A assaults a pregnant woman B, causing injuries to her unborn child C. C is born alive, but dies soon afterwards from the injuries sustained while in the womb. Can A be prosecuted for the death of C? In a number of cases where this situation has arisen, it has been held that A can be prosecuted, notwithstanding that C did not have an independent life at the time of the attack.

This point was accepted in *Senior* (1832), where a midwife was convicted of manslaughter having negligently injured a child during delivery who died soon after birth. It was also applied in *R. v Kwok Chak Ming* (1963). Here, a pregnant woman was stabbed several times during an attack. Her unborn child was injured by these stab wounds, was born alive nevertheless, but died shortly after from these injuries. In that case, the Hong Kong Court of Appeal held that the attacker could be convicted of either murder or manslaughter, depending on whether he had the intention necessary for each crime.

More recently, the issue came before the House of Lords in *Attorney General's Reference No. 3 of 1994* (1998). In this case, M was a young woman who was between 22 and 24 weeks pregnant. Her partner, and the father of the child, stabbed her several times with a kitchen knife. This injured her severely, and also injured her unborn child and caused her to give birth prematurely. The child died 121 days later from complications associated with the premature birth but not connected directly to the stabbing. The defendant had already pleaded guilty to the offence of attacking M, but when the child died he was charged again, this time with the murder of the child.

The House of Lords approved of *Senior*, and held (*per* Lord Goff) that:

> "Violence towards a foetus which results in harm suffered after the baby has been born alive can give rise to criminal responsibility even if the harm would not have been criminal (apart from statute) if it had been suffered in utero."

However, the House of Lords also had to consider the issue of *mens rea*. In this case, it appeared that the intention of the defendant was to injure the mother, not the unborn child, so that the defendant lacked the necessary intention for murder as regards the child. Consequently, the defendant could not be found guilty of murder unless either the mother and unborn child could be treated as a single victim for the purpose of *mens rea*, or the doctrine of transferred malice applied. The House of Lords rejected both arguments, however, holding that the unborn child was a unique organism, distinct from the mother, and that it would be stretching the doctrine of transferred malice too far to apply it in these circumstances.

This decision will make it very difficult to prosecute for murder in these situations, since it requires that the defendant intends to harm not only the mother but also the unborn child. It does not, however, prevent such a defendant from being prosecuted for manslaughter, since the *mens rea* for manslaughter does not require an intention directed towards a particular individual.

(e) "under the King's Peace"

This phrase indicates that the killing of enemy aliens during a time of war under battle conditions will not amount to murder.

(f) "with malice aforethought"

This refers to the *mens rea* for the crime of murder. At common law the *mens rea* was originally described as being "malice aforethought". This is now, however, a misleading phrase. It suggests that malice (*i.e.* spite, hatred, or ill-will) should be present, and also suggests that there should be planning or premeditation. As the common law developed, both requirements were dropped, so that eventually neither malice nor premeditation were required for murder. A mercy killing would amount to murder, despite the absence of what we would ordinarily understand by "malice"; similarly, an impulsive attack would amount to murder, despite the lack of premeditation.

The common law *mens rea* was changed in Ireland by the Criminal Justice Act 1964. The *mens rea* required for murder is now set out in s.4, which provides:

> "(1) Where a person kills another unlawfully the killing shall not be murder unless the accused *intended to kill, or cause serious injury* to, some person, whether the person actually killed or not.
>
> 2) The accused person shall be presumed to have intended

> the natural and probable consequences of his con-
> duct; but this presumption may be rebutted." (empha-
> sis added.)

Consequently, in order for murder to be established, it must be shown that the defendant intended to kill or cause serious injury. Any lesser intention will not suffice. For example, suppose that A slaps B, intending merely to bruise him. B, however, suffers from a rare medical condition, and dies soon after as a result. In this case, the defendant should not be convicted of murder, since he lacked an intention to kill or to cause *serious* injury.

On the other hand, if, as in *People (DPP) v Doohan* (2002), A inflicted a "punishment beating" on B, intending that B would receive "a couple of broken arms or legs", this would be sufficient to show an intention to cause serious injury, and a death resulting from such a beating would be murder, notwithstanding that there might not be an intention to cause death.

(g) "either expressed by the party or implied by law"

At common law, the *mens rea* for murder was extremely wide. In addition to an (express) intention to kill or cause serious harm, the necessary intention was also deemed to be present (*i.e.* implied) if the defendant killed (even accidentally) while committing any felony. This was known as the doctrine of constructive malice, or the felony murder rule. For example, suppose that A, while carrying out a robbery, accidentally drove into and killed B. Under the felony murder rule, this would amount to the crime of murder, notwithstanding the lack of any intention to harm B.

The reasoning behind this harsh rule was summarised by Wrottesley J. in *R. v Jarmain* (1946):

> "We think that the object and scope of this branch of the law is at least this, that he who uses violent measures in the commission of a felony involving personal violence, does so at his own risk and is guilty of murder if those violent measures result even inadvertently in the death of the victim."

This rule was criticised on the basis that it could lead to results which were arbitrary and disproportionate. It also conflicted with the general modern view that persons ought not to be punished for outcomes which they neither intended or foresaw. In many jurisdictions it has now been repealed, and in Ireland it was abolished by s.4(1) of the Criminal Justice Act 1964, which we have already dealt with.

(h) "so as the party wounded or hurt, etc. die of the wound or hurt, etc. within a year and a day after the same"

We have already considered the year and a day rule above.

5.2.1 Attempted murder

The *mens rea* for attempted murder differs from that for murder. Murder is a result crime, in that it can only be committed where the result of the defendant's conduct is death. In order to convict a person of attempted murder, it must be shown that they intended to bring about that result—*i.e.* that they intended to kill. An intention to cause serious injury is not enough. See *People (DPP) v Douglas and Hayes* (1985).

For example, suppose that A fires a gun at B, intending to wound but not to kill. If A hits, and kills B, the crime of murder is committed. If A misses, however, he will be guilty of an attempt to cause serious harm, but not attempted murder.

This point is considered further in Chapter 13 in relation to the *mens rea* required for attempts generally.

5.2.2 Aggravated murder

Until 1964, a verdict of murder carried a mandatory death sentence. By that stage, however, public sentiment was turning against the death penalty, and the death sentence was generally commuted to a sentence of life imprisonment. The Criminal Justice Act 1964 recognised this shift by abolishing the death penalty for most killings, but retaining an offence of capital murder punishable by death as a deterrent in respect of certain, particularly reprehensible killings.

The most well known of these is the killing of a member of the Garda Síochána acting in the course of their duty. As was pointed out by Henchy J. in *People (DPP) v Murray* (1977), the purpose behind this offence was "to give an added protection to the members of an unarmed police force by making death the penalty for murdering one of its members on duty." The crime also extended, however, to other killings, such as the murder of foreign leaders or diplomats.

Since then, the death penalty has been abolished entirely by s.1 of the Criminal Justice Act 1990. However, that Act still recognises the need to treat particular killings as being especially serious, and therefore creates (in s.3) an offence of aggravated murder.

This is essentially identical to the former crime of capital murder and applies to:

(a) the murder of a member of the Garda Síochána acting in the course of his duty;

(b) the murder of a prison officer acting in the course of his duty;

(c) murder in the course of specified offences under the Offences Against the State Act 1939, or in the course of the activities of an unlawful organisation under that Act;

(d) the murder of the head of a foreign state, or a member of the government of a foreign state, or a diplomat of a foreign state, when the murder is committed within the State, for a political motive.

Section 3(2)(a) deals with the *mens rea* required for aggravated murder, and puts in legislative form the holding in *People (DPP) v Murray* (1977):

"a person shall not be convicted ... unless it is proved that he knew of the existence of each ingredient of the offence ... or was reckless as to whether or not that ingredient existed."

In summary, therefore, the offence of aggravated murder is the offence of murder, with the aggravating factor of the identity of the victim, or the subversive nature of the activities being carried out, together with the fact that the defendant knew or was reckless as to the existence of the aggravating factor.

Aggravated murder, like murder, carries a mandatory life sentence. In addition, however, aggravated murder requires (ss.4 and 5) that the defendant must serve at least 40 years before becoming eligible for remission, commutation of sentence or temporary release.

5.2.3 Murder and the defences

There is a complicated interaction between the crime of murder and the various defences. Each defence will be dealt with in more detail in Chapters 11 and 12, but it should be noted at this point that two

defences are *unavailable* to a charge of murder (duress and
necessity), while two other defences are available *only* to a charge
of murder, and operate to reduce the crime to manslaughter
(provocation and excessive self defence).

5.2.4 Punishment for murder

Murder carries a mandatory sentence of imprisonment for life. In
practice, however, life does not mean life. It is open to the Minister
for Justice, advised by the Parole Board, to grant temporary or early
release to life sentence prisoners. After seven years, a life sentence
prisoner may have his situation reviewed by the Parole Board, which
will interview the prisoner and make a recommendation to the
Minister. In deciding whether to recommend temporary or early
release, the Parole Board will take into account factors including:

    (1) whether the prisoner's release would constitute a
          threat to the community;

    (2) whether it is reasonable to grant early/temporary
          release in view of the nature and circumstances of
          the offence committed;

    (3) whether the offender warrants release, taking into
          account his or her behaviour in custody;

    (4) whether there are there any compelling compassionate
          grounds which merit special consideration

    (5) whether the offender has engaged constructively with
          the prison-based therapeutic services to combat his/
          her offending behaviour.

The role of the Board is advisory, and the final decision on release is
the Minister's. However, in the majority of cases to date (over 70
per cent) the Minister has implemented the recommendations of the
Board in full or in part.

    The average time served before release was (as of March 1999)
between 8 and 12 years. (Charleton, Dermott and Bolger, *Criminal
Law* (1999), p.542). More recently, though, this has been increasing.
The current Minister (Michael McDowell TD, SC) and the chairman
of the Parole Board have both indicated that, even where there are
no aggravating factors, murderers should expect to serve a term of
at least 12 to 14 years before being considered for release.

(O'Donnell, "When has a prisoner been punished enough?" *Irish Times*, July 14, 2004.) The Minister has also indicated that murders in the course of other violent crime such as robbery, gangland activity or drug crime will see a minimum of 15 to 20 years imprisonment before release is considered.

Where early release is granted, it is always conditional and on licence. Restrictions may be imposed, such as a requirement to report regularly to a particular Garda station, or to live at a particular address. If these restrictions are breached, or the released prisoner is thought to present a risk, they can be rearrested and taken back into custody.

Academic commentators (such as O'Malley, "Sentencing murderers: the case for relocating discretion" (1995) *Irish Criminal Law Journal* 31) have raised doubts about the appropriateness of a mandatory sentence for the crime of murder. O'Malley points out that it is very difficult to plan a programme of rehabilitation for a prisoner whose release date is so uncertain; that a mandatory sentence is a blunt instrument when applied to difficult cases such as so-called mercy killings or those who kill under duress; and that vesting discretion in the executive arguably violates the constitutional vision of the separation of powers. On this last point, it has also been said that vesting this discretion in a politician may lead to popular sentiment controlling the early release system, with decisions being made for electoral advantage rather than on the merits.

Mandatory life sentences have been abolished in several Australian states. In England, both the House of Lords Select Committee on Murder and Life Imprisonment and the Penal Reform Trust Committee have recommended that the mandatory life sentence for murder should be replaced by determinate sentencing. In this jurisdiction, the call for reform has also been joined by a number of judges, including the former Chief Justice, Keane C.J., who has suggested that the mandatory life sentence for murder might be replaced by a system where judges would decide the appropriate sentence for murderers. The Law Reform Commission has also taken a position against the mandatory sentence for murder, suggesting in its 1996 Report on Sentencing that the trial judge should be given a discretion.

The issue of the mandatory life sentence for murder ties in with the question of whether we should retain the distinction between murder and manslaughter, which we will consider next.

5.2.5 *The murder/manslaughter distinction*

In addition to the debate over sentencing for murder, there is a debate over whether the law should merge both murder and manslaughter into a single offence of unlawful killing. Suggestions of a merger are not new. In *Hyam v DPP* (1975), Lord Kilbrandon said:

> "There does not appear to be any good reason why the crimes of murder and manslaughter should not both be abolished, and the single crime of unlawful homicide substituted; one case will differ from another in gravity, and that can be taken care of by variation of sentences downwards from life imprisonment. It is no longer true, if ever it were true, to say that murder as we now define it is necessarily the most heinous example of unlawful homicide."

Proponents of a merger argue that the distinction between murder and manslaughter is often arbitrary and unclear, and that a less serious murder might well deserve to be treated more leniently than a more serious case of manslaughter. (Bacik, "'If It Ain't Broke' — A Critical View of the Law Reform Commission Consultation Paper on Homicide: The Mental Element in Murder" (2002) 12 *Irish Criminal Law Journal* 6).

Proponents also argue that there would be practical benefits. Carney J. has noted that in the overwhelming majority of murder trials, the defence accepts that the accused unlawfully killed the deceased and would be willing to plead to manslaughter. However, defendants are unwilling to plead to murder because of its mandatory life sentence. He argues that since:

> "the unlawful killing of the deceased by the accused is scarcely ever in issue suggests that if the crimes of murder and manslaughter were merged in a crime to be known as unlawful homicide ... the contested murder trial might become a rarity ... There would be no reason why there should not be a plea of guilty in almost every case."

Carney J. goes on to argue that this would have significant benefits in clearing backlogs before the criminal courts and creating substantial savings. He also suggests that a desirable side effect would be to spare the relatives of victims "the disappointment and trauma occasioned to them by a manslaughter only verdict", suggesting that relatives feel that a finding of manslaughter means that they have not "got justice". (Carney, Decriminalising Murder? NUI Galway Faculty of Law 2 Law CPS 2003.)

The Law Reform Commission, on the other hand, has recently recommended against abolishing the distinction. In its *Consultation Paper on Homicide: The Mental Element in Murder* (2001), the Commission argued that the law should distinguish between more serious and less serious killings, so that a merged offence would "lump together into a single category the most cold-blooded killers with the least blameworthy manslaughters". The Commission took the view that murder is popularly understood as the most serious crime, and carries a unique stigma which emphasises the gravity of the offence and may also have deterrent value. The Commission also expressed concern that abolishing the distinction would effectively shift the centre of gravity of homicide trials to the sentencing stage, marginalising the role of the jury. Finally, the Commission noted that many of the difficulties associated with the distinction could be dealt with by means other than abolition, including the removal of the mandatory life sentence for murder.

The current Minister has made similar points in response to Carney J.:

"The suggestion that amalgamating the crimes of murder and manslaughter into a crime of homicide would lead to more pleas of 'guilty' thereby saving court time ignores several fundamental problems. To take away from juries the function of deciding whether a crime of homicide was intentional but to allow a judge alone to impose radically different sentences by reference to a judge-only determination of the same factual issue decision might be convenient but would be very doubtful in constitutional terms. The question of intention is a central question of fact which must surely be left to juries. Otherwise trial by jury in homicide cases would be reduced to simply deciding the identity of the culprit and causation. Pleas of guilty under such a system would be followed by hugely lengthy hearings on sentencing in which the accused, once convicted, would be 'on the back foot' disputing the issue of intention. Instead of solving a problem, we would be just moving it around." (Address to the First Edward O'Donnell McDevitt Annual Symposium—"Sentencing in Ireland" on February 28, 2004.)

5.3 Suicide

5.3.1. Legality of suicide

Suicide itself is no longer a crime, having been decriminalised by s.2(1) of the Criminal Law (Suicide) Act 1993, a piece of legislation which finally recognises the absurdity of criminalising conduct which, by definition, leaves the offender beyond the jurisdiction of any court. This reform of the law is somewhat belated, coming more than 30 years after the Suicide Act 1961, which decriminalised suicide in England.

5.3.2 Suicide pacts and assisted suicide

However, the decriminalising of suicide does not entirely remove the criminal law from the field of voluntary decisions to die: there are still difficulties when more than one person is involved. It is still murder to kill another intentionally, notwithstanding that the killing was done at the request and with the consent of that person. Consent is not a defence to murder. If, therefore, a doctor administers a fatal dose of morphine, with the intention of killing, that doctor is guilty of murder, notwithstanding that the fatal dose was administered at the request of the patient.

This rule of law has harsh results in the area of suicide pacts. Suppose A and B both decide to commit suicide, with each agreeing to inject the other with a fatal drug. They carry out their plan, but only B dies. A is found in time and an antidote administered. In this jurisdiction, A is guilty of murder, notwithstanding the surrounding circumstances. By comparison, in England s.4(1) of the Homicide Act 1957 recognises a lesser offence in this situation by providing that:

> "It shall be manslaughter, and shall not be murder, for a person acting in pursuance of a suicide pact between him and another to kill the other or be a party to the other killing himself or being killed by a third party."

The position is different if A merely supplies B with the means by which B can kill himself. Suppose, for example, that A purchases drugs for B, knowing that B intends to take an overdose. In these circumstances, it would not be appropriate to charge A with murder or manslaughter, since it cannot be said that his act caused the death of B. The act which causes the death of B is the act of B himself, not the act of A. There is an intervening decision on B's part, breaking the chain of causation.

Nor, in these circumstances, would A face any criminal liability as an accessory under s.7 of the Criminal Law Act 1997, as suicide is no longer a crime. (Section 7 is limited to the case of a person who aids, abets, counsels or procures the commission of *any crime*.)

Section 2(2) of the Criminal Law (Suicide) Act 1993 anticipates this situation by creating an offence of assisted suicide:

> "A person who aids, abets, counsels or procures the suicide of another, or an attempt by another to commit suicide, shall be guilty of an offence and shall be liable on conviction on indictment to imprisonment for a term not exceeding fourteen years."

Since the terminology used in this section is identical to that used in s.7 of the 1997 Act, case law on what constitutes aiding, abetting, counseling or procuring under s.7 would also be relevant in this context.

There are also, however, authorities specifically relating to the case of suicide. In *Dunbar v Plant* (1997) (a civil case) it was held that a woman aided and abetted the suicide of her fiancé where both she and her fiancé simultaneously attempted to hang themselves, she unsuccessfully. Similarly, in *Wallis* (1983), a defendant pleaded guilty to aiding and abetting the suicide of a flatmate in circumstances where the defendant bought the necessary tablets and alcohol, sat with the flatmate while she took the mixture, and refrained from calling an ambulance until the flatmate was dead.

The potential scope of the offence is shown by *Attorney General v Able* (1984), where an injunction was sought restraining the publication of a pamphlet by the Voluntary Euthanasia Society entitled "A Guide to Self-Deliverance" which, as the title indicated, provided practical advice on killing oneself. Although the application was ultimately unsuccessful, it was accepted by Woolf J. that supplying this information could amount to an offence where:

- the pamphlet was supplied to a person contemplating suicide;
- the supplier acted with the intention of assisting or encouraging a person to commit suicide;

- a person did in fact read it and as a result was assisted in or encouraged to commit or attempt suicide; and
- that person did in fact commit or attempt suicide.

In summary, therefore: if A kills B at the request of B, the appropriate charge is one of murder; while if A assists B in killing (or attempting to kill) himself, the appropriate charge is one of aiding, abetting, counseling or procuring B's suicide under the Criminal Law (Suicide) Act 1993.

5.4 Manslaughter

Murder is committed when the accused intends to kill or cause serious injury, and death results. Manslaughter, which is also an offence at common law, is committed when unlawful death is caused, but the *mens rea* falls short of that required for murder. This is the case either where there is no intention to kill or cause serious injury, or where there is such an intention, but culpability is lessened by the defences of provocation or excessive self-defence being available.

The lower level of culpability is reflected in a lower level of punishment. Manslaughter, unlike murder, does not carry a mandatory life sentence. While it carries a maximum penalty of life imprisonment, in practice sentences tend to be substantially lower. In fact, it is not unusual for suspended sentences to be imposed for manslaughter convictions where there are mitigating circumstances.

Manslaughter has never been defined by statute and covers a wide variety of killings, from the deliberate to the accidental, making it impossible to offer a single, comprehensive definition of the crime. Instead, it is customary to divide manslaughter into a number of categories. In this jurisdiction, the classification usually adopted is that set out by Charleton, who describes cases of manslaughter as coming under 5 categories:

1. Where A kills B intending to kill or cause serious injury, but where the defence of *provocation* applies;
2. Where A kills B intending to kill or cause serious injury, believing he was acting in self defence, but where the force used was excessive (*excessive self defence*);
3. Where A kills B without intending to kill or cause serious injury, but by virtue of *criminal negligence*;
4. Where A kills B without intending to kill or cause serious injury, but as a result of an *assault*;

5. Where A kills B without intending to kill or cause serious injury, but as a result of a *criminal and dangerous act*. (Charleton, *Criminal Law—Cases and Materials* (Butterworths, London, 1992) p.356.)

Categories 1 and 2 are usually described as cases of *voluntary manslaughter*, while categories 3, 4 and 5 are described as cases of *involuntary manslaughter*. This description is misleading, since the distinction has nothing to do with voluntariness or the defence of automatism. Instead, the distinction relates to whether the accused intended to kill or cause serious injury. If he did, but can rely on provocation or excessive self-defence, this is voluntary manslaughter. If he did not have this intention, this is involuntary manslaughter.

Categories 1 and 2 are dealt with in Chapter 11. Here we will deal with the three forms of involuntary manslaughter.

5.4.1 Manslaughter by criminal negligence

This crime is committed where a person causes death by virtue of conduct which is criminally or grossly negligent: that is, so negligent that any reasonable person would have realised that the conduct created a high degree of risk of serious injury to others. This is an objective test and differs from the subjective test applied to intention and recklessness; for manslaughter by criminal negligence, it is not necessary to show that the accused *realised* that he was creating such a risk. It is, therefore, something of an anomaly in Irish law: an accused can be convicted of this very serious crime without having any element of subjective fault or actual awareness that he was creating a risk. Given this anomalous status, it is important to remember that criminal negligence is a much higher standard than the standard of negligence in tort.

The leading Irish case defining criminal negligence is *People (AG) v Dunleavy* (1948). Here, the accused was charged with manslaughter, having killed a cyclist while driving without lights on the wrong side of a busy city road. The jury was directed that it was to decide whether the conduct of the accused showed such a disregard for the lives and safety of others as to amount to a crime deserving punishment, but were not explicitly directed as to what degree of negligence was required. The Court of Criminal Appeal held that this direction was inadequate: the jury should have been directed as to the different degrees of negligence, and as to the very high degree of negligence which is required in the case of manslaughter. The jury should be told that the negligence required goes beyond a mere matter of compensation, showing a disregard for the life and safety of others, and that the negligence required must be:

> "of a very high degree and of such a character that any reasonable driver, endowed with ordinary road sense and in full possession of his faculties, would realise, if he thought at all, that by driving in the manner which occasioned the fatality he was, without lawful excuse, incurring, in a high degree, the risk of causing substantial personal injury to others." (*per* Davitt J. at pp.101–102).

This definition is an extension of the definition which was previously laid down in the case of *R. v Bateman* (1926). In that case, a doctor was charged with the manslaughter of a woman who had died while giving birth. Hewart C.J. stated (at p.732) that the jury should be told that the negligence required: "went beyond a mere matter of compensation and showed such disregard for the life and safety of others as to amount to a crime against the State and conduct deserving punishment", but did not also require that the jury be directed as to the very high degree of negligence required.

Although *People (AG) v Dunleavy* sets a high standard for criminal negligence manslaughter, there have been several cases since where this standard has been met. For example, in *People (AG) v Crosby* (1961) a motorist was found guilty of manslaughter where he was very drunk, approached a bridge at high speed on the wrong side of the road, striking three pedestrians. Similarly, in *People v O'Neill* (1964) a motorist was found guilty of manslaughter where he caused an accident by driving at excessive speed, on the wrong side of the road, approaching a blind bend.

The most recent Irish case in this area is *DPP v Cullagh* (1999). The appellant was convicted of manslaughter at a fairground in Tipperary which he owned and operated. The victim was killed when the chairoplane she was being carried in became detached from the metal arm holding it to the central equipment, causing her to fall to the ground. At trial it was shown that the ride was over 20 years old, had not been properly inspected or maintained, had lain in a field for several years, and was in "appalling condition".

The Court of Criminal Appeal approved of the trial judge's

direction that the standard of negligence required was "gross negligence", not the ordinary standard of civil negligence, and that mere inadvertence, which would attract liability in a civil action, was insufficient. The court also noted that the test was objective, acknowledging that "the particular factor which caused the tragedy would not have been apparent to Mr. Cullagh", but going on to say that he should have been aware of it nevertheless, particularly since he "was making available for entertainment equipment which was of its nature to some degree hazardous and undoubtedly old".

A similar approach is taken in English law. The leading English case on this type of manslaughter is *R. v Adomako* (1995). The appellant was an anaesthetist who failed to notice for six minutes that a tube supplying oxygen to his patient had become disconnected. The patient suffered a heart attack and died as a result. The appellant was convicted of manslaughter by gross negligence, and appealed on the basis that the trial judge had misdirected the jury on the definition of gross negligence.

The House of Lords held that the appellant was properly convicted. *Per* Lord Mackay L.C., the ingredients of gross negligence manslaughter were fourfold:

1. The defendant must owe the victim a duty of care;
2. There must be a breach of that duty;
3. Which causes the death of the victim; and
4. The breach must amount to gross negligence.

In relation to the fourth point, Lord Mackay stated that the jury should be told to consider whether the defendant's conduct was "so bad" as to deserve a criminal conviction, not merely to require the payment of compensation:

> "gross negligence [depends] on the seriousness of the breach of the duty committed by the defendant in all the circumstances in which he was placed when it occurred. The jury will have to consider whether, having regard to the risk of death involved, the conduct of the defendant was so bad in all the circumstances as to amount in the jury's judgment to a criminal act or omission".

This definition was criticised by counsel for the appellant on the basis that it was circular, since "the jury [is] being told in effect to convict of a crime if they thought a crime had been committed".

Lord Mackay acknowledged that there was an element of circularity in the definition, but stated that whether negligence rises to the standard of gross negligence is a question of degree, and ultimately the jury must decide whether the negligence involved is such that it should attract a criminal sanction.

5.4.2 Manslaughter as a result of an assault

"It is manslaughter for the accused to kill the victim by an assault where the accused intends to hurt or cause the victim more than trivial harm." (Charleton, *Offences Against the Person* (Round Hall Press, 1992), p.83.)

This charge is appropriate where the accused did not intend to cause serious injury, but did intend to injure. In many cases, the accused will have been "unlucky", in that a seemingly minor crime will have had the unforeseen effect of the victim's death. An example is *R. v Holzer* (1968). In that case, the accused got into a fight with the victim and punched the victim in the face. The victim fell backwards and hit his head on the road. The victim later died. The accused testified that he did not intend to cause serious injury, but only to "cut his lip or bruise his lip or something". It was held that unless the physical injury intended was merely trivial or negligible, such as a scuff or a slap to the hand, then assault resulting in death would be manslaughter:

"[A] person is guilty of manslaughter if he commits the offence of [assault] on the deceased and death results directly from that offence and the beating or other application of force was done with the intention of inflicting on the deceased some physical harm not merely of a trivial or negligible character, or, it would seem with the intention of inflicting pain, without more injury or harm to the body than is involved in the infliction of pain which is not merely trivial or negligible." (*Per* Stephen J. at p.482).

Note that the word "assault" is used in this context in the modern sense, to include both assault and battery. This modern usage has now been followed in the Non-Fatal Offences Against the Person Act 1997, which uses the term assault for what would before, strictly speaking, have been battery. Consequently, it seems that a defendant may be guilty of manslaughter by assault even though he might not have struck the deceased, but merely threatened to do so.

For example, suppose that A runs towards B with a knife, shouting threats. B, trying to escape, falls, hits his head, and dies soon afterwards. Since A's actions would amount to an assault, it would seem that A could be convicted of manslaughter as a result of an assault.

DPP v Daley and McGhie (1980) supports this view. In that case, the defendants chased the victim and threw stones at him. In attempting to escape, he tripped and fell and was subsequently found to be dead. It was unclear whether the fatal injury had been caused by the stones or the fall. The defendants were convicted of manslaughter. On appeal to the Privy Council, it was held that the trial judge was correct in directing the jury that:

> "where one person causes in the mind of another by violence or the threat of violence a well-founded sense of danger to life or limb as to cause him to suffer or to try to escape and in the endeavour to escape he is killed, the person creating that state of mind is guilty of at least manslaughter."

5.4.3 Manslaughter as a result of a criminal and dangerous act

> "For the accused to kill the victim by intentionally doing an unlawful act which was also objectively dangerous, is manslaughter."(Charleton, *Offences Against the Person* (Round Hall Press, 1992), p.105.)

This category overlaps with manslaughter by criminal negligence and manslaughter by assault: an assault resulting in death may well be manslaughter under each of these three headings.

What forms of unlawful acts does this category apply to? It is not enough for an act to be illegal or tortious: it must amount to a criminal and objectively dangerous offence. Otherwise, every negligent killing would amount to manslaughter. This is illustrated by *People (AG) v Maher* (1937), where the accused, while driving a car without having a licence, killed a man without any evidence of negligence. It was held that there was insufficient evidence to convict for manslaughter. The mere fact that the driving of the car was unlawful was not enough—it had to be shown that the act was both criminal and dangerous.

Another example is *People (AG) v Crosbie and Meehan* (1966). The victim, a docker, died from a knife wound in the course of a fight in a crowded room. It was not clear how the wound was inflicted or with what intention: the defendant had brought the knife in self-defence (or so he claimed), and stated that while waving the knife around to frighten off attackers he must have accidentally hit the victim. This would not, therefore, amount to manslaughter by assault (although it might amount to manslaughter by criminal negligence). Could it amount to manslaughter by a criminal and dangerous act?

The Court of Criminal Appeal held that it could. If the knife was produced to frighten or intimidate, and not in self-defence, then the crime of assault was committed. Waving the knife around in a crowded room was an objectively dangerous act (even if the defendant did not realise it). If death resulted, that death would be manslaughter as a result of a criminal and dangerous act:

> "A person who produces a knife with the intention of intimidating or frightening another and not for self-defence commits an assault and the act done is therefore unlawful. When a killing results from an unlawful act ... the act causing death must be unlawful and dangerous to constitute the offence of manslaughter. The dangerous quality of the act must however be judged by objective standards and it is irrelevant that the person did not think that the act was dangerous." (*Per* Kenny J. at p.495.)

In *R. v Pagett* (1983), the accused was convicted of manslaughter when he forcefully used a girl as a shield to protect himself from shots fired by the police, causing her to be killed by police bullets. The court held that the accused had committed two unlawful and dangerous acts: the act of firing at the police and the act of using the girl as a shield when the police might fire in his direction in self-defence. Either act was deemed to constitute the *actus reus* of manslaughter.

This category of manslaughter does not apply where the act carried out is normally lawful, and becomes unlawful only because negligently carried out: *People (AG) v Dunleavy* (1948). Otherwise, every death due to careless or inconsiderate driving (which are offences, albeit minor offences) would be manslaughter.

It is not necessary that the unlawful and dangerous act be aimed at or directed towards the deceased. In *R. v Mitchell* (1983), the accused attempted to skip a queue in a post office and hit a man who objected. The man fell against an old woman who suffered a broken femur necessitating an operation. While recovering from surgery, she died suddenly as a result of a blood clot of the left leg veins caused by the fracture to the femur. The accused was convicted of manslaughter.

5.4.4 Death on the roads

Cases such as *People (AG) v Dunleavy* (1948), *People (AG) v Crosby* (1961) and *People v O'Neill* (1964) demonstrate that while killing in the course of driving may amount to manslaughter, the prosecution must show a very high standard of negligence.

However, this high standard is not appropriate for all cases of negligence on the roads; there is a need for an intermediate offence which will address cases where death is caused due to negligent driving which falls short of criminal negligence.

Consequently, s.53 of the Road Traffic Act 1961 creates an offence of causing death by dangerous driving. The standard of carelessness which is required for dangerous driving is intermediate between "ordinary" negligence and criminal negligence: the test is objective, and dangerous driving occurs where a person drives in a manner which a reasonable man "would clearly recognise as involving a direct and serious risk of harm to the public" (*per* Judge Barra Ó'Briain, then President of the Circuit Court, in *People v Quinlan* (1962)). This test is the settled practice in directing juries in dangerous driving cases, and has been explicitly approved by the Court of Criminal Appeal in *People (DPP) v Connaughton* (2001).

In deciding whether driving is dangerous, s.53 directs that all the circumstances of the case must be taken into account, including speed, the condition of the vehicle, the nature and condition of the place, and the amount of traffic. This offence carries a maximum penalty of ten years imprisonment, and often results in a custodial sentence. Hardiman J. has noted that:

> "Experience shows that it is almost unique, amongst offences not requiring a specific intent, in carrying a real

possibility of a significant custodial sentence for a convicted
person of good character." (*Bowes v DPP* (2003))

5.5 Infanticide

It is well established that mothers, shortly after giving birth, face
special challenges, both physical and psychological. Physical
circumstances include the physical exhaustion of pregnancy and birth,
and consequent hormonal changes, as the body readjusts.
Psychological factors, meanwhile, include what is now known as
post-natal depression, the stresses inherent in being responsible for
a new life, new financial and relationship pressures, and, in some
cases, the added strain attached to being a single mother. When a
mother facing those circumstances kills her child, the law recognises
that a murder conviction may not be appropriate.

A separate crime of infanticide is, therefore, created by the
Infanticide Act 1949. This offence is unusual, in that it operates both
as an offence and a defence. A defendant may be charged with
infanticide; alternatively, if a defendant is charged with murder she
can raise infanticide as a defence—if successful, she will be convicted
of infanticide rather than murder, and will face a lesser punishment.
Where a defendant raises this defence, the burden of proof is on the
prosecution to establish, beyond a reasonable doubt, that the killing
amounts to murder and not infanticide.

The elements of the offence are as follows:

- A mother kills her child;
- Within 12 months of its birth;
- In circumstances which would otherwise have
  amounted to murder; and
- At the time of the killing the balance of her mind was
  disturbed by reason of either:
  (i) not having fully recovered from giving birth to the
  child, or
  (ii) the effect of lactation after the birth of the child.

The most important element in that definition is that the balance of
the mother's mind must have been disturbed. This does not mean
that the mother's condition must rise to the level of the insanity
defence; a lesser degree of disturbance will suffice. An example of
the type of disturbance required can be seen in *R. v Sainsbury*

(1989). The defendant was a young girl who gave birth on her own in a bathroom, took the baby and (with her boyfriend) wrapped it in a blanket and drowned it in a river. She pleaded guilty to infanticide, and the trial judge accepted that plea, noting that:

> "Even without the stresses of pregnancy and child-birth, you were emotionally and intellectually a very immature fourteen-year-old. You were a woman in body but a child in mind. You were quite unable to cope with pregnancy and unable to understand its full implications. You were too frightened to confide in your parents or anyone else who could help you. When you had this baby you were not prepared for the consequences and at a loss as to what to do. It is clear on the evidence that the effect of giving birth to this baby left the balance of your mind disturbed so as to prevent rational judgment and decisions."

The advantage of a verdict of infanticide is that the offender may be sentenced as if she had been found guilty of manslaughter, thus avoiding a mandatory life sentence. As such, infanticide is comparable to the defence of diminished responsibility available in English law under s.2(1) of the Homicide Act 1957: in each case there is a mental disturbance which does not eliminate *mens rea* but does mitigate culpability.

It should be noted that infanticide is only available in the case of mothers who kill; fathers who deliberately kill (for example, the boyfriend in *R. v Sainsbury*) will still face a charge of murder, notwithstanding that they might be subject to similar stresses.

Further Reading:

Law Reform Commission, *Consultation Paper on Homicide: The Mental Element in Murder* (L.R.C. 17–2001); Law Reform Commission, *Report on Sentencing* (L.R.C. 53–1996), Chap.5; O'Malley, "Sentencing murderers: the case for relocating discretion" (1995) I.C.L.J. 31

6. SEXUAL OFFENCES

This is an area of the criminal law that has always been heavily influenced by prevailing attitudes and standards. It is not surprising, therefore, that there has been reform of many sexual offences in recent years as new areas of protection were identified and traditional attitudes became increasingly regarded as outmoded.

6.1 Rape

Two distinct forms of rape exist in Irish law. The first is usually called "common law rape" since it was originally a common law offence, although it is now contained in s.2(1) of the Criminal Law (Rape) Act 1981 which provides:

> "A man commits rape if:
> (a) he has sexual intercourse with a woman who at the time of the intercourse *does not consent to it*, and
> (b) at the time *he knows that she does not consent* to the intercourse *or he is reckless* as to whether she does or does not consent to it."

This section is a useful example of the division between the *actus reus* and *mens rea* of an offence, with (a) containing the former and (b) the latter.

6.1.1. Actus reus *of common law rape*

The *actus reus* of common law rape is sexual intercourse with a woman who does not consent to it. At common law there was a rule that a wife by her marriage gave irrevocable consent to intercourse, and therefore a husband could not be guilty of the rape of his wife. The 1981 Act appeared to recognise this rule by referring to "unlawful sexual intercourse", *i.e.* intercourse outside marriage. This rule was widely criticised as being both outmoded and demeaning to women and was abolished in this jurisdiction by s.5 of the Criminal Law (Rape) Amendment Act 1990. The 1990 Act removed the word "unlawful" from the definition of rape, and provided that "any rule of law by virtue of which a husband cannot be guilty of the rape of his wife is hereby abolished". However, s.5(2) goes on to provide that any criminal proceedings for marital rape must have the consent of the DPP.

The statutory definition of rape in England also contained the phrase "unlawful sexual intercourse" and was also assumed to recognise the common law rule. However, in *R v R* (1991) the House of Lords held that the word "unlawful" was simply redundant and that the statutory definition therefore applied to marital rape. The Lords agreed with the Court of Appeal decision that the marital exemption in relation to rape was "a common law fiction which has become anachronistic and offensive" (at p.490). The position in both jurisdictions is therefore that rape within marriage is unlawful.

Sexual intercourse for common law rape means vaginal intercourse only. Some degree of penetration by the penis, however slight, is required (s.1(2) Criminal Law (Rape) (Amendment) Act 1981). Ejaculation is not required (*People (Attorney General) v Dermody* (1951)). Forced oral or anal intercourse and penetration by an object are now covered by s.4 rape.

Penetration is a continuing act and failure by an accused to withdraw when he realises that the other is not consenting amounts to rape: *Kaitamaki v R.* (1985). The argument cannot be made in those circumstances that *actus reus* and *mens rea* did not coincide.

6.1.2 Section 4 rape: difference between common law rape and section 4 rape

It was recognised that the common law definition of rape, now contained in s.2 of the Criminal Law (Rape) Act 1981, was inadequate since it did not deal with anal or oral rape or rape by an object, all of which are as degrading to the victim as common law rape. Section 4(1) of the Criminal Law (Rape) (Amendment) Act 1990 was therefore introduced and it provides that:

> "In this Act 'rape under section 4' means a sexual assault that includes-
> (a) the penetration (however slight) of the anus or mouth by the penis, or
> (b) penetration (however slight) of the vagina by any object held or manipulated by another person."

The *actus reus* of s.4 rape is, therefore, a *sexual assault* accompanied by certain acts of penetration. We have yet to look at the definition of sexual assault; however, for the moment, it is enough to know that it is an assault with "circumstances of indecency" and consent is a defence just as in common law rape. The *mens rea* for this offence is also essentially the same as for sexual assault or rape, which will be dealt with later.

What are the differences between common law rape and s.4 rape? Common law rape can only be committed by a man, while s.4 rape can be committed by either sex (rape with an object). Common law rape can only be committed against a woman, while s.4 rape can be committed against either sex (it includes anal or oral rape of a man).

6.2 Consent

Failure to struggle or put up a fight does not amount to consent, despite misconceptions to the contrary. Absence of violence is not presence of consent. The Criminal Law (Rape) (Amendment) Act 1990 sought to put this beyond doubt by providing in s.9 that:

> "It is hereby declared that in relation to an offence that consists or includes the doing of an act to a person without the consent of that person any failure or omission by that person to offer resistance to the act does not of itself constitute consent to the act."

At first glance, consent seems a clear-cut issue: it is either present or not. Problems arise, however, when consent results from fraud. In the case of *R. v Williams* (1923) a singing teacher persuaded his 16-year-old pupil that intercourse was a necessary operation to improve her breathing control. Can it be said that there was consent in that case? It was held that there was not: fraudulently misrepresenting the nature of the act meant that the apparent consent was not real. Similarly, in *Flattery* (1877) the accused had intercourse with a girl under the guise of performing an operation. She submitted to what was being done under the belief that he was treating her medically, but the accused was convicted of rape as he had fraudulently induced that belief. In *R. v Dee* (1884), meanwhile, it was held that there was no real consent where a man induced a woman to have intercourse with him by pretending to be her husband. This position is also laid down by statute: s.4 Criminal Law Amendment Act 1885; s.20 Criminal Law Amendment Act 1935.

However, in *R. v Linekar* (1995), it was held that consent was present despite fraud. In that case, the defendant approached a prostitute and agreed to pay £25 for intercourse. He had no intention of paying, and subsequently made off without paying. Was the consent of the victim real? The Court of Appeal held it was: fraud as to a collateral matter did not undermine consent, although fraud as to the nature of the act or the identity of the actor would mean that apparent consent was not real.

Consent may also be vitiated by fear, as illustrated by *R. v Olugboja* (1982). The defendant told a 16-year-old girl that he had met at a disco in Oxford that he was going to rape her and she complied because of fear. The defendant's friend was also in the vicinity, and he had raped the girl's companion a short time earlier. The girl was pushed onto a settee in a darkened room and did not struggle, resist, scream or cry for help. The Court of Appeal emphasised (at p.332) that "there is a difference between consent and submission; every consent involves a submission but it by no means follows that a mere submission involves consent."

It is clear that there is no consent where the victim is *incapable* of giving consent. In *People (DPP) v X* (1995), a man was convicted of rape for having intercourse with a woman while she slept. Similarly, the defendant in *Malone* (1998) was convicted of raping an intoxicated 16-year-old girl who gave evidence that she had been unable to resist because of her condition.

6.3 *Mens rea* of sexual offences

Absence of consent is a prerequisite before most sexual offences can be made out. The *mens rea* of the offence, therefore, will be that the defendant intended to commit the acts in question either *knowing* that the victim did not consent, or *being reckless* as to whether or not the victim consented. The first requires that the defendant is *conscious* of the lack of consent; the second that the defendant was aware that the victim might not be consenting. This *mens rea* is explicitly set out by statute in the case of common law rape (Criminal Law (Rape) Act 1981, s.2(1) (b)), and has been held by the courts to apply also in the case of sexual assault (*R. v Kimber* (1983)).

6.3.1 Honest but unreasonable belief in consent

However, one difficulty arises. Suppose that a defendant *honestly believes* that a victim is consenting, *but his belief is unreasonable*. Should the defendant be found guilty of a crime? Two approaches to this situation are possible. An objective approach would find a defendant liable if he honestly believed that there was consent, but he had no reasonable grounds for his belief. A subjective approach would acquit the defendant, looking solely at his honest belief and not at whether it was reasonable of him to hold that belief.

In *DPP v Morgan* (1975), this precise issue came before the House of Lords. In a bizarre set of facts, a husband invited three drinking partners back to his house to have sexual intercourse with his wife. He told them that she would put up a struggle, but that this would be simply an act and that she would in fact welcome having intercourse with them. The men went back to his house and each had sex with her while she was held down, fighting and screaming. The defence of each of the three men was that they had honestly, though obviously unreasonably, believed that the victim had consented to intercourse. The trial judge directed the jury that this could not amount to a defence unless the defendants had reasonable grounds for their belief. The defendants were convicted.

·   On appeal to the House of Lords, it was held (by a majority) that the defendants could not be convicted of rape if they had genuinely believed that the victim was consenting. *Per* Lord Hailsham L.C. (at p.361):

> "Once one has accepted ... that the prohibited act in rape is non-consensual sexual intercourse, and that the guilty state of mind is an intention to commit it, it seems to me to follow ... that there is no room either for a 'defence' of honest belief or mistake ... Either the prosecution proves that the accused had the requisite intent, or it does not. In the former case it succeeds, and in the latter it fails. Since honest belief clearly negatives intent, the reasonableness or otherwise of that belief can only be evidence for or against the view that the belief and therefore the intent was actually held ..."

Outrage followed this decision, which was described by the tabloids as "A Rapists' Charter". Pressure was exerted to change the *mens rea* of rape to an objective test, asking whether the accused had reasonable grounds for his belief that the victim was consenting. However, this was not done. The English Advisory Group on the Law of Rape accepted that *DPP v Morgan* (1975) was correct in principle. Nevertheless, the Advisory Group did advise that legislation should clarify that:

1. An *honest belief* in consent would negative *mens rea*; and
2. This belief *did not need to be based on reasonable grounds*; but
3. The jury *may take into account whether reasonable grounds existed in deciding whether the belief was honest.*

English legislation adopted this approach in the Sexual Offences (Amendment) Act 1976, s.1(1), and this approach was also adopted in Ireland in the Criminal Law (Rape) Act 1981, s.2(2) of which states:

> "It is hereby declared that if at a trial for a rape offence the jury has to consider whether a man believed that a woman was consenting to sexual intercourse, the presence or absence of reasonable grounds for such a belief is a matter to which the jury is to have regard, in conjunction with any other relevant matters, in considering whether he so believed."

This approach is a common sense compromise: the accused is entitled to claim a genuine belief in consent but the jury is entitled to consider whether such a belief would have been reasonable in deciding whether the accused did in fact have that belief. For the sake of comparison, consider the New Zealand approach, where the test is objective: an accused must believe in consent "on reasonable grounds" (s.128(3) Crimes Act 1961; Crimes (Amendment) Act 1985).

It is not necessary that the jury should be directed on the provisions of s.2(2) of the 1981 Act in every case where rape is charged; such a direction only becomes necessary where the defence raised is one of mistaken belief in consent. This was confirmed by the Supreme Court in *People (DPP) v McDonagh* (1996). In that case, the defendants were charged with rape. Their defence was that the complainant had consented to sexual intercourse in return for payment. They were convicted. On appeal, it was argued that the trial judge had erred in failing to explain to the jury the effect of s.2(2). This was a somewhat novel line of argument: s.2(2) had clearly been intended to facilitate prosecutions and had been enacted in response to *R. v Morgan* (1975). It was, therefore, ironic that the defendants were arguing in favour of an interpretation which would have the effect of facilitating defendants. It was held by Costello J. that s.2(2) was limited in its effect to cases where the defence mounted was one of mistaken belief in consent: it had no application in cases such as the present one, where the defence was the existence of actual consent.

6.3.2 *Recklessness as to consent*

Recklessness in this context has the same meaning as in *People (DPP) v Murray* (1977): the accused must be consciously aware of the possibility that the victim is not consenting. Objective recklessness is not enough.

6.4 Sexual assault

Until 1990 the majority of sexual attacks which did not amount to rape amounted to indecent assault. Although statute provided maximum penalties for each offence, there was no statutory definition of either.

There was dissatisfaction with this situation. The differentiation between indecent assault upon a male and upon a female was anachronistic. Until 1981 there were different maximum penalties depending on the sex of the victim. (This was remedied by the Criminal Law (Rape) Act 1981.) In addition, each offence covered a wide span of behaviour, from relatively minor offences to violent sexual attacks. Consequently, it was felt that the label of indecent assault and the maximum sentence available were inadequate for the more serious offences which were included in the definition of indecent assault.

The solution came in the Criminal Law (Rape) (Amendment) Act 1990. This combined the offences of indecent assault upon a male and upon a female into one offence, to be known as sexual assault, having a single maximum penalty of five years regardless of the sex of the victim. In addition, the more serious cases of sexual attack are now dealt with in two ways. Those involving penetration will now amount to s.4 rape, while other serious sexual attacks fall into a new category of aggravated sexual assault. This is a gender-neutral offence carrying a maximum penalty of life imprisonment.

The penalty is the same as that for common law rape and s.4 rape, reflecting the fact that some attacks not involving penetration can be just as grave as those involving penetration.

The following sections are relevant:

> "s. 2(1) The offence of indecent assault upon any male person and the offence of sexual assault upon any female person shall be known as sexual assault.(2) A person guilty of sexual assault shall be liable on conviction on indictment to imprisonment for a term not exceeding 5 years.
>
> s. 3(1) In this Act 'aggravated sexual assault' means a sexual assault that involves serious violence or the threat of serious violence or is such as to cause injury, humiliation or degradation of a grave nature to the person assaulted.(2) A person guilty of aggravated sexual assault shall be liable on conviction on indictment to imprisonment for life."

It should be noted that the 1990 Act does not define indecent or sexual assault but simply prescribes a new name and range of penalties for an existing offence at common law. It was argued after the passage of the 1990 Act that there was in fact no offence of indecent assault known to Irish law. If so, then the 1990 Act would have been ineffective as purporting to rename and give new penalties for an offence which did not exist. This argument was, however, rejected by O'Hanlon J. in *Doolan v DPP* (1993) and by the Supreme Court in *People (DPP) v EF* (1994), both of which held that an offence of indecent assault existed at common law and that it was permissible to rename the offence and provide new penalties for it without re-enacting it. The 1990 Act therefore creates a mixed statutory and common law offence in much the same way as s.4 of the Criminal Justice Act 1964 does with regard to murder. This means that to define sexual assault we have to consider what constituted indecent assault at common law.

6.4.1 Indecent assault at common law

> "An indecent assault has been defined as an assault (including psychic assault) accompanied with circumstances of indecency." (Charleton, *Offences Against the Person* (Round Hall Press, 1992), p.286.)

What is an assault? An assault is an act by which one person
intentionally or recklessly causes another to apprehend immediate,
unlawful personal violence or to sustain such violence. (For the
definition of assault see the Non-Fatal Offences Against the Person
Act 1997, discussed further in chapter 7 on Offences Against the
Person.) For an assault to take place, it is not necessary that there
should be any element of hostility or aggression. Instead, "violence"
simply means any unlawful touching of a victim without consent or
lawful excuse: *Faulkner v Talbot* (1981).

The difficulty lies in defining "circumstances of indecency".
Some circumstances will be obviously indecent (an attempt to remove
another's clothes) while others may or may not be indecent depending
on the circumstances. In *R. v Court* (1988), the accused was a shop
assistant and struck a 12-year-old girl in the shop several times on
her buttocks, outside her shorts. Later asked why he did so, he replied
"buttock fetish". Were there circumstances of indecency, given that
the girl was unaware of his motive? The House of Lords upheld the
conviction of the accused, laying down the following criteria:

1. The assault component of indecent assault includes
    not just physical violence, but conduct which causes
    another to fear immediate and unlawful physical
    violence;

2. Some circumstances are objectively incapable of being
    regarded as indecent, regardless of the motive of the
    accused: for example, to remove another's shoe is
    not capable of being regarded as indecent, even if the
    accused is a shoe fetishist;

3. Some circumstances are inherently indecent,
    regardless of the motive of the accused: for example,
    to remove a victim's clothes against her will amounts
    to indecent assault, regardless of whether the accused
    had a sexual intention, or simply intended to embarrass
    or humiliate the victim;

4. In other circumstances, the jury may consider all the
    surrounding factors in deciding if an assault is in fact
    indecent, including the relationship between the parties
    and the motive of the accused; (For example, for a
    parent to spank a child is not indecent.) and

5. It is not necessary to show that the victim was aware

of the circumstances of indecency. It was no defence
that the victim was unaware of the accused's buttock
fetish. An indecent assault can obviously take place
on a sleeping or unconscious victim.

6.4.2 Aggravated sexual assault

Section 3(1) of the 1990 Act defines aggravated sexual assault to
mean:

"a sexual assault that involves *serious violence or the
threat of serious violence* or is such as to cause *injury,
humiliation or degradation of a grave nature* to the
person assaulted". (Emphasis added.)

Where these factors are present the maximum penalty is life
imprisonment, reflecting the gravity of the offence.

6.5 Incest

Incest is a crime governed by the Punishment of Incest Act 1908.
The offence consists of sexual intercourse with a close blood relative.
The majority of cases are violent or abusive, but this is not an element
of the crime: consensual intercourse between close relatives will
still amount to incest. In other words, consent is not a defence. The
bulk of incest cases concern fathers abusing daughters and, for that
reason, different considerations apply to incest by a male and incest
by a female.

6.5.1 Incest by a male

"A male who has sexual intercourse with a woman who is
to his knowledge his mother, sister, daughter or
granddaughter commits incest." (O'Malley, *Sexual
Offences: Law, Policy and Punishment* (Round Hall
Sweet and Maxwell, 1996), p.114.)

Vaginal intercourse must be established: other forms of abuse or
exploitation do not amount to incest. Brother and sister include half-
brother and half-sister (*i.e.* where there is one parent in common)
but not step-brother and step-sister, since the offence is one limited
to blood-relations. Consequently, it follows that sexual abuse by
adoptive parents does not amount to the crime of incest.

Until the enactment of the Criminal Law (Rape) (Amendment) Act 1990, there was a conclusive presumption that a boy under 14 years of age could not commit incest. This has now been abolished. On this point, see further the defence of infancy, Chapter 12.

6.5.2 Incest by a female

"A female of or above the age of 17 years who with consent permits her father, grandfather, brother or son to have sexual intercourse with her commits incest provided she is aware of the relevant relationship between herself and the male." (O'Malley, *Sexual Offences: Law, Policy and Punishment* (Round Hall Sweet and Maxwell, 1996), p. 118.)

The offence is the same as incest by a male, except that the female is not criminally liable until she reaches the age of 17, on the assumption that she is the victim of any incestuous intercourse before that age.

6.5.3 Punishment of incest

Committed by a male, the maximum penalty is life imprisonment (s.1, Punishment of Incest Act 1908; s.12, Criminal Law Amendment Act 1935; s.5(1), Criminal Law (Incest Proceedings) Act 1995). Committed by a female, the maximum penalty is 7 years imprisonment (s.2, 1908 Act).

6.5.4 Reform

It is well-recognised that the crime of incest should be extended to adoptive relationships and step-children and that it should encompass sexual acts falling short of intercourse. See, for example, the discussion in Department of Justice, Equality and Law Reform, *The Law on Sexual Offences: A Discussion Paper* (Stationery Office, 1998).

6.6 Sexual offences against the mentally handicapped

Until 1993, the only offence of this type was contained in s.4 of the Criminal Law Amendment Act 1935 which made it an offence punishable by two years' imprisonment to have unlawful sexual intercourse with a woman who was "an idiot or an imbecile or feeble-minded". This was unsatisfactory, as it employed what is now regarded as offensive terminology and offered no protection against other forms of sexual exploitation of the mentally handicapped. The Criminal Law (Sexual Offences) Act 1993 replaces s.4 of the 1935 Act. Section 5 of the 1993 Act creates three distinct offences:

(1) Sexual intercourse with a mentally impaired person (10 years' imprisonment; 3 years' for attempt (first conviction); 5 years' for attempt (subsequent conviction);

(2) Buggery of a mentally impaired person (penalties as intercourse); and

(3) Commission of an act of gross indecency by a male with a male who is mentally impaired. (2 years' imprisonment).

The 1993 Act defines "mentally impaired" as follows:

"Suffering from a disorder of the mind, whether through mental handicap or mental illness, which is of such a nature or degree as to render a person incapable of living an independent life or of guarding against serious exploitation." (s.5).

There is a defence where a defendant is married to a mentally impaired person. A defence is also provided where an accused can show that at the time of the alleged commission of the offence he did not know and had no reason to suspect that the person in respect of whom he is charged was mentally impaired. However, consent is *not* a defence, even assuming that the victim has sufficient mental capacity to give consent.

It should be noted that the 1993 Act is designed for situations where a mentally impaired person is capable of giving consent: if a victim is so mentally disabled as to be incapable of consenting then the accused will also be guilty of rape or sexual assault if he has the necessary *mens rea*. The necessary mental capacity to give consent is expressed by Glanville Williams to be as follows:

"[T]he woman must both know the physical facts and know that the connection is sexual; failing either knowledge, she does not consent in law." (*Textbook of Criminal Law* (2nd ed., London, 1983), p.571.)

The Law Reform Commission in its 1990 Report on Sexual Offences Against the Mentally Handicapped emphasised the balance that must be achieved between guarding against sexual exploitation and facilitating mentally handicapped people's sexual expression. However, the current legislation has been criticised by organisations representing the handicapped. It has been argued that many people who are unable to live independently because of mental handicap are capable of guarding against exploitation. The legislation creates a serious difficulty for those people in their sexual relationships. The Law Reform Commission Report concluded that the test of whether a person was capable of living an independent life did not add anything to the definition of the category of persons who should be protected, but the legislators did not follow that recommendation.

6.7 Sexual abuse of children

6.7.1 Sexual assault

There is no specific offence, as such, of sexual abuse of children. However, sexual activity with children may amount to an offence where the child is not old enough to consent to that activity. A person of either sex under 15 years of age cannot consent to activity amounting to a sexual assault by virtue of s.14 of the Criminal Law Amendment Act 1935.

6.7.2 Unlawful carnal knowledge

Similarly, a girl under the age of 17 years cannot consent to sexual intercourse. Under ss.1 and 2 of the 1935 Act, unlawful carnal knowledge of a girl under 15 is an offence punishable by life imprisonment, while unlawful carnal knowledge of a girl aged between 15 and 17 is an offence punishable by five years' imprisonment. This prohibition applies regardless of the age of the offender: where two 16-year-olds are involved, then the male has committed an offence. Arguably, it would be more appropriate to criminalise sexual intercourse with under-age children on a gender-neutral basis, reflecting the fact that a graver offence is committed where a middle-aged man has sex with a 16-year-old girl than where two teenagers have sex.

In this context, carnal knowledge simply means vaginal intercourse and unlawful means that the parties must not be married. Otherwise, neither consent nor mistake on the part of the man as to age provides any defence. As regards consent, Maguire C.J., in *AG (Shaughnessy) v Ryan* (1960), stated that the sections "were designed to protect young girls, not alone against lustful men, but against themselves" (at p.183). Regarding mistake as to age, see *R. v Prince* (1875), where even a reasonable mistake as to age was held not to amount to a defence. The accused was charged with the offence of abducting an unmarried girl under the age of 16 out of the possession of her lawful guardian contrary to s.55 of the Offences Against the Person Act 1861. The girl was 14 but looked older than 16 and had told the accused that she was 18. He believed her and it was held that this belief was reasonable. Blackburn J., however, held that a reasonable belief did not amount to a defence as the offence was one of strict liability: "The man who has connection with a child relying on her consent does so at his peril if she is below the statuable age."

6.7.3 Child sex tourism

The Sexual Offences (Jurisdiction) Act 1996 was passed to deal with the increasing international trend for people to travel abroad to procure children for sexual activity. This legislation applies to Irish citizens and to those ordinarily resident in the country. It provides that Irish courts have jurisdiction to try people suspected of committing sexual offences against children in a foreign country. The activity must have been a criminal offence in the foreign jurisdiction and also be an offence under Irish criminal law. The Act defines children as being under the age of 17 years.

6.7.4 Child trafficking and pornography

The Child Trafficking and Pornography Act 1998 was enacted to combat international paedophile rings. It became obvious in Europe during the 1990s that children were being kidnapped or brought from developing countries to richer countries for the purposes of sexual exploitation. It was also realised that there was a significant international market for child pornography and that this market was growing with more widespread access to the internet. The offences set out in the Act include child trafficking; taking a child for sexual exploitation; allowing a child to be used for pornography; producing and distributing child pornography; and possession of child pornography. Defendants convicted of offences under this Act may also be subject to the provisions of the Sex Offenders Act 2001.

In *People (DPP) v Muldoon* (2003), the applicant appealed against the severity of his sentence. He had been convicted of being in possession of and advertising child pornography and was sentenced to two and a half years' imprisonment. The trial judge exercised his jurisdiction under the Sex Offenders Act 2001 to require post-release supervision of the applicant by a probation officer for a period of 11 years. The trial judge imposed a further condition restraining the applicant from having control over a personal computer or from having internet access from his home for the 11-year period. The applicant was only to have access to a personal computer or to the internet under supervision. This was the aspect of the sentence which was appealed on grounds of severity. Keane C.J. dismissed the appeal. He emphasised that the offences were of a very serious nature. The evidence was that the applicant, a person skilled in computer science, had been engaged in effectively advertising the provision of images involving child pornography which were described as being of a horrific nature. Whilst the restrictions imposed would seriously impinge on the applicant's right to earn a living from his skills in information technology, this was a restriction that he had brought about himself as a result of his criminal activity.

6.7.5 Law Reform Commission Report on Child Sexual Abuse

The Law Reform Commission *Report on Child Sexual Abuse* made a series of proposals on reform of the law relating to sexual abuse of children. In relation to statutory rape, it proposed the lowering of the age limit for the more serious offence in s.1 to 13 but that the offence should remain punishable by a maximum of life imprisonment. It recommended that the maximum sentence for an offence under s.2 be seven years. A further recommendation was that it should not be an offence for a male to have intercourse with a girl aged over 15 years of age unless he is either five years or more older than her or is a person in authority, *i.e.* any person having even temporary responsibility for her education, supervision or welfare. The existing strict liability in relation to statutory rape was criticised and the Law Reform Commission recommended that if the accused genuinely believed that the girl was over 17 he should have a complete defence unless he was a person in authority or was five years or more older than the girl. If the defendant could demonstrate a reasonable belief that the girl was over 13 but under 15, he should be liable to a maximum sentence of seven years' imprisonment.

The Law Reform Commission expressed concern about the offence of indecent (now sexual) assault on a person under 15 years of age in s.14 of the Criminal Law Amendment Act 1935. The offence does not cover situations where an adult, without force or threat or touching, induces a child to undress before the adult or to touch him or her indecently. The Commission recommended a new definition of child sexual abuse or sexual exploitation to cover such scenarios. The Department of Justice *Discussion Paper on The Law on Sexual Offences* sought views on the above.

6.7.6. Sex Offenders Act 2001

The Sex Offenders Act 2001 has significantly altered the way sexual offenders are treated by the criminal justice system. It establishes a register of sex offenders, with particular reference to those who have committed offences against children. Such offenders are required to notify gardaí of their names and addresses. A risk assessment will be made of those on the register, and the gardaí are empowered to disclose the names of offenders where necessary to prevent an immediate risk of crime or to alert members of the public to a particular danger. Sex offenders coming into the jurisdiction from abroad are also required to register. A civil sex offenders order is also available against sex offenders whose behaviour in the community gives rise to reasonable concern that such an order is necessary to protect the public. The order is available to prohibit conduct which is not criminal but is nevertheless undesirable, *e.g.* loitering around school playgrounds. The act also creates a new offence where sex offenders seek or accept work involving unsupervised contact with children without first notifying the employer of their conviction.

The constitutionality of the Act was challenged unsuccessfully in *Enright v Ireland* (2003). The plaintiff was convicted of sexual offences in 1993 and the Sex Offenders Act 2001 came into force prior to his release. The Act applies to persons convicted before the legislation came into force providing they were still serving a sentence when the Act came into force. The High Court held that the fact that a provision had a punitive or deterrent element did not necessarily mean that it should be considered to be part of the criminal penalty of the offence. The registration requirements under the Act did not constitute a penalty for the sexual offences committed, therefore their imposition could not be regarded as inconsistent with a constitutional right under Art.38.1 not to have a penalty imposed which did not exist at the time of the offence. The court remarked that although the notification requirements provided by the Act imposed a burden on the sex offender, they did not restrain him in his movements or place him under a disability. It noted that the Oireachtas, in enacting the Sex Offenders Act 2001, was required to weigh up the constitutional rights of convicted persons with the constitutional rights of other citizens who might be at risk of attack from such persons following their release from prison. It was necessary to consider whether this balance was so contrary to reason and fairness as to constitute an unjust attack on the plaintiff's right to fair procedures. The court held that it was not.

6.8 Procedural aspects of sexual offences

6.8.1 Corroboration

Special procedural safeguards apply to cases of sexual offences. Some are protective of the alleged victim, while some are protective of the accused. An example of the latter was the rule that a jury should be warned that it is dangerous to convict on the uncorroborated evidence of a complainant in a sexual offence unless there exists independent corroborative evidence. Thus, in situations where it came down to one word against another, the accused enjoyed protection. Examples of corroborative evidence would include medical evidence of forcible intercourse, or proof that the accused was lying on a material issue because of a realisation of guilt.

This rule did not mean that the jury *could not* convict on uncorroborated evidence, merely that they should be warned that it was *dangerous to do so*. The rule was regarded as outdated because it put victims of sexual offences in a position where they were automatically regarded as untrustworthy. Section 7(1) of the Criminal Law (Rape) (Amendment) Act 1990 has now abolished this rule and provides that whether or not the case warrants such a warning being given is at the discretion of the judge.

6.8.2 Publicity

Section 7 of the Criminal Law (Rape) Act 1981 (as amended by s.17(2) Criminal Law (Rape) (Amendment) Act 1990) provides that matters tending to reveal the identity of a complainant shall not be published or broadcast except in limited circumstances relating to safeguards for the defence, or if anonymity imposes a substantial and unreasonable burden on the reporting of the trial, and it is in the public interest to remove the restriction. Section 8 of the 1981 Act guarantees the anonymity of an accused in a sexual case in a similar way until after he is convicted. Even then, as a result of s.7, the identity of the convicted person cannot be published if that would be likely to identify the complainant. There is a special regime for anonymity in incest cases: Criminal Law (Incest Proceedings) Act 1995.

As regards trials being held in public, there is a constitutional requirement in Art.34.1 that justice should be administered in public save in such special and limited cases as may be prescribed by law. Trials of sexual offences are one such case, and s.6 of the Criminal Law (Rape) Act 1981 (as amended by s.11 Criminal Law (Rape) (Amendment) Act 1990) provides that in the trial of certain sexual offences (cases involving rape and aggravated sexual assault) the judge shall exclude the public from court, except for bona fide representatives of the media. The complainant is entitled to have a parent, relative or friend in court, as is the accused if the accused is under 18 years of age. Verdict and sentence must, however, be announced in open court.

The 1981 Act does not extend to sexual assault and other such crimes. However, under s.20 of the Criminal Justice Act 1951, the court may exclude the public if the offence is one of an "indecent or obscene nature". In other words, the court has a discretion to exclude as regards sexual offences other than rape.

6.8.3 Cross-examination of complainant

At common law, cross-examination of the complainant about her previous sexual history was considered to be relevant to the credibility of the complainant. However, cross-examination of the accused could be used as a tool to put the complainant herself on trial or to mount an unwarranted intrusion on the complainant's private life. In addition, it was an example of outmoded ideas of morality to assume that sexual intercourse with others in the past meant that the complainant was more likely to have consented to the specific act forming the basis of the trial.

The legislative response was s.3 of the 1981 Act as amended by s.13 of the 1990 Act. This prohibits evidence being given or questions asked about the previous sexual experience of the complainant with any person except with the leave of the judge. The judge is to give leave to ask such questions only if satisfied that it would be unfair to the accused to refuse to allow the questions to be asked; if the effect of allowing evidence to be given or questions to be asked might be to create a reasonable doubt in the mind of the jury as to the guilt of the accused.

6.8.4 Evidence by persons under 17 years

Another feature which is relevant, although not limited to cases involving sexual offences, is s.12 of the Criminal Evidence Act 1992. This provides for evidence to be given through television link by persons under 17 years in any criminal proceedings. Section 13 allows for the evidence of such a witness to be conducted through an intermediary provided the court is satisfied that this is appropriate due to the age or mental condition of the witness. Section 18 extends the above provisions to persons with a mental handicap who have reached the age of 17 years. Evidence via a television link was challenged as being unconstitutional in *Donnelly v Ireland* (1998). The appellant argued that he had a constitutional right to confront his accuser in open court or, alternatively, that this was a vital element of his constitutional right to cross-examine witnesses. The Supreme Court held that there was no constitutional right to confront a witness in Irish law and noted that similar television link provisions had been upheld in the United States despite the express right to confront accusers in the United States Constitution.

6.8.5 Doctrine of recent complaint

The common law required that the victim of a rape case "raise hue and cry" by complaining about the rape as immediately as possible. Although this is no longer a prerequisite to a successful prosecution for rape, the rationale for the doctrine of recent complaint is based on that ancient principle. Under the doctrine, evidence of an earlier complaint by a victim of a sexual offence (to another individual, not a formal complaint to the Gardaí) is inadmissible unless it can be characterised as a "recent complaint"; a complaint made at a time shortly after the alleged offence took place. Such evidence is very important from a prosecution point of view to establish consistency and credibility. It is also an exception to the general rule that witnesses must not be asked if they have made a prior consistent statement. For those reasons, the defence will often argue that a complaint made by the alleged victim does not fall within the doctrine and cannot therefore be admitted. It should be noted, however, that a complaint by the victim at the first opportunity does not amount to corroboration. The complaint should be made at the earliest opportunity that reasonably afforded itself and must have been made voluntarily and not as a result of leading questions.

In *People (DPP) v Brophy,* the complaint to a father and some friends was held not to fall within the doctrine and was therefore inadmissible. The allegation was of sexual assault during a one-hour period which the complainant spent at the accused's house. He gave her a lift to a shopping centre afterwards and the complainant showed no distress and said "I'll see you tomorrow." She then met her mother but did not complain to her, only later in the afternoon complaining to her father and some companions. In *People (DPP) v Kiernan* (1994), the complainant did not complain to her parents or boyfriend at first but did complain to her boyfriend the following day. She claimed to have been too frightened to tell her family. She stated that she knew her boyfriend had a much older brother and that she would receive good advice from him. However, she did not make any complaint on the first day and went out to dinner with her boyfriend, her sister and her sister's boyfriend that evening. Had she complained to her boyfriend on the day of the incident, the court would have been satisfied that such a complaint would have been made "as speedily as could reasonably be expected." However, the complaint made the following day was not made at the first reasonable opportunity and evidence of the complaint was therefore inadmissible.

The subsequent decision of *People (DPP) v DR* (1998) took a more liberal view of when complaints could be said to have been made as soon as was reasonably possible. The incident took place on a Sunday evening. The complainant had the opportunity to complain to her husband that night or the following morning. She also had the opportunity to complain to her husband's sister, with whom she was staying. However, the defendant was in a relationship with her husband's sister. It was also accepted that the defendant had a violent temper which he had difficulty in controlling, and the complainant was afraid that there would be a violent confrontation if she told her husband. In addition, the complainant said she had been "frozen" by the incident and had difficulty in talking about it. She did not tell her husband when they were driving home on the Monday morning but told him later that day when she was sitting at home in her garden. She began by saying that their host was "no gentleman" and her husband questioned her and eventually the whole story came out. The court found that her complaint was not the result of answering leading questions—her husband had merely assisted her in saying something which she herself wished to say. It was held that the complaint had been made as soon as was reasonably possible.

6.8.6 Legal representation for complainant

There has recently been a groundswell of opinion in favour of the view that complainants should have separate legal representation. This view was expressed by, for example, the Working Party on the Legal and Judicial Process, which took the view that this would provide support for complainants, render the trial process less traumatic for them and would help bring about an increase in the reporting of rape.

However, there has been equally strong opposition to such a proposal. In part, this is based on the view that such representation would unfairly prejudice the defendant. The Law Reform Commission took the view in its Consultation Paper on Rape (1987) that:

> "It might indeed be constitutionally suspect, since it tilts the balance of the criminal process significantly in favour of the prosecution in a defined range of offences by permitting a dual representation hostile to the interests of the accused, thereby depriving him of one of the long standing benefits of a criminal trial conducted 'in due course of law' as that phrase was plainly understood at the time of the enactment of the Constitution." (at p.70)

Similarly, Flood J., in *People (DPP) v MC* (1995), indicated that s.5 of the Criminal Justice Act 1993 (giving a victim a right to give evidence of the impact of the offence on her) did not make the victim an independent party in the criminal trial and took the view that "the constitutional validity of a statutory provision to that effect would be very doubtful".

Other opinion has been to the effect that separate legal representation would simply muddy the waters of the criminal trial, confusing the issue to the point where the jury might give up and return an unjustified acquittal.

Consequently, the recent trend has been towards other measures to improve the conditions of complainants (for example, the limitations on examination on prior sexual history, the grant of free legal aid for victims of rape or aggravated sexual assault to allow a complainant to consult a legal aid solicitor who may accompany the complainant into court (s.26(3) Civil Legal Aid Act 1995), the victim impact rights created by the Criminal Justice Act 1993, greater access to Gardaí and prosecution lawyers, automatic giving of copies of statements to complainants).

More recently, however, the Sex Offenders Act 2001 has introduced a limited form of separate legal representation for complainants in rape and other serious sexual assault cases. This representation applies during applications to adduce evidence of or to cross-examine the complainant on her previous sexual history. It is felt that representation limited to such applications does not pose constitutional difficulties, as such applications are made in the absence of the jury and the representation therefore cannot impinge on the jury's view of the case.

Further Reading:

O'Malley, *Sexual Offences: Law, Policy and Punishment* (Round Hall Sweet and Maxwell, 1996); Charleton, *Offences Against the Person* (Round Hall Press, 1992), pp.262–337; Department of Justice, Equality and Law Reform, *The Law on Sexual Offences: A Discussion Paper* (Stationery Office, 1998); Charleton, "Criminal law—Protecting the Mentally Sub-Normal against Sexual Exploitation" (1984) 6 D.U.L.J. *(ns)* 165; Law Reform Commission Report, *Sexual Offences Against the Mentally Handicapped* (L.R.C. 1990); Law Reform Commission Consultation Paper, *Child Sexual Abuse* (L.R.C. 1989); Law Reform Commission Consultation Paper, *Rape* (L.R.C. 1987); Law Reform Commission Report, *Rape* (L.R.C. 1988), Ní Raifeartaigh, *Doctrine of Fresh Complaint in Sexual Cases* (1994) 12 I.L.T. 160; Gillespie, "Tackling Child Grooming on the Internet: The UK Approach" (2005) 10 (1) Bar Review 4; Conroy, "Sentencing under the Child Pornography and Trafficking Act 1998" (2004) 14(2) I.C.L.J. 8.

7. OFFENCES AGAINST THE PERSON

7.1 Background

Until 1997, the law of non-fatal offences against the person was made up of a variety of statutory and common law offences, the bulk of which were contained in the Offences Against the Person Act 1861. There was a wide range of very specific offences: assault, assault occasioning actual bodily harm, unlawful wounding, wounding with intent, suffocation or strangulation, and so on. The definition of each offence was highly technical, and unduly complex. The variety of offences available also caused problems for prosecutors, with cases being lost because the wrong offence was chosen.

The law on this topic has now been comprehensively overhauled by the Non-Fatal Offences Against the Person Act 1997. This Act largely follows the recommendations of the Law Reform Commission made in the *Report on Non-Fatal Offences Against the Person* (Dublin, 1994), and creates a simplified hierarchy of offences including assault, assault causing harm, causing serious harm, syringe offences, false imprisonment, coercion, harassment and endangerment.

7.2 Assault

Prior to the 1997 Act, there were two separate offences: assault and battery. Assault was defined as an action causing the victim to *fear* that force would be immediately inflicted upon him, while battery was the *actual infliction* of force. For example, if A threatened B, and then struck B, A would have committed an assault when B was caused to fear the imminent use of force, and would have committed a battery when he went on to strike B.

Section 2 of the 1997 Act merges both offences under a single offence of assault. Assault is now defined as follows:

> "A person shall be guilty of the offence of assault who, without lawful excuse [*e.g. in the course of making a lawful arrest*], intentionally or recklessly -
>
> (a) directly or indirectly applies force to or causes an impact on the body of another, or

(b) causes another to believe on reasonable grounds that he or she is likely immediately to be subjected to any such force or impact, without the consent of the other."

Section 2(a) (applying force) corresponds to the old offence of battery, while s.2(b) (causing another to believe that force will be applied) corresponds to the old offence of assault. It is important to note that this legal definition of assault does not correspond with the ordinary meaning of the word. Usually, when a person speaks of an "assault" they will have in mind some form of physical contact. Under s.2, however, an assault is committed even where there is no physical contact, provided that the victim was put in fear of imminent unlawful contact.

7.2.1 Consent

Absence of consent is a part of the crime. Consent will be implied in circumstances such as contact sports, where each participant implicitly consents to the use of a certain level of force as part of the sport. As regards ordinary day to day conduct (for example, tapping a person on the shoulder to attract their attention) s.2(3) provides that no offence is committed if:

- the force or impact is not intended or likely to cause injury; and
- the contact in question is generally acceptable in the ordinary conduct of daily life; and
- the defendant did not know or believe that it was in fact unacceptable to that particular person.

This last point is important, as even innocuous conduct will amount to an assault if a defendant knows that it is unacceptable to a particular person. Suppose that A has a phobia about germs, causing him to shun all physical contact. B, knowing this, proceeds to tap him on the shoulder, causing distress to A. B would be guilty of assault.

7.2.2 Corporal punishment

At common law, parents (or persons *in loco parentis*) have long been allowed to use reasonable force for the chastisement or discipline of their children, and the 1997 Act does not affect this immunity. Until recently, teachers also were immune from punishment in respect of reasonable corporal punishment. This rule has now, however, been abolished by s.24 of the 1997 Act, which provides:

> "The rule of law under which teachers are immune from criminal liability in respect of physical chastisement of pupils is hereby abolished."

7.2.3 Force

"Force" is defined in s.2(2) to include application of heat, light, electric current, noise or any other form of energy, or application of matter in any form. This definition is extremely wide—it could, for example, amount to an assault if A were to deliberately shine a torch into the eyes of B.

The term "force" can be misleading. In its everyday meaning, it might suggest a requirement of hostility or aggression, and in the past it was sometimes stated that battery was committed only where the contact was "angry, or revengeful, or rude, or insolent" (1 Hawk. P.C. 263). However, in modern law it is clear that there is no such requirement—so that if A were to affectionately stroke B's hair, without B's consent, this could be an assault: *Faulkner v Talbot* (1981).

There is no minimum threshold for the amount of force required (implied consent to ordinary day-to-day conduct excluded): the slightest touching without consent can amount to an assault, regardless of whether the victim is in fact injured. So in *Collins v Wilcock* (1984) it was held to be a battery where a police officer took hold of a woman's arm without her consent. *Per* Goff J.:

> "The fundamental principle, plain and incontestable, is that every person's body is inviolate. It has long been established that any touching of another person, however slight, may amount to a battery ... The effect is that everybody is protected not only against physical injury but against any form of physical molestation."

The force need not be applied directly to the body of the victim—it is sufficient if the defendant touches something which is worn or carried by the victim. In *R. v Thomas* (1985), for example, a battery was committed where a defendant touched a woman's skirt, though not her body. In that case the victim did not realise what the defendant was doing, illustrating the point that the victim need not be aware of the contact. An assault could be committed, for example, where the victim is asleep or unconscious.

7.2.4 Immediacy

Section 2 retains the effect of the prior case law that, for an assault (as distinct from a battery) to occur, the victim must believe that he will be *immediately* subjected to force or impact. Threats to use force at some future date do not amount to assault, although they may amount to other offences. For the same reason, conduct which would otherwise amount to an assault may be negatived by circumstances which show that force is not about to be immediately used. In the renowned case of *Tuberville v Savage* (1669), it was alleged that the plaintiff had placed his hand on his sword while saying "If it were not assize time, I would not take such language from you". This was held not to be an assault: placing of the hand on the sword would indicate immediate use of force, but the words indicated that the plaintiff would not act, and so the defendant could not have believed that force was immediately to be used.

Equally, if I were to wave a knife at a person who was on the other side of a gorge, and to shout that I intended to kill him, no assault would be committed if the circumstances were such that the person was safely out of my range: the person would not be put in fear of the *immediate* application of force.

7.2.5 Causes another to believe

On the same point, an assault is not committed if the victim does not *in fact* apprehend immediate and likely force. Suppose that A is on one side of a gorge and B on the other. A points a gun at B and threatens to shoot. B is, however, aware that the gun is merely a replica, and knows that he is in no danger. In this situation, A has not committed an assault, since B did not apprehend the immediate use of force.

7.2.6 Can words alone amount to an assault?

Before the 1997 Act there was some confusion as to whether words alone, unaccompanied by "menacing gestures" or any physical act, could amount to an assault. For example, in *R. v Meade &* Belt (1823) (at p.185) it was said that that "No words or singing are

equivalent to an assault, nor will they authorise an assault in return."
On the other hand, in *R. v Wilson* (1955) (at p.745), Lord Goddard
C.J. held that shouting "Get out the knives" would be an assault.

This supposed rule was often criticised as illogical and arbitrary,
and in England it was abolished in *R. v Ireland* (1998). In that case,
the defendant was alleged to have committed an assault by making
silent telephone calls to three women, putting them in fear of violence.
It was argued for the defendant that since words alone could not
amount to an assault, neither could mere silence. The House of Lords
rejected this argument, however, holding (*per* Lord Steyn) that:

> "The proposition that a gesture may amount to an assault,
> but that words can never suffice, is unrealistic and
> indefensible. A thing said is also a thing done. There is no
> reason why something said should be incapable of causing
> an apprehension of immediate person violence, e.g. a man
> accosting a woman in a dark alley saying, 'Come with me
> or I will stab you.' I would, therefore, reject the proposition
> that an assault can never be committed by words."

In this jurisdiction, the rule was criticised by the Law Reform
Commission, and it is clear that the 1997 Act is drafted in such a
way as to abolish it. The terms of s.2 ("causes another to believe on
reasonable grounds") make it clear that words alone can now amount
to an assault, provided that the words amount to reasonable grounds
for the belief that the application of force or impact is immediately
likely.

7.2.7 Indirect use of force?

Before 1997, the case law was unclear as to whether assault was
committed where a person *indirectly* applied force to another, for
example by digging a pit for a victim to fall into, or by derailing a
train. On balance, it seemed that it was: as in the case of *DPP v K*
(1990) in which a schoolboy was held to commit assault where he
poured acid into a hot air dryer in a bathroom, injuring the next user
who switched on the dryer. Section 2 now puts this point beyond
doubt and makes it clear that assault can be committed by either the
direct or indirect application of force.

This issue recently arose in England in *Haystead v Director of
Public Prosecutions* (2000). In that case, the defendant punched a
woman twice in the face, causing her to drop her child. The child

struck his head on the floor. The defendant was charged with battery in respect of the injury to the child. He argued that battery at common law could be committed only where there was a direct application of force to the victim. After a comprehensive review of the cases, the court held that battery could be committed indirectly, provided that the physical injury was the direct consequence of the defendant's actions, and the chain of causation was not broken by some *novus actus interveniens.*

7.2.8 Punishment

Simple assault is a summary offence only and carries a maximum fine of €1,500 and/or imprisonment for up to six months.

7.3 Assault causing harm

The next offence created by the Act is contained in s.3, which provides that: "A person who assaults another causing him or her harm shall be guilty of an offence". Harm is defined in s.1 as "harm to body or mind and includ[ing] pain and unconsciousness". This offence is, therefore, an aggravated form of assault, made up of the components of assault together with the infliction of harm.

It is significant that harm is defined to include harm to body *or mind*: an assault which causes the victim no physical harm may nevertheless cause the victim psychological harm, and this would seem to fall within the terms of s.3.

Consider *R v Ireland* (1998). In that case, a defendant's silent telephone calls caused a number of victims to suffer psychiatric illness, including severe depression. The House of Lords accepted that this constituted assault causing actual bodily harm, under the 1861 Act, on the basis that "the body" included all the organs, including the brain.

7.3.1 Punishment

Assault causing harm is punishable by an unlimited fine and/or imprisonment for up to five years.

7.4 Causing serious harm

Section 4 creates the offence of causing serious harm:

> "A person who intentionally or recklessly causes serious harm to another shall be guilty of an offence".

Serious harm is defined in s.1 as meaning:

> "injury which creates a substantial risk of death or which causes serious disfigurement or substantial loss or impairment of the mobility of the body as a whole or of the function of any particular bodily member or organ."

It is important to note that this does not follow the recommendations of the Law Reform Commission, which advocated the creation of an offence of *assault* causing serious harm. Instead, the 1997 Act simply adopts the concept of *causing* serious harm: it is not necessary that the conduct which causes the harm should also amount to an assault. (For example, suppose A knows he is HIV positive; he has unprotected intercourse with B without informing B of this status. B falls ill. In these circumstances there is no assault, since B consented to the intercourse: nevertheless, if A has the requisite intention, then A's conduct may amount to the offence of causing serious harm to B.)

The offence is one of intentionally or recklessly causing serious harm, and the requirement of *mens rea* applies, therefore, both to the conduct in question and to foresight of serious harm. Again, the principles laid down in *People (DPP) v Murray* (1977) apply: the defendant must intend serious harm, or be subjectively reckless as to whether it results.

7.4.1 Is consent a defence to causing serious harm?

Absence of consent is a constituent part of assault under s.2. Since assault causing harm is an aggravated form of assault, absence of consent is also a constituent part of assault causing harm contrary to s.3. However, s.4, causing serious harm, contains no reference to consent being a defence. Should we treat consent as a defence notwithstanding this omission?

Before the 1997 Act consent could only be a defence to the causing of bodily harm under the Offences Against the Person Act 1861 in limited circumstances: consent was not a general defence. The report of the Law Reform Commission on Non-Fatal Offences Against the Person recommended that there should be a statutory scheme for determining when consent would be a defence to the infliction of serious harm; however, this recommendation was not followed in the 1997 Act. Consequently, one must look to the case law to see when consent will be a defence.

The issue of consent as a defence to serious harm has generally arisen in three main contexts. The first is that of sport, where players consent to physical contact within the rules of the sport. This will seldom result in serious harm, except in the case of boxing. The second is that of dangerous exhibitions: stunts and the like. The third is that of sadomasochistic sexual activities.

When will consent be a defence in each context? The leading authority is the case of *R. v Brown* (1993). In this case, the defendants had consensually and in private inflicted various sadomasochistic tortures on each other. They were unwise enough to video these activities; the video tape fell into the hands of the police, and they were charged with occasioning actual bodily harm on each other. The question presented was whether lack of consent was an essential part of the offence.

It was held by the House of Lords that, in the circumstances, consent was irrelevant. As a general rule, a person could not consent to bodily harm: in the words of an earlier case involving a consensual fist fight (*Attorney General's Reference, Number 6 of 1980* (1981)): "it is not in the public interest that people should try to cause or should cause each other actual bodily harm for no good reason". The House of Lords accepted the decisions in earlier cases that consent was a defence in cases of "properly conducted games and sports, lawful chastisement or correction, reasonable surgical interference, dangerous exhibitions, etc. These apparent exceptions can be justified as involving the exercise of a legal right, in the case of chastisement or correction, or as needed in the public interest, in the other cases." (*Attorney General's Reference, Number 6 of 1980* (1981))

It therefore appears that consent is a defence only where the conduct in question is "in the public interest": needless to say, the House of Lords did not accept that the "gratification of sadomasochistic desires" was in the public interest. In general, therefore, it seems that the court will look to the public utility of the act in determining whether consent can amount to a defence. In particular, it should be noted that *R. v Brown* (1993) accepted the legality of boxing, notwithstanding that the participants in boxing certainly do intend to inflict on each other actual or serious bodily harm.

7.4.2 Punishment

Causing serious harm may be punished by an unlimited fine and/or life imprisonment.

7.5 Threats to kill or cause serious harm

Section 5 of the 1997 Act deals with threats other than in the context of assaults and provides that:

> "A person who, without lawful excuse, makes to another a threat, by any means intending the other to believe it will be carried out, to kill or cause serious harm to that other or a third person shall be guilty of an offence."

This section is entirely distinct from assault, even though the same conduct might at the same time amount to both assault and an offence under s.5. For example, if A stands in front of B with an upraised knife and shouts "I'm going to kill you" then this would probably amount to both and assault and an offence under s.5. However, if A phones B and says "I'm going to kill you", but B knows that A is in another country, then this will not amount to assault: the necessary element of immediacy is lacking. It will, however, amount to an offence under s.5.

This section is also distinct from assault as regards the state of mind of the victim. The crime of assault is established only where a victim actually believes that he is likely to be subjected to immediate force or impact. It is not established where a victim does not so believe. Suppose A threatens B with a replica firearm. If B knows that the firearm is a replica, then B may not believe that this is likely. The crime of assault may not have been established. On the other hand, an offence under s.5 will be established: A has made a threat, intending B to believe that it will be carried out, to kill or cause serious injury to B. Under s.5, the subjective state of mind of the victim is irrelevant.

7.5.1 Punishment

Threats to kill or cause serious injury may be punished by an unlimited fine and/or imprisonment for up to ten years.

7.6 Syringe attacks and related offences

During the passage of the 1997 Act there was a wave of public concern about robberies carried out by drug users involving syringes, needles and blood. These robberies appeared especially threatening because of the risk of infection associated with these items. Consequently, s.6 was inserted to create a number of distinct offences relating to syringes, blood and contaminated blood. Before looking at each, terms must be defined. Section 1 defines these as follows:

> "'contaminated blood' means blood which is contaminated with any disease, virus, agent or organism which if passed into the bloodstream of another could infect the other with a life threatening or potentially life threatening disease;"

> "'contaminated fluid' means fluid or substance which is contaminated with any disease, virus, agent or organism which if passed into the bloodstream of another could infect the other with a life threatening or potentially life threatening disease;"

> "'contaminated syringe' means a syringe which has in it or on it contaminated blood or contaminated fluid;" and

> "'syringe' includes any part of a syringe or a needle or any sharp instrument capable of piercing skin and passing onto or into a person blood or any fluid or substance resembling blood."

The offences are then created as follows. First is the offence created by s.6(1) in two components. The first component is injuring another by piercing the skin of that other with a syringe, or threatening to so injure the other with a syringe. The second is that the defendant intends the victim to believe, or it is likely that the victim will be caused to believe, that he may become infected with disease as a result.

Second is the offence created by section 6(2), which is again in two parts. The first is spraying, pouring or putting onto another, blood or any substance resembling blood, or threatening to do so. The second is the same as in s.6(1): that the defendant intends the victim to believe, or it is likely that the victim will be caused to believe, that he may become infected with disease as a result.

Third is the offence created by s.6(3):

> "A person who in committing or attempting to commit an offence under section 6(1) or section 6(2)-
>
>> (a) injures a third person with a syringe by piercing his or her skin, or
>> (b) sprays, pours or puts onto a third person blood or any fluid or substance resembling blood, resulting in the third person believing that he or she may become infected with disease as a result of the injury or action caused shall be guilty of an offence."

This is a secondary offence, which comes into play only once a person is committing or attempting to commit an offence under s.6(1) or s.6(2), and covers the situations where A threatens or attacks B, but manages to also injure C. In these circumstances, A is guilty of an offence.

Finally, there are the offences created by s.6(5). These offences are distinguished from the preceding offences in that they involve actual (not merely threatened) attacks with contaminated blood or syringes, and therefore a real risk of actually causing disease. Under s.6(5)(a) it is an offence to intentionally injure another by piercing the skin of that other with a contaminated syringe. Under s.6(5)(b) it is an offence to intentionally spray, etc., another with contaminated blood. Under s.6(5)(c) it is an offence, similar to that created by s.6(3), to injure a third person while committing or attempting to commit an offence under s.6(5)(a) or (b).

7.6.1 Punishment

For each of the offences created by subs.(1), (2) and (3), the maximum penalty is an unlimited fine and/or imprisonment for up to ten years. The maximum penalty for the subs.(5) offence is an unlimited fine and/or life imprisonment.

7.6.2 Possession of syringes

Section 7 creates an offence of possession of a syringe, etc., with intention to cause or to threaten injury or to intimidate another. The maximum penalty for this offence is an unlimited fine and/or imprisonment for up to seven years.

Section 8 creates two distinct offences of placing or abandoning syringes in places where they are likely to injure another. The less serious offence (subs.(1)) is committed where a person: "places or abandons a syringe in any place in such a manner that it is likely to injure another and does injure another or is likely to injure, cause a threat to or frighten another". This carries a maximum penalty of an unlimited fine and/or imprisonment for up to seven years. The more serious offence is defined by subs.(2), and applies where a person "intentionally places a contaminated syringe in any place in such a manner that it injures another". This requires three distinct elements—there must be an intention to injure, there must be an injury, and the syringe must in fact be contaminated. This carries a maximum penalty of an unlimited fine and/or life imprisonment.

This section would cover, for example, leaving a syringe hidden in a seat with the intention that the next occupant should injure themselves.

7.7 Coercion

The 1997 Act creates a general offence of coercion in s.9. Before 1997 there had been only one specific offence of coercion, which was limited in its scope. Section 9 is wider, and covers various forms of harassment and intimidation intended to coerce:

> "A person who, with a view to compel another to abstain from doing or to do any act which that other has a lawful right to do or to abstain from doing, wrongfully and without lawful authority -
>
> > (a) uses violence to or intimidates that other person or a member of the family of the other, or
> > (b) injures or damages the property of that other, or
> > (c) persistently follows that other about from place to place, or
> > (d) watches or besets the premises or other place where that other resides, works or carries on business, or happens to be, or the approach to such premises or place, or
> > (e) follows that other with one or more persons in a disorderly manner in or through any public place,
>
> shall be guilty of an offence."

The offence has two constituent parts: the intention to compel, and the use of unacceptable means to do so. However, it seems that the offence will not be committed by, for example, a creditor who resorts to following a debtor around to secure payment: in that case, it cannot be said that the debtor has a lawful right to abstain from payment.

7.7.1 Punishment

The maximum penalty for this offence is an unlimited fine and/or imprisonment for up to five years.

7.8 Harassment

The Law Reform Commission in its Report identified a need for a new offence to cover acts of harassment that interfere with a person's right to a peaceful and private life, even though those acts might not give rise to a fear of violence. The essence of this offence is not the individual actions (which might not in themselves be illegal) but the distress caused by their repetition.

Suppose, for example, that A engages in what is commonly described as stalking—persistently following B, making silent telephone calls to B, and/or sending B numerous letters, with the result that B becomes upset and distressed. Prior to the 1997 Act, this conduct would have been difficult to prosecute. In particular, unless B was put in fear of violence, no assault was committed. (Although in *R. v Burstow* (1997) the House of Lords took a creative approach to this problem, and held that acts of harassment which resulted in psychological injury could amount to the infliction of grievous bodily harm, contrary to s.20 of the Offences Against the Person Act, 1861, since that section penalised the infliction of harm irrespective of whether the harm was caused by way of an assault.)

The result of this gap in the law was that victims generally had to resort to civil actions for their protection. An example of this can be seen in *Royal Dublin Society v Yates* (1997), where the defendant appeared to become besotted by an employee of the plaintiff society, and pursued her by way of (*inter alia*) flowers, poems, letters and even paintings depicting her. He also frequented the premises of the plaintiff and the streets outside, and at one point had to be forcibly ejected from those premises. The court accepted that this behaviour amounted to the tort of nuisance and granted an injunction restraining the defendant from communicating with the victim in this case, or with any other employees of the plaintiff.

The recommendation of the Law Reform Commission was followed in s.10 of the 1997 Act, which provides:

> "(1) Any person who, without lawful authority or reasonable excuse, by any means including by use of the telephone, harasses another by persistently following, watching, pestering, besetting or communicating with him or her, shall be guilty of an offence.
>
> (2) For the purposes of this section a person harasses another where -
>
> (a) he or she, by his or her acts intentionally or recklessly, seriously interferes with the other's peace or privacy or causes alarm, distress or harm to the other, and
>
> (b) his or her acts are such that a reasonable person would realise that the acts would seriously interfere with the other's peace and privacy or cause alarm, distress or harm to the other."

7.8.1 Mens rea

The *mens rea* for this offence presents an unusual problem. In many cases a stalker is likely to be unaware of the effect of his conduct. Typically, the offender may be somewhat unbalanced and will pursue what he perceives to be a romantic interest, being unaware that his conduct is unwelcome. Will this person have the necessary intention to be found guilty of harassment, given that he is genuinely oblivious to the effect of his actions?

Under s.10, the offence is committed by a person who "by his or her acts *intentionally or recklessly*, seriously interferes with the other's peace or privacy or causes alarm, distress or harm to the other". In addition, the actions must be "such that *a reasonable person would realise* that the acts would seriously interfere with the other's peace and privacy, or cause alarm, distress or harm". This wording refers to the defendant's *acts* as being intentional or reckless, rather than the *effect* of those acts. Instead, the effects are judged according to the standard of the reasonable person. Although this wording is cumbersome, it appears clear that it is intended to cover a person who does not realise the effect of his actions, provided that a reasonable person would so realise.

Suppose, for example, a besotted individual stalks his victim while believing that he is merely pursuing her romantically, or that his behaviour is actually welcome to the victim. Section 10 will cover this situation, notwithstanding the absence of understanding on the part of the offender. Indeed, under any other interpretation the most persistent and dangerous offenders might escape liability on the basis that they did not appreciate the effects of their actions.

7.8.2 *"Persistently"*

The section applies only where a defendant "persistently" harasses another. Consequently, a single incident will not be sufficient to establish the crime. Instead, the prosecution must show a number of incidents over a period of time. This may present some problems in borderline cases.

Suppose, for example, that A telephones B several times over the space of an hour. Would this conduct be persistent, given that it takes place over a relatively short period of time and might arguably be described as one incident? Alternatively, suppose that A confronts B on two occasions, several months apart, in relation to two separate issues. Would this amount to persistent conduct, given the small number of incidents, the length of time which separates them, and the lack of any apparent link between the two incidents?

There is, as yet, no Irish case considering this point. However, a number of English decisions have considered the similar requirement under the Protection from Harassment Act 1997 that a defendant's actions must amount to a "course of conduct".

For example, in *Kelly v DPP* (2003), it was held that a defendant who left three messages on the victim's voice mail in the space of five minutes had engaged in a course of conduct for the purposes of that act: the court was entitled to treat each message as separate and distinct, notwithstanding the defence argument that in reality the three telephone calls amounted to a single incident. It will be interesting to see whether this approach would be followed by an Irish court: arguably, the word "persistently" would require that the conduct extend over a longer period of time.

In *R. v Hills* (2001), the defendant had attacked his partner on two separate occasions, six months apart. Between the two attacks, however, the defendant and the victim had reconciled and lived together. The charge of harassment was dismissed, on the basis that the two attacks did not amount to a course of conduct. The court was particularly influenced by the fact that there were only two incidents, a substantial period of time had elapsed between the two attacks, and the two attacks could not be described as linked to each other by anything other than the identity of the parties.

7.8.3 *"Lawful authority or reasonable excuse"*

There is an exception for conduct which is carried out either under lawful authority or with reasonable excuse. For example, overt surveillance by the Gardaí will not be criminalised. The offence is, therefore, not intended to cover situations where there is a good reason for what might otherwise amount to harassment. Another example given by the Law Reform Commission was that of the creditor who pursues a debtor seeking payment:

> "The question may also arise as to whether a creditor who repeatedly seeks to have a bill paid should be guilty of an offence. The answer would seem to be that, while clearly the point can be reached where persistence becomes harassment, the legitimacy or justifiability of the intrusion is a factor to which weight should be attached in determining whether the conduct was worthy of criminal sanction. For this reason we recommend that it should be necessary to prove that the conduct was without lawful authority or reasonable excuse. We appreciate that this introduces an element of uncertainty, but without a proviso on these lines the offence would seem overbroad." (Law Reform Commission, *Report on Non-Fatal Offences Against the Person* (Dublin, 1994), p.258.)

7.8.4 *Non-contact orders*

If a person is convicted of harassment, the court has the power to order that he not communicate with the victim or approach closer than a specified distance to the victim's home or workplace, for such period as the court determines (s.10(3)). It is an offence to fail to comply with such an order (s.10(4)). Remarkably, the court is also given the power to make such an order even if the defendant is not convicted, provided that it considers it to be "in the interests of justice to do so" (s.10(5)). This would seem to include cases where the prosecutor meets the civil standard of proof but not the criminal standard, or where the defendant is dealt with under the Probation

Act. However, there must be a question mark over the constitutionality of a power to restrict a defendant's liberty where that person has been acquitted of an offence.

In the first conviction under this section (and the only reported decision on harassment to date), *People (DPP) v Ramachchandran* (2000), the court considered the extent of this power. In that case, the accused was convicted of harassment of a woman and her daughter. However, his trial was compromised by a number of factors stemming from his insistence on representing himself. The Court of Criminal Appeal overturned his conviction, but held that notwithstanding his acquittal the court was satisfied on the balance of probabilities that the two victims were in need of the protection of the court, and therefore granted a non-contact order against him. That case accepts, therefore, that such orders may be made even where there is no conviction, and establishes that the standard of proof for such orders is the civil standard rather than the criminal standard. It also illustrates how wide such orders may be: amongst other things, the defendant was ordered to remain outside an area three miles in radius, centred on Eyre Square in Galway, thus effectively barring the defendant from the entire city.

7.8.5 Punishment

The maximum penalty for this offence is an unlimited fine and/or imprisonment for up to seven years.

7.9 Demands for payment of debts

Section 11 of the 1997 Act deals with the special case of demands for the payment of a debt. These may amount to coercion (if the debt is not in fact due) or harassment (depending on their nature) but will also be subject to this section which provides:

> "A person who makes any demand for payment of a debt shall be guilty of an offence if -
> (a) the demands by reason of their frequency are calculated to subject the debtor or a member of the family of the debtor to alarm, distress or humiliation, or
> (b) the person falsely represents that criminal proceedings lie for non-payment of the debt, or
> (c) the person falsely represents that he or she is

authorised in some official capacity to enforce payment, or
(d) the person utters a document falsely represented to have an official character."

This is a summary offence only, and carries a maximum fine of £1,500.

7.10 Poisoning

Section 12 creates an offence of poisoning:

"A person shall be guilty of an offence if, knowing that the other does not consent to what is being done, he or she intentionally or recklessly administers to or causes to be taken by another a substance which he or she knows to be capable of interfering substantially with the other's bodily functions."

The section goes on to specify that "a substance capable of inducing unconsciousness or sleep is capable of interfering substantially with bodily functions" (s.12(2)). Note that the section covers both administration of a substance as well as causing it to be taken—if, for example, A were to spike B's drink with a sedative, this could amount to poisoning, notwithstanding that A did not *directly* administer it to B.

The maximum penalty for this offence is an unlimited fine and/ or imprisonment for up to three years.

7.11 Endangerment

Prior to the 1997 Act, Irish law recognised a number of specific offences involving the creation of a risk, without any actual injury being caused. It was, for example, an offence to interfere with the railways in a way which created a risk, or to lay a man-trap. There was, however, no general offence of endangerment.

The Law Reform Commission argued that the deliberate or reckless creation of a risk was itself deserving of punishment, notwithstanding that no injury might actually be caused, and therefore recommended that a wider offence of endangerment should be created:

"Moreover, the right to bodily integrity would be given more comprehensive and consistent protection by the creation of such an offence. In the first place, it would cover the gap in existing law arising from the fact that a person who recklessly creates a risk of serious injury commits no offence although he may be prosecuted for attempt where he does so intentionally, or for causing serious injury where such injury results. In certain cases, where the evidence of intent is insufficient, it may provide a valuable alternative to a charge of attempted murder or attempting to cause serious injury.

[…]

In such cases of advertent risk-taking, where the risk of serious injury or death may be said to be 'substantial', there is clearly a strong case for facilitating early intervention by authority to prevent the occurrence of actual harm. The creation of a general offence of endangerment would also give effect to the principle that the wanton disregard of others' safety is in itself deserving of condemnation and sanction as a serious infringement of basic values, irrespective of the manner in which such a risk is taken." (*Report on Non Fatal Offences Against the Person,* pp. 294–295)

This recommendation was followed in s.13 which creates a general offence of endangerment:

"A person shall be guilty of an offence who intentionally or recklessly engages in conduct which creates a substantial risk of death or serious harm to another."

Serious harm is defined in s.1 as:

"injury which creates a substantial risk of death or which causes serious disfigurement or substantial loss or impairment of the mobility of the body as a whole or of the function of any particular bodily member or organ."

Examples of endangerment would include, according to the Commission, a builder who constructs a building in a way which he knows to be unsafe and to create a risk of collapse. Charleton, McDermott and Bolger have also suggested that endangerment might be committed in circumstances similar to the Blood Transfusion Board Scandal, where officials were aware that blood products were contaminated but failed to take steps to recall the products or warn the users of the products. (*Criminal Law* (1999), p.736).

The only cases to date on endangerment are the Court of Criminal Appeal decisions in *People (DPP) v McGrath* (2004) and *People (DPP) v Cagney* (2004). These two related cases arose out of a late night drunken brawl involving the victim, Langan, and the two defendants. During this brawl McGrath attempted to attack Langan, but was held back by a friend. McGrath then shouted at Cagney to hit Langan for him. Cagney did so, striking Langan with two blows to the head. Langan fell to the ground, hitting his head. Langan ultimately died from the effects of the fall.

McGrath and Cagney were charged with manslaughter and endangerment. Both were acquitted of manslaughter, but convicted of endangerment. In the case of Cagney, this verdict presented little difficulty—striking somebody in the head is clearly conduct which creates a substantial risk of serious harm, and the court accepted that:

> "even if the [defendant] did not intend the endangerment … he may be guilty of endangerment if he was reckless as to whether his conduct, his physical activity, would have that effect."

In the case of McGrath, a more difficult issue was presented. Could McGrath be said to be guilty of endangerment in circumstances where he merely ran after, shouted at, and threatened the victim? The defence argued that this was a mere "expression of anger and aggression" and was insufficient to come within the statute. The prosecution, however, argued that McGrath had endangered the victim, and in particular by roaring the words "hit him" had caused the blows that were struck by Cagney.

The court accepted that McGrath could be found guilty of endangerment, holding that his conduct in pursuing the victim in an aggressive manner, shouting at and threatening the victim, and shouting to Cagney in an aggressive manner to hit the victim, together would entitle the jury to find that he had created a substantial risk of serious harm to the victim.

An argument was also made in that case that the offence of endangerment was not appropriate where injury was in fact caused. The court rejected this argument, however, holding that:

> "The court is satisfied that the offence of endangerment, on the clear words of the section, may exist even if no injury occurs. Further, the court does not consider that the offence is excluded when injury has occurred."

7.11.1 Punishment

The maximum penalty for endangerment is an unlimited fine and/or seven years' imprisonment.

7.12 Endangering Traffic

Related to the s.13 endangerment offence, s.14 creates a more specific offence of endangering traffic:

> "A person shall be guilty of an offence who -
> (a) intentionally places or throws any dangerous obstruction upon a railway, road, street, waterway or public place or interferes with any machinery, signal, equipment or other device for the direction, control or regulation of traffic thereon, or interferes with or throws anything at or on any conveyance used or to be used thereon, and
> (b) is aware that injury to the person or damage to property may be caused thereby, or is reckless in that regard."

The maximum penalty is the same as for the general offence of endangerment, even though the *mens rea* is lesser: under s.14, a person need only be reckless as to the possibility of *any* injury or damage to property, while under s.13 a person must be reckless as to the possibility of *serious* injury.

7.13 False imprisonment

Before 1997 there were two distinct offences related to restraints on personal liberty: kidnapping and false imprisonment. The offence of kidnapping was a common law offence, and was committed where a person was taken by force or fraud against his will. The offence of false imprisonment was also a common law offence, and was committed where the accused "unlawfully impose[d], for any time, a total restraint on the personal liberty of another". Both were declared to be felonies punishable by life imprisonment by s.11 of the Criminal Law Act 1976.

The 1997 Act amalgamates the two offences, reflecting what was happening in practice, with prosecutors relying on the charge of false imprisonment because of ambiguities in the offence of kidnapping. (Charleton, *Offences Against the Person* (Round Hall Press, 1992), p.244.) Section 15 therefore provides:

> "(1) A person shall be guilty of the offence of false imprisonment who intentionally or recklessly -
> (a) takes or detains, or
> (b) causes to be taken or detained, or
> (c) otherwise restricts the personal liberty of,
>
> another without that other's consent.
>
> (2) For the purposes of this section, a person acts without the consent of another if the person obtains the other's consent by force or threat of force, or by deception causing the other to believe that he or she is under legal compulsion to consent."

The provision regarding consent is important: consent is vitiated by force, but is only vitiated by fraud if this causes the victim to believe that there is a legal obligation to consent. It is pointed out by the Law Reform Commission that:

> "In other cases of deception, the victim is free to withdraw consent at any time without fear of force being used, so that his or her liberty cannot be said to be totally restrained." *(Report on Non-Fatal Offences Against the Person* (Dublin, 1994), p.319.)

As regards the restraint on personal liberty, it is clear that s.15 retains the common law position that a person can be falsely imprisoned without being aware of the fact: *Dullaghan v Hillen and King* (1957). So a person can be falsely imprisoned although asleep, or mentally handicapped so as to be unable to appreciate the fact.

How severe must the restraint on personal liberty be to amount to false imprisonment? At common law, the imprisonment must be total: that is, a person must be confined within fixed bounds, so as to prevent movement in all directions. (However, those fixed bounds could be quite large: imprisonment in a room, a house, or a vast country estate all would amount to a crime.) It did not take place where a person was walled in on three sides, but free to walk away through the fourth. However, a person was not required to take an unreasonable risk (for example, of personal injury) or to undergo some major humiliation to avoid an obstacle created by the defendant. (For example, a person would be falsely imprisoned if their clothes were taken away, so that while they were free to leave they would have to appear in public naked.)

Section 15 at first glance appears to be wider in scope, in that it refers to "restricting personal liberty", which might be read to include situations where a person's freedom of movement was constrained in some directions, but not in others. However, the Law Reform Commission did not recommend such a radical change in the law, and it therefore seems that imprisonment must still be total: a mere obstruction in a person's path will not amount to false imprisonment. For the same reason, there is no false imprisonment where a person is under close surveillance which does not actually confine them. In *Kane v Governor of Mountjoy Prison* (1988), the applicant was kept under extremely close Garda surveillance while a warrant for his extradition was pending. He alleged that he had in effect been detained by this surveillance. This argument was rejected by the Supreme Court: the surveillance had not interfered with his ability to go where he chose, which was the essence of detention.

7.13.1 Punishment

False imprisonment carries a maximum penalty of life imprisonment.

7.14 Child abduction

The 1997 Act creates two distinct offences of child abduction. The first, contained in s.16, relates to the abduction of a child by a parent or guardian, who takes the child out of the State either in defiance of a court order or without court approval or the consent of each guardian of the child. It does not apply where the person is a parent but is not a guardian. It is a defence that the person was unable to communicate with the other persons from whom consent is required but believed that they would consent; it is also a defence that the person did not intend to deprive others of their rights in relation to the child. The sensitivity of this offence is reflected in the fact that proceedings cannot be instituted without the consent of the DPP.

The second relates to abduction of children by other persons. Section 17 makes it an offence for a person other than one to whom s.16 applies (parents, guardians and persons having custody) to intentionally take or detain or cause to be taken or detained a child under the age of 16 so as to remove or keep the child from the lawful custody of another person having control of the child. This offence does not require that the child be taken out of the jurisdiction. Belief that the child is 16 or over is a defence. The consent of the child is irrelevant for both this offence and the offence under s.16: the offences are designed to protect parents as well as children, who will not be in a position to give an informed consent, particularly where the child is quite young.

7.14.1 *Punishment*

Both the s.16 and s.17 offences carry an unlimited fine and/or imprisonment for up to seven years.

7.15 Assault with intent to cause bodily harm or commit an indictable offence

This offence is created by s.18 of the Criminal Justice (Public Order) Act 1994, and is another form of aggravated assault:

> "Any person who assaults any person with intent to cause bodily harm or to commit an indictable offence shall be guilty of an offence."

The maximum penalty for this offence is an unlimited fine and/or imprisonment for up to five years.

7.16 Blackmail

Section 17(1) of the Criminal Justice (Public Order) Act 1994 creates the offence which is generally described as blackmail:

> "It shall be an offence for any person who, with a view to gain for himself or with intent to cause loss to another, makes any unwarranted demand with menaces."

An unwarranted demand is defined by s.17(2)(a):

> "a demand with menaces shall be unwarranted unless the
> person making it does so in the belief -
>
>> (i) that he has reasonable grounds for making the
>> demand, and
>> (ii) that the use of the menaces is a proper means of
>> reinforcing the demand."

This is a two-stage test: for a defendant to escape liability he must
believe both that the demand is reasonable and that the menaces are
reasonable. Threatening to publish nude photographs of a person
could not be believed to be a proper way of reinforcing an otherwise
legitimate demand for payment of a debt, for example.

In addition, s.7(2)(b) specifies that the nature of the act
demanded is immaterial, as is whether the menaces relate to action
to be taken by the person making the demand. In other words, it
does not matter what is demanded, nor whether the defendant's
threat relates to something to be done by him or by others.

The components of the offence are therefore:

> (1) an unwarranted demand;
> (2) with menaces; and
> (3) made with a view to gain for the defendant, or to
> cause loss to another.

"Menaces" are not defined in the 1994 Act and therefore we must
look to the case law on the previous offences of blackmail under
ss.29–31 of the Larceny Act 1916. These cases originally defined
menaces as threats of injury to the person or to property, but later
cases gave menaces a wider meaning, with Lord Wright stating that:

> "the word menace is to be liberally construed, and not as
> limited to threats of violence but as including threats of any
> action detrimental to or unpleasant to the person addressed."
> (*Thorne v Motor Trade Association* (1937))

In that case, the defendant was a trade association who demanded
that a member pay a fine for breach of the rules of the association
(selling at below an agreed price); failure to pay the fine would result
in the member being boycotted by other members. It was held that

this did not constitute the offence of demanding money with menaces without reasonable or probable cause (under the 1916 Act) since it did not go beyond the promotion of lawful business interests. However, the definition of menaces will encompass, for example, the threat of publication of details of a person's sexual life. So, in *R. v Tomlinson* (1895) the victim was caught with a woman who was not his wife, and the defendant threatened to tell the world. This was held to come within the meaning of menaces, notwithstanding that neither the conduct of the victim nor the activity of the defendant in revealing this conduct would itself be illegal.

7.16.1 Punishment

This offence carries a maximum penalty of an unlimited fine and/or imprisonment for up to 14 years.

Further Reading:

Law Reform Commission, *Report on Non-Fatal Offences Against the Person* (L.R.C. 45–1994); Law Reform Commission, *The Law Relating to Dishonesty* (L.R.C. 43–1992), pp.115–120, 297–307.

8. Offences Against Property

The offences discussed in this chapter include Arson, Criminal Damage and the offences set out in the Criminal Justice (Theft and Fraud Offences) Act 2001.

8.1 Arson and criminal damage

The offences of arson and criminal damage were formerly dealt with under the Malicious Damage Act 1861, a notoriously badly drafted piece of legislation, in that it created a number of extremely specific offences with highly technical differences between them. The Law Reform Commission therefore recommended (*Report on Malicious Damage* (L.R.C. 26–1988)) that these should be replaced by generic offences of criminal damage, capable of being carried out by means of arson. These recommendations were implemented by the Criminal Damage Act 1991.

This Act creates three distinct offences: damaging property *simpliciter*, damaging property with an intention to endanger life or recklessness as to whether life is endangered, and damaging property with intent to defraud. Each of these offences may be committed by damaging property by fire, in which case they shall be charged as arson. If committed by arson, each offence carries a higher penalty, reflecting the danger to third parties which arson represents:

> "Fire is capable of inflicting enormous injury and damage. It respects no legal boundaries. Anyone who starts a fire with the intention of damaging or destroying property is engaging in an act that may be considered distinctively different (at least in its potential implications) from damaging or destroying a house (or other property) by other means." (Law Reform Commission, *Report on Malicious Damage* (L.R.C. 26–1988), p.27). (Although the Law Reform Commission went on to recommend that arson should not carry a higher penalty than other means of damaging property, this recommendation was not followed.)

8.1.1 Elements common to each offence

"Property" is defined in s.1 as including both property of a tangible nature and data.

"Damage" is defined in s.1 so as to include destroying, defacing, dismantling, rendering inoperable and preventing the operation of tangible property. In relation to data, damage is defined as including adding to, altering, corrupting, erasing or moving that data, or doing any act contributing to such addition, alteration, etc. This element of the definition is significant: the activities of computer hackers will almost invariably fall within the offence of damaging property; where they do not, s.5 of the Act creates the offence of unauthorised accessing of data.

"Lawful excuse" is dealt with in s.6, and shall include situations where the defendant:

> "believed that the person ... he believed to be entitled to consent to or authorise the damage to ... the property in question had consented, or would have consented ... if he ... had known of the damage ... and its circumstances", or

> "[caused the damage] in order to protect himself or another or property belonging to himself or another or a right or interest in property which was or which he believed to be vested in himself or another and ... he believed -

> (i) that he or that other or the property, right or interest was in immediate need of protection, and

> (ii) that the means of protection adopted ... were or would be reasonable having regard to all the circumstances."

The meaning of "lawful excuse" was considered in *Jaggard v Dickinson* (1980). The appellant, late at night and while drunk, broke two windows and damaged a curtain in another person's house while attempting to break into the house, believing it to be the house of a friend in the same street. The two houses were identical, and the appellant's relationship with the friend was such that she had his consent to treat the house as if it were her own. There was a defence under the relevant English legislation of honestly believing that one had a lawful excuse for damaging the property in question. It was held that the legislation specifically required the court, when deciding whether there was an honest belief that there was a lawful excuse to damage property, to consider the defendant's actual state of belief, and that belief could be honestly held even though it was induced by intoxication. (*Majewski* was not followed in this case).

Another case concerning the meaning of "lawful excuse" is *R. v Denton* (1982). The defendant, who was employed at a cotton mill, set fire to machinery in the mill and the machinery and building were damaged. He was charged with arson but claimed that his employer had asked him to set fire to the machinery so he could make a fraudulent insurance claim. He argued that he therefore had a lawful excuse pursuant to the relevant legislation, which afforded him a good defence, as he had believed that "the person entitled to consent to the damage to the property in question had consented". It was held that the defendant had not committed the offence of arson. This case has been criticised by commentators; Charleton remarks at p.754 that: "It is difficult to see how subjective integration into a common design to destroy property for the purposes of fraud could possibly constitute a lawful excuse."

Lloyd v DPP (1992) concerned the cutting of padlocks on a clamped vehicle. The appellant parked his car in a private car park which he was not entitled to use. His car was later immobilised by a security company by the use of wheel clamps. The appellant cut two padlocks and removed the wheel clamps. He was charged with criminal damage to the padlocks. He argued that he had a defence of lawful excuse as, *inter alia*, the clamping was an unlawful act. It was held that, at best, the appellant had a remedy in civil law against the clampers. Self-help involving the use of force could only be contemplated where there was no reasonable alternative. There was no lawful excuse for damaging the wheel clamps since the appellant had the choice of paying the fine under protest, removing his car and then taking civil action against the security company.

In *Johnson v DPP* (1994), the appellant was a squatter who had damaged the door frame of a house he was occupying by chiselling off the locks and replacing them with a lock of his own. When charged with criminal damage, he argued that he had a defence of lawful excuse because he had caused the damage in order to protect his property, had believed the property to be in immediate need of protection and that the means he adopted were reasonable having regard to all the circumstances. It was held that the damage to the door was not done to protect property and that the appellant had no belief that his property was in immediate need of protection. The test to be applied was whether he believed he had to do something which would otherwise be a crime in order to prevent the immediate risk of something worse happening.

8.1.2 *Damaging property*

Section 2(1):

> "A person who without lawful excuse damages any property belonging to another intending to damage any such property or being reckless as to whether any such property would be damaged shall be guilty of an offence."

8.1.3 *Damaging property with intent to endanger life*

Section 2(2):

> "A person who without lawful excuse damages any property, whether belonging to himself or another-
>
> (a) intending to damage any property or being reckless as to whether any property would be damaged, and
> (b) intending by the damage to endanger the life of another or being reckless as to whether the life of another would be thereby endangered,
> shall be guilty of an offence."

Note the overlap between this offence and endangerment contrary to s.13 of the Non-Fatal Offences Against the Person Act 1997: s.13 covers a larger spectrum of behaviour than damaging property. It is also broader because it is not necessary that a defendant intended or was reckless as to the outcome *(i.e.* the required level of harm to the injured party)—it is sufficient the harm occurred.

The English decision of *R. v Webster and Warwick* (1995) concerned the offence of damaging property with intent to endanger life. Two separate appeals considered the charge. In the first case, the appellants pushed a heavy stone from the parapet of a railway bridge onto a passenger train passing below. The passengers were showered with material from the damaged train roof but no physical injury was caused. In the second case, the appellant drove a stolen car from which a passenger threw bricks at a pursuing police car. One of the bricks smashed the rear window of the police car, showering the officers with broken glass. The appellant then rammed his car into the police car several times. It was held that the prosecution had to prove that the danger to life resulted from the destruction of or damage to property and that it was not sufficient for the prosecution to prove that the danger to life resulted from the defendant's act which caused the destruction or damage. The words "destruction or damage" referred to the destruction or damage which the defendant intended to cause or to the risk of which he was reckless, not to the destruction or damage which in fact occurred. What had to be considered was not whether and how life was in fact endangered, but whether and how it was intended by the defendant to be endangered or if there was an obvious risk of it being endangered.

Where a defendant dropped a stone from a bridge, if he intended that the stone itself would crash through the roof of the train thereby directly injuring passengers or was reckless whether he did, the charge would not be made out if only the roof material fell on the passengers. However, if he intended that the stone would smash the roof so that material from it would or might descend upon passengers or was reckless whether it did, thereby endangering life, he was guilty of the offence. Where a defendant threw a brick at the windscreen of a moving vehicle and caused some damage to the vehicle, the question whether he committed the relevant offence did not depend on whether the brick hit the windscreen, but on whether he intended to hit it and intended or was reckless as to whether any resulting damage would endanger life.

8.1.4 Damaging property with intent to defraud

Section 2(3):

> "A person who damages any property, whether belonging to himself or another, with intent to defraud shall be guilty of an offence."

This offence is intended to deal with, for example, the problem of insurance fraud, and therefore applies even where a person damages his own property.

8.1.5 Arson

Section 2(4): "An offence committed under this section by damaging property by fire shall be charged as arson." It has already been noted that this is not a separate offence but the same offence committed in a particular way and therefore charged differently and resulting in a more severe penalty.

8.1.6 Threats to damage property

Section 3 provides that an offence is committed by somebody who threatens to damage property belonging to some other person or who threatens to damage his own property in a way which is likely to endanger the life of another person. The threat must have been one intended to cause fear that it would be carried out. It is not necessary that the person to whom the threat is directed be the owner of the property or the person whose life is endangered—the offence is still made out if a third party either owns the property or is being endangered. For example, A makes a threat to B that he will damage his own boat, thereby jeopardising the life of C who is on board. A intends the threat to cause B fear.

8.1.7 Possessing any thing with intent to damage property

It is an offence under s.4 if a person having any thing in his custody or under his control intends, without lawful excuse, to use it or to cause or permit another to use it to damage property belonging to himself or the intended user or a third party in a manner likely to endanger life, or with intent to defraud. For example, A intends to use a hammer to damage the steering mechanism of B's car/to damage the steering mechanism of his own car for the purpose of making a fraudulent insurance claim.

8.1.8 Unauthorised accessing of data

Computer-hacking is criminalised in s.5. This provides that a person who without lawful excuse operates a computer (a) within the State with intent to access any data kept either within or outside the State, or (b) outside the State with intent to access any data kept within the State, shall, whether or not he accesses any data, be guilty of an offence.

8.1.9 Compensation orders

Section 9 of the Act provides that:

> "On conviction of any person of an offence under section 2 of damaging property belonging to another, the court, instead of or in addition to dealing with him in any other way, may, on application or otherwise, make an order (in this act referred to as a 'compensation order') requiring him to pay compensation in respect of that damage to any

person (in this section referred to as the 'injured party')
who, by reason thereof, has suffered loss (other than
consequential loss)."

This jurisdiction parallels the right of action of a victim against the
offender; the amount of the compensation order may not exceed the
amount which would be payable if the victim were to take an action
in tort. For example, A destroys B's taxi and as a result B is unable
to work for three weeks while he gets a new taxi. B can recover the
price of the taxi under this section but not the lost income. The lost
income is not allowable because it is classed as "consequential loss",
and this type of loss is expressly excluded under s.9.

8.2 Criminal Justice (Theft and Fraud Offences) Act 2001

8.2.1 Introduction

This legislation radically alters Irish law relating to dishonesty. It
sets out a new framework for such offences The pre-2001 law was
to be found primarily in the common law and also in numerous statutes
such as the Larceny Acts of 1861, 1916 and 1990 and the Forgery
Acts of 1861 and 1913. The 2001 Act was intended to modernise
the area and to place a new emphasis on white collar crime and
computer-related crime. It completely repeals most of the earlier
legislation in this area.

8.2.2 Theft

The offence of theft is set out in s.4: " ... a person is guilty of theft
if he or she dishonestly appropriates property without the consent of
its owner and with the intention of depriving its owner of it." This
definition is different to the definition of stealing in s.1 of the Larceny
Act 1916: "A person steals who, without the consent of the owner,
fraudulently and without a claim of right made in good faith, takes
and carries away anything capable of being stolen with intent, at the
time of such taking, permanently to deprive the owner thereof."

(i) "Dishonestly". The 2001 Act defines "dishonestly" as meaning
"without a claim of right made in good faith." The Theft Act 1968
(UK) is premised on a test of dishonesty but the statute does not
define what is meant by dishonesty. There have been numerous

English cases, however, interpreting the term. The interpretation given in *R. v Feely* (1973) was that dishonesty should be judged by the "current standards of ordinary decent folk." The later decision of *R. v Ghosh* (1982) set out a two-fold test: (1) what was done was dishonest according to the ordinary standards of reasonable and honest people; (2) the accused realised that what he was doing was dishonest according to those standards. The 1992 Law Reform Commission Report on Dishonesty remarked that there are numerous potential definitions of dishonesty and recommended that dishonesty should be defined in terms of the absence of a claim of legal right.

(ii) "Appropriates". This is defined in the Act as usurping or adversely interfering with the proprietary rights of the owner of the property. Property is not appropriated without the consent of the owner if either of the following applies: "the person believes that he or she has the owner's consent, or would have the owner's consent if the owner knew of the appropriation of the property and the circumstances in which it was appropriated", the person "appropriates the property in the belief that the owner cannot be discovered by taking reasonable steps". Consent obtained due to intimidation or deception is invalid. Section 4(4) provides that judges or juries, when considering whether the defendant believed that he or she had acted dishonestly, or that the owner of the property had consented or would have consented to its appropriation, or that the owner could not be discovered by taking reasonable steps, should have regard to the presence or absence of reasonable grounds for such a belief.

The Larceny Act 1916 required the physical taking and carrying away of the property. The new offence of theft does not require this carrying away or asportation and is defined in such a way that a person in possession can steal property. For example, A gives a valuable string of pearls to B for safekeeping during a trip around the world. B is therefore in possession of the pearls. He can, however, steal the pearls if he decides not to give the set back to A on his return. This is because he will thereby be interfering with A's right to the jewellery. Under the old law he would have been charged with fraudulent conversion instead of larceny, as he did not physically grab the pearls and run off with them—he always had the pearls to begin with, albeit for the specific purpose of keeping them safe for their absent owner.

(iii) "Depriving". This phrase in s.4 is construed as meaning "temporarily or permanently depriving". Under the old law of larceny the property had to be permanently taken; borrowers of property could not be regarded as having committed larceny. This was the reason why the offence of joyriding was never prosecuted under the Larceny Acts but was instead an offence under the Road Traffic Acts. The Law Reform Commission recommended the removal of the requirement to permanently deprive the owner of property. It remains the position under English law that permanent deprivation is necessary. However, under English legislation, borrowing may amount to treating the thing as one's own and therefore equate to intending to permanently deprive the owner of the thing if the borrowing or lending of it is for a period and in circumstances making it equivalent to outright taking or disposal.

8.2.3 *Making gain or causing loss by deception*

Section 6 provides that a person who "dishonestly, with the intention of making a gain for himself or herself or another, or of causing loss to another, by any deception induces another to do or refrains from doing an act ...". The former offence of obtaining by false pretences did not adequately address this situation. That offence required that the defendant obtain property, whereas under s.6 the offence can be committed if the defendant did not receive any benefit from his deceit provided that loss was caused to another. Furthermore, obtaining by false pretences only covered situations where the false representation made was one of past or present fact and did not extend to statements of opinion and promises as to future conduct. The English legislation still limits the deception to present intentions, but the 2001 Act is not so qualified and encompasses "any" deception. The Law Reform Commission recommended that it should constitute deception to make a false statement as to future intentions. A person who campaigns for a non-existent charity would be guilty of this offence.

8.2.4 *Obtaining services by deception*

The former offence of obtaining by false pretences was only made out where property was obtained as a result. It did not extend to situations where services were dishonestly obtained. Section 7 fills this lacuna and provides that it is an offence for any person to obtain services by deception. The defendant must have obtained the services "dishonestly, with the intention of making a gain for himself or herself or another or of causing loss to another." Obtaining services from another is defined as inducing another to "confer a benefit on some person by doing some act, or causing or permitting some act to be done, on the understanding that the benefit has been or will be paid for." Section 7 is similar to the equivalent offence under English law. A person pretending to be a member of a gym and thereby using its facilities would be guilty of an offence under this section.

8.2.5 Making off without payment

Section 8 makes it an offence for a person, knowing that payment on the spot is required or expected, to dishonestly make off without paying for the goods or services with the intention of avoiding payment on the spot. This offence is broadly similar to the equivalent English provision. Judicial interpretation of the phrases "on the spot" and "making off" is awaited. The definition of what constitutes the "spot" is hugely important, as is whether a defendant who only realises that he has left without paying when he arrives home has "made off". *Actus reus* and *mens rea* must coincide for the offence to be made out, so it is vital to know what constitutes the spot (and by corollary whether the person has left the spot, *i.e.* made off) in order to know whether the *mens rea* was present when the *actus reus* took place. Consider the case of a person who leaves a petrol station having filled his car and only realises that he has forgotten to pay when the reaches home. Is he deemed to have made off from the spot?

8.2.6 Unlawful use of computer

The offence of unlawful use of a computer is provided for in s.9. It is an offence to dishonestly, within the State or outside the State, operate or cause to be operated a computer within the State with the intention of making a gain for oneself or for another or causing a loss to another. Section 5 of the Criminal Damage Act 1991 provided for the offence of computer hacking, but this was inadequate to fully address other scenarios of dishonesty involving computers. One of the policy reasons behind the enactment of the 2001 Act was to criminalise such behaviour. This offence is more significant than the offence of unauthorised access (hacking) as it is indictable and carries a substantial penalty, whereas the s.5 offence is summary only. In addition, it involves an element of making a gain or causing a loss which is not required under the Criminal Damage Act.

8.2.7 *False accounting*

This was an important aspect of the white collar crime the 2001 Act was designed to combat. Section 10 provides for an offence of false accounting. It is an offence to do any one of the following with the intention of making a gain for oneself or another or of causing loss to another: destroying, defacing, concealing or falsifying accounts or any document made or required for any accounting purpose; failing to make or complete accounts or documents; and furnishing false or misleading accounts or documents. The making of misleading or false entries and the omission of relevant particulars may amount to falsifying accounts for the purpose of s.10.

8.2.8 *Suppression etc. of documents*

Section 11 concerns the dishonest use of valuable securities and other documents in order to realise a benefit or cause a loss. It is an offence under this section to dishonestly destroy, deface, conceal or procure the execution of certain documents with the intention of making a gain for oneself or another or causing a loss to another. For example, A burns a will belonging to a deceased member of his family in order that he will inherit part of the estate or in order to thwart another person's inheritance.

8.2.9 *Burglary*

Section 12 sets out the offence of burglary. Burglary is committed by entering a building as a trespasser, intending to commit an arrestable offence, or by being present as a trespasser committing or attempting to commit such an offence. The new offence of burglary is wider than the old offence contained in s.23A of the Larceny Act 1916. Under the old law, burglary could only be committed by entering as a trespasser with intent to steal, inflict grievous bodily harm, rape or do unlawful damage, or, having entered as a trespasser, stealing or attempting to steal or inflicting grievous bodily harm or attempting to inflict grievous bodily harm. Under the old legislation, entry with intent to rape or do unlawful damage amounted to burglary, whereas entry and a subsequent decision to rape or do unlawful damage did not. This lacuna is filled by s.12, as it refers to the category of arrestable offences rather than specifying various offences. The defendant must still enter as a trespasser, however, so case law on the definition of "trespassing" and of "entering" remains relevant.

Trespass also takes place where a person exceeds his right of entry or enters for a purpose other than that for which permission was given. In *R. v Jones and Smith* (1976), the two accused entered the home of the father of one of them, intending to steal from it. The father had given the son unreserved permission to enter the house at any time, and it was therefore argued that the accused had not been trespassing. This was rejected by the Court of Appeal: a person is a trespasser if he enters for a purpose other than the one for which the permission was granted. In *DPP v McMahon* (1987), the defendants each owned a licensed premises and were charged with offences contrary to the Gaming and Lotteries Act. Evidence was given that the gardaí entered the premises in plain clothes without a search warrant and proceeded to gather evidence. The Supreme Court held that the Garda Síochána did not have any statutory authority to enter the premises and, by reason of their intention in so doing, were outside the implied invitation of the owner of the licensed premises. They were therefore trespassers, and the evidence which they obtained by inspecting the use of gaming machines within these premises was evidence obtained by unlawful means. However, no constitutional rights were infringed and a court had discretion whether to admit such evidence in the circumstances.

What amounts to entering? Has a person entered where part only of his body has passed the threshold? At common law entry was governed by highly technical rules, and an entry could be effected either by an instrument or by the accused putting any part of his body, however slight, over the threshold. The amendment of the law seems to have been intended to do away with these refinements, and in England the test has been stated to be whether an entry is "effective". So, in *R. v Brown* (1985), the accused was charged with burglary, having broken a shop window, leaned in and rummaged around the shop front display. Could this amount to entering? It was held by the Court of Appeal that it could. There was no requirement that a person wholly enter the building. Instead, whether an entry had taken place was a matter for the jury to decide, and they should be directed to consider whether an effective entry had taken place.

What is a building? The leading case is *B & S v Leathley* (1979), which accepted that a freezer container which was resting on old railway sleepers was a building, since it was "a structure of considerable size intended to be permanent or to endure for a considerable time". However, in *Norfolk Constabulary v Seekings and Gould* (1986), truck trailers supplied with electricity and used as temporary storage space were held not to be buildings.

Burglary can also take place where a person enters part of a building as a trespasser, which is an important qualification. Consider the case of a person who is invited to apartment 1 and then breaks into the adjoining apartment 2. Clearly, he did not enter the apartment block as a trespasser; nevertheless, he enters apartment 2, which is a part of the building, as a trespasser and so may be guilty of burglary. This may be extended further: in *R. v Wilkington* (1979), the accused was present in a department store and entered the area inside a three-sided counter area, in which there was a till. It was held that the area inside this counter area was capable of being a "part of a building", and since it was part of the store from which the public were excluded it was open to the jury to find that the accused had entered that part of the building as a trespasser.

The offence can be committed by entry with the intention of committing a specified offence. What form of intention is necessary? Is it enough that a person enters with a conditional intent, such as an intention to steal if there is anything worth stealing? In *R. v Wilkington* (1979), the accused went behind the counter area and opened a till to see if there was anything in it worth stealing; if there had been he would have taken it. This form of conditional intent was held to be sufficient for the crime of burglary; it was irrelevant that, unknown to the accused, there was nothing worth taking.

8.2.10 Aggravated burglary

This offence, contained in s.13, is burglary committed where the defendant has with him at the time a firearm, imitation firearm, weapon of offence or explosive. The definition of aggravated burglary is the same as it was under the Larceny Act.

8.2.11 Robbery

Section 14 sets out this offence. A person who steals is guilty of robbery if, at the time or immediately before the stealing and in order to do so, he uses force or puts or seeks to put any person in fear of being then and there subjected to force. This definition is broadly similar to that set out in the Larceny Acts. The Theft Act retains the concept of "force" rather than "violence". Violence was the term used before the Larceny Act was amended in 1976. The distinction between the terms is that actions that amount to force do not always amount to violence. For example, wrenching a shopping basket from a victim's hand can amount to force, although one might have difficulty describing it as violence *(R. v Clouden* (1987)).

The main case on this point is *R. v Dawson and James* (1977). Here, the defendants pickpocketed a sailor by nudging him until he lost his balance, when one of them reached into his pocket and took his wallet. Was there sufficient evidence of robbery to be put before the jury? The Court of Appeal held that there was; the word "force" had been chosen to eliminate the technicalities inherent in the previous term "violence". The word is a common one, and one which the jury can apply based on common sense. As a matter of law, the conduct of the defendants could amount to force. There is therefore an element of overlap between robbery and larceny from the person.

The element of force required is, significantly, not quite the same as that required for assault. For assault, what is required is either the actual use of force or causing another to apprehend the immediate use of force. For robbery, what is required is either the actual use of force, or causing or *seeking* to cause another to apprehend the immediate use of force. The distinction can be illustrated by an example. If A threatens B with the immediate use of force, but B does not believe the threat, then assault is not committed; B must actually experience fear. But if A threatens B with the immediate use of force in order to steal, and does steal, then robbery is committed even where B does not believe the threat, since A *sought* to put B in fear of being subjected to force.

8.2.12 Possession of certain articles

The possession, when a person is not in his or her own residence, of any article intending to use it in conjunction with certain offences is an offence under s.15. These offences include theft, burglary, certain offences involving deception, blackmail, extortion and unauthorised taking of a vehicle. The possession, without lawful authority or excuse, of any article made or adapted for use in the commission of any of these offences is also criminalised.

8.2.13 Handling etc., stolen property and other proceeds of crime

The offence of handling stolen property is set out in s.17. This offence is committed by a person who, knowing or being reckless as to whether property is stolen, receives it or undertakes to assist in its retention, removal, disposal or realisation. Where this is done in circumstances where it is reasonable that the person knew it was stolen or was reckless as to whether it was stolen, then the defendant will be taken to have known or to have been reckless, unless the court is satisfied that there is a reasonable doubt. Stolen property includes property that has been unlawfully obtained, *i.e.* the proceeds of the disposal of stolen property.

The offence of handling is now broader than it was under the Larceny Acts. The *mens rea* required prior to the Larceny Act 1990 was knowing that the goods were stolen; belief was not sufficient. The 1990 Act widened this to knowing or believing that the goods were stolen. Under the 2001 Act, the *mens rea* also extends to recklessness as to whether property was stolen. The equivalent English legislation requires knowledge or belief and does not include recklessness. Recklessness is defined in the 2001 Act as disregarding a substantial risk that the property is stolen. "Substantial risk" means risk of such a nature and degree that, having regard to the circumstances in which the person acquired the property and the extent of the information then available to him or her, its disregard involves culpability of a high degree.

Under the Larceny Acts, a prosecutorial dilemma arose where people were found in possession of stolen property but it was unclear whether they had actually stolen the goods themselves or merely handled them. It was necessary for the prosecution on a charge of handling to prove that the goods had been stolen by a person other than the accused. The result was that people arrested in possession of stolen goods sometimes failed to be convicted of either larceny or handling. This problem is solved by s.18. This section sets out a new offence of possession of stolen property where a person, without lawful authority or excuse, possesses stolen property knowing or being reckless as to whether it was stolen. The defendant who has stolen property in his possession, where it is reasonable to conclude that he knew or was reckless as to whether it was stolen, will be presumed to have known or to have been reckless unless the court is satisfied that there is a reasonable doubt. Section 19 provides for an offence of withholding information regarding stolen property. Failure or refusal to give an account to gardaí, when demanded, of property in a person's possession is an offence where there are reasonable grounds for believing that an offence of theft or handling stolen property has been committed.

8.2.14 Money laundering

It is an offence under s.21 to do any of a number of things in relation to property, knowing or believing or being reckless as to whether the property is or represents the proceeds of criminal conduct. The actions prohibited include converting, transferring, handling or removing the property from the State intending to conceal its true nature.

8.2.15 Forgery

The Forgery Act 1913 was extremely complex, was primarily concerned with documents and did not cover all tangible things. The Law Reform Commission advised that it be extended to cover all tangible things and recommended the adoption of the definition of "instrument" in the equivalent English legislation. It also recommended that cash and credit cards should be specifically included. The 2001 Act provides that a person who makes a false instrument intending it to be accepted as genuine, resulting in prejudice to the person accepting it, will be guilty of forgery. "Instrument" includes any document, disc, tape, postage stamp, revenue stamp, social services card, cheque card, credit card and admission ticket. It is also an offence to use a false instrument knowing or believing it to be false, intending to induce a person to accept it as genuine and thereby causing that person to suffer some loss. Similarly, copying a false instrument knowing or believing it to be false, intending to pass it as genuine and thereby causing loss to another is an offence. It is also an offence to use a copy of a false instrument knowing or believing it to be false, intending that it should pass as genuine and thereby causing loss to any person accepting it as genuine. The offence of forgery includes having custody or control of false instruments intending to pass them off as genuine thereby causing loss to another and having custody or control of such instruments without lawful authority or excuse.

8.2.16 Counterfeiting

The 2001 Act simplifies the offence of counterfeiting. It is an offence to make a counterfeit currency note or coin intending that it pass as genuine. It is also an offence to pass or tender as genuine a counterfeit or to deliver a counterfeit to another intending it to be passed as genuine, to have custody or control of such a counterfeit without lawful authority or excuse and to make or have in one's custody or control anything intending to use it or permit another to use it to make a counterfeit. The Act also criminalises the doing of any of the above acts by a person outside the State and the importation and exportation of a counterfeit of a currency note or coin from a member of the European Union.

Further reading:

McGreal, *Criminal Justice (Theft and Fraud Offences) Act 2001* (Round Hall, 2003); Law Reform Commission, *Report on the Law Relating to Dishonesty* (1992); Law Reform Commission, *Report on Receiving Stolen Property*, (1987); McMullan,"The Criminal Justice (Theft and Fraud Offences) Act 2001: An Overview" (2003) 13 (1) I.C.L.J. 8.

9. OFFENCES AGAINST THE ADMINISTRATION OF JUSTICE

9.1 Perjury

Perjury is an offence at common law, which can be punished by an unlimited fine and/or imprisonment. O'Connor, *Justice of the Peace* (1911) defines the offence as follows (at p.920):

> "Perjury is the making on oath or affirmation, before a competent court or authority in the course of a judicial proceeding, of any assertion, material to the matter in question in such proceeding which to the knowledge of such person is false, or which, whether true or false, he does not believe to be true, or as to which he knows himself to be ignorant."

We will look at each of these elements in turn.

9.1.1 On oath or affirmation

The statement must be made in the course of giving evidence on oath or affirmation (an affirmation being the secular equivalent of the religious oath). Statements not on oath or affirmation, even if they are made during court proceedings and are deliberately false, will not amount to perjury. For example, if during legal argument a party were to make a deliberately false statement then this would not be perjury.

9.1.2. Before a competent court or authority in the course of a judicial proceeding

For perjury to be committed, the statement must be made in the course of a judicial proceeding before a court or an equivalent body. False statements in other contexts, while they might well amount to some other crime, will not amount to perjury. For example, it would not be perjury to lie to the police in the course of a criminal investigation. (Although it might amount to the offence of attempting to pervert the course of justice: see *People (DPP) v Paul Murtagh* (1990)).

The term "judicial proceedings" is very wide. A comprehensive definition is given by the Law Reform Commission:

> "'Judicial proceedings', in this context, includes, in addition to the courts established under the Constitution and special criminal courts, other complementary proceedings (e.g. commissions established by order of the court to take evidence), all statutory tribunals at which evidence must be given an oath, and proceedings before persons who are authorised by law to hear, receive and examine evidence on oath. Preliminary proceedings in connection with judicial proceedings (e.g. affidavits, depositions, answers to interrogatories, and examinations) are included, as are proceedings before every officer, arbitrator, commissioner, or other person having, by law or by consent of the parties, authority to hear, receive and examine evidence on oath."
> (*Report on Oaths and Affirmations* (L.R.C. 34-1990), p.21)

9.1.3 Material to the matter in question

The false evidence given must be *material*—that is, relevant to the determination of the matter. It is not perjury for a vain witness to lie about her age, unless of course her age is relevant to the proceedings.

9.1.4 Which to the knowledge of such person is false, or which, whether true or false, he does not believe to be true, or as to which he knows himself to be ignorant.

A defendant commits perjury if he knows his evidence to be false—but also where he is reckless as to whether it is true or false.

Further reading:

Law Reform Commission, *Report on Oaths and Affirmations* (L.R.C. 34–1990), Chap. 2.

9.2 Contempt of court

Contempt of court refers to activities which prejudice the administration of justice. At common law, contempt of court (such as disruption of court proceedings) is a crime which can be prosecuted summarily or on indictment.

The law in this area is, however, complicated by two factors. First, not all contempts are criminal. Some forms of interference with the administration of justice—such as a party refusing to obey an injunction—are treated as a less serious *civil* contempt of court and not as a crime. We must, therefore, be able to distinguish between civil and criminal contempts.

Second, criminal contempt of court has some unusual procedural aspects. It can be prosecuted by the DPP in the same way as any other crime—but in some cases it is also open to the court to deal with a contempt of its own motion and without a full hearing, and without some of the procedural safeguards (such as trial by jury) which would otherwise apply to a criminal trial.

9.2.1 *Civil v criminal contempt*

The leading Irish case on the distinction between civil and criminal contempt is *State (Keegan) v De Burca* (1973). In that case, the defendant had refused to answer a question of the court, and had been sentenced to imprisonment until she purged her contempt: that is, until she agreed to comply with the order of the court to answer the question. The effect was to impose imprisonment for an indefinite period.

This would have been the appropriate result if the contempt had been civil; but she argued that the contempt was criminal, and so she should have been sentenced to a definite period of imprisonment, or a fine. In differentiating between the two forms of contempt, Ó Dálaigh C.J. stated:

"Criminal contempt consists in behaviour calculated to prejudice the due course of justice, such as contempt *in facie curiae* [*in the face of the court*], words written or spoken or acts calculated to prejudice the due course of justice or disobedience to a writ of *habeas corpus* by the person to whom it is directed - to give but some examples of this class of contempt. Civil contempt usually arises where there is a disobedience to an order of the court by a party to the proceedings and in which the court generally has no interest to interfere unless moved by the party for whose benefit the order was made. Criminal contempt is a common law misdemeanour and, as such, is punishable by both imprisonment and fine at discretion, that is to say, without statutory limit, its object is punitive: see the judgment of this Court in *In Re Haughey* (1971). Civil contempt, on the other hand, is not punitive in its effect but coercive in its purpose of compelling the party committed to comply with the order of the court, and the period of committal would be until such time as the order is complied with or until it is waived by the party for whose benefit the order was made." (At p.227.)

It was then held by the Supreme Court that the refusal to answer a question constituted criminal contempt in the face of the court for which a determinate sentence should have been imposed.

Similarly, in *State (Commins) v McRann* (1977) Finlay P. stated that:

"The major distinction which has been established over a long period and by a long series of authority between criminal and civil contempt of court appears to be that the wrong of criminal contempt is the complement of the right of the court to protect its own dignity, independence and procedures and that, accordingly, in such cases, where a court imposes sentences of imprisonment its intention is primarily punitive. Furthermore, in such cases of criminal contempt the court moves of its own volition, or may do so at any time.

In civil contempt, on the other hand, a court only moves at the instance of the party whose rights are being infringed and who has, in the first instance, obtained from the court the order which he seeks to have enforced. It is clear that in such cases the purpose of the imposition of imprisonment is primarily coercive; for that reason it must of necessity be in the form of an indefinite imprisonment which may be terminated either when the court, upon application by the person imprisoned, is satisfied that he is prepared to abide by its order and that the coercion has been effective or when the party seeking to enforce the order shall for any reason waive his rights and agree, or consent, to the release of the imprisoned party." (At p.89)

Analysing these two decisions, the Law Reform Commission has indicated that:

> "The primary purpose of civil contempt proceedings is coercive, whereas for criminal contempt the primary purpose is punitive; moreover in civil contempt proceedings the court moves only at the instance of the party whose rights have been infringed whereas no similar inhibition applies in respect of criminal contempt." (*Consultation Paper on Contempt of Court,* p.176)

9.2.2 Types of criminal contempt

Criminal contempt is generally divided into four categories:

(1) Contempt in the face of the court

This refers to conduct which is so direct and immediate as to be deemed to be "in the personal knowledge of the court": *The State (DPP) v Walsh*, (1981) at p.432 (*per* Henchy J). In most cases, these contempts will literally be "in the face of" the court—that is, they will occur in front of the judge. It is not essential, however, that the contempt take place before the judge, provided that there is a sufficiently close connection in time or space with the court proceedings. For example, where a party in litigation threatened a lawyer for the other side in the public waiting area out of court, this was held to constitute contempt in the face of the court. (In *Re Goldman* (1968)).

Contempt in the face of the court will include cases where individuals set out to disrupt or interrupt court proceedings. For example, in *Morris v The Crown Office* (1970) criminal contempt was committed where students protesting in favour of the Welsh language took over a court in session. It will also include threats or abuse directed to the judge (as in *U.S. v Lumumba* (1984), where a lawyer stated in court that a judge was an "outstanding bigot" and a "racist dog"). It will also include cases where a witness refuses to answer questions. An example is *Re O'Kelly* (1974). In that case a journalist employed by RTE was called as a prosecution witness in a trial of a defendant for membership of an illegal organisation. He refused to answer certain questions arising out of an interview with the defendant, claiming a journalistic privilege. He was found guilty of contempt and sentenced to three months' imprisonment. On appeal, it was held that journalists did not enjoy any special privilege as regards information received by them in confidence, and his conviction for contempt in the face of the court was upheld.

(2) Scandalising the court

This outdated term refers to conduct (usually media comment) calculated to reduce public confidence in the administration of justice. There is a tension here between the right of freedom of expression (including the right to criticise the courts and the judiciary) and the supposed public interest in preventing attacks on the courts, such as allegations of corruption, which undermine public confidence in the judiciary. In *Re Kennedy and McCann* (1976) O'Higgins C.J. stated that:

> "The right of free speech and the full expression of opinion are valued rights. Their preservation, however, depends on the observance of the acceptable limit that they must not be used to undermine public order or morality or the authority of the State. Contempt of court of this nature carries the exercise of these rights beyond this acceptable limit because it tends to bring the administration of justice into disrepute and to undermine the confidence which the people should have in judges appointed under the Constitution to administer justice in our Courts." (At pp.385–386)

In that case, therefore, two journalists were found to be in contempt of court where they published "biased and inaccurate" reports of custody proceedings (in breach of an order prohibiting publication), including allegations that the court had ignored the statutory rules on custody and had acted for an improper purpose.

Comparable allegations were made about the Special Criminal Court in *State (DPP) v Walsh* (1981). The defendants, members of a group called Association for Legal Justice, issued a statement to the media in relation to the trial of Noel and Marie Murray for capital murder of a Garda. In that statement, they said that the court was made up of "Government-appointed judges having no judicial independence which sat without a jury and which so abused the rules of evidence as to make the court akin to a sentencing tribunal". The Supreme Court found that this allegation of bias or corruption amounted to a "classical example" of the offence of scandalising the court.

Similarly, in *AG v Connolly* (1947), an editor was found guilty of contempt where he published comments on a murder trial before the Special Criminal Court, including statements suggesting that the court had prejudged the case. The offending comments included statements that the defendant "was fast approaching his martyrdom" and that "now he awaits his death which sentence will inevitably be passed on him after the mockery of a trial". The High Court found that this was a wild charge, going far beyond legitimate criticism, and as such amounted to scandalising the court.

In those cases, the abuse amounted to allegations of corruption or bias. However, the offence can also be committed by other types of attacks, including mere abuse. One famous example is the English case of *Gray* (1900). In that case there was some tension between local newspapers and Darling J., which resulted in Darling J. issuing a warning to the press from the bench. Shortly afterwards, the defendant, editor of a local newspaper, published an article criticising Darling J., including the following words:

> "The terrors of Mr Justice Darling will not trouble the Birmingham reporters very much. No newspaper can exist except upon its merits, a condition from which the Bench, happily for Mr Justice Darling, is exempt. There is not a journalist in Birmingham who has anything to learn from the impudent little man in horsehair, a microcosm of conceit and empty headedness, who admonished the Press yesterday."

It was accepted that this article, albeit mere scurrilous abuse, amounted to a criminal contempt of court, in that it was an attack on a judge in his capacity as a judge. (On the other hand, had it been an attack on a judge in his personal capacity—discussing, for example, his private life—it would not have been contempt. The doctrine of scandalising the court applies only to attacks on judges in their role as judges.)

We should note, however, an important limitation: it is not contempt to subject the courts to legitimate discussion and criticism. Lord Atkin has said, in a well known passage in *Ambard v Attorney-General for Trinidad and Tobago* (1936) that:

> "But whether the authority and position of an individual judge, or the due administration of justice, is concerned, no

wrong is committed by any member of the public who
exercises the ordinary right of criticising, in good faith, in
private or in public, the public act done in the seat of justice.
The path of criticism is a public way: the wrongheaded are
permitted to err therein: provided that members of the public
abstain from imputing improper motives to those taking part
in the administration of justice, and are generally exercising
a right of criticism, and not acting in malice or attempting to
impair the administration of justice, they are immune. Justice
is not a cloistered virtue: she must be allowed to suffer the
scrutiny and respectful, even though outspoken, comments
of ordinary men."

This has been accepted as a correct statement of the law by the
Supreme Court in *Re Hibernia National Review Ltd.* (1976),
although in that case the court found that the allegations made by
the defendants went beyond good faith criticism, particularly since
they involved serious misrepresentations of the facts of the case.
Similarly, in *Re Kennedy and McCann,* O'Higgins C.J. stressed
that "reasonable criticism" of the courts could not be regarded as
contempt.

(3) Breach of the *sub judice* rule

A matter is *sub judice* if it is currently before a court. In order to
prevent outside pressure on, or manipulation of, court proceedings, it
is a criminal contempt to publish material which tends to interfere
with particular proceedings which are *sub judice*. This is particularly
important in relation to criminal proceedings, where the liberty of an
accused person is at stake, where there may be a risk of "trial by
media", and where juries might be swayed by irrelevant or prejudicial
material, such as disclosure of previous convictions which would not
be admissible in evidence. As with the offence of scandalising the
court, this creates a tension between freedom of expression and the
public interest in ensuring fair trials. The test here is whether a
particular publication creates a real risk (not merely a remote
possibility) of interference with the administration of justice in
particular proceedings. It is not necessary to show that the publication
did *in fact* impair the proceedings; the risk of interference is enough.

In order for the *sub judice* rule to apply, the proceedings must
be *pending*. This has created difficulties in relation to criminal
proceedings which are "imminent". Suppose, for example, that a

newspaper publishes a story about a suspect implicating him in a particular crime shortly before that suspect is arrested and charged. Clearly such a story is capable of prejudicing a trial. But can a prosecution be said to be pending before a person has been charged? There is some Northern Irish authority suggesting that the jurisdiction extends to matters which are "imminent": *R. v Beaverbrook & Associated Newspapers Limited* (1962). However, Kelly J. has recently confirmed, in *DPP v Independent Newspapers* (2003), that the contempt jurisdiction only attaches once a person has been brought before the court to be charged.

One of the most serious forms of contempt consists of publications likely to prejudice a jury against an accused. It is contempt to publish details of previous convictions of an accused, or even (if sufficiently prejudicial) to reveal an accused's previous bad character. For example, in *R. v Thomson Newspapers Limited, ex parte AG* (1968) the defendant newspaper was in contempt where it published a story in which the accused was described as a brothel-keeper, procurer and property racketeer.

More recently, photographs of defendants have created problems. In *People (DPP) v Davis* the Court of Criminal Appeal held that publishing photographs of the accused in handcuffs, during a murder trial, could amount to a contempt of court, in that it was likely to prejudice the jury against the accused, and tended to deprive the accused of the "dignity associated with the presumption of innocence".

It will also be contempt to publish material which prejudges a case. An example is *R. v Parnell* (1880), where a newspaper, the Dublin Evening Mail, was found in contempt for publishing a story during a trial alleging that the case against the defendants (Charles Stuart Parnell and others, accused of conspiracy to induce tenants to withhold rent) was overwhelming, and that any acquittal would be against the evidence and could only be procured by intimidation.

In the majority of cases, this form of contempt will arise in respect of trials before a jury, particularly since juries are seen as especially susceptible to outside pressure. However, the rule also applies to matters decided by a judge sitting alone. For example, the Supreme Court, in *Kelly v O'Neill* (1999), has recently held that the rule applies to publications about defendants after conviction but before sentence, even though the decision on sentencing is made by a judge alone. The Supreme Court in that case acknowledged that judges are, by their training and experience, less susceptible to outside influences, but held that nonetheless there was a possibility that judges could be prejudiced by unnecessary exposure to irrelevant material, and also held that (in relation to sentencing) there was a risk that judges might be perceived as imposing sentences in response to popular demand.

4. Other acts which interfere with the course of justice
This catch all category covers other actions which tend to prejudice the administration of justice. Examples of this form of contempt include attempts to intimidate witnesses or counsel: In *Re Kelly and Deighan* (1984) and *Brown v Putnam* (1975). Similarly, it would be contempt of court to interfere with a jury: In *Re MM and HM* (1933).

9.2.3 Mens rea and criminal contempt

Do the various forms of criminal contempt require an intention to interfere with the administration of justice? Would it be sufficient that the defendant was reckless as to the possibility of interference? Or is criminal contempt an offence of strict liability? The *mens rea* required for contempt is a difficult issue, and it seems that *mens rea* may differ as between the various forms of criminal contempt.

It is unclear whether *mens rea* is required for contempt in the face of the court. As regards acts, other than publication, which interfere with the course of justice, the *mens rea* issue is also unclear. Breach of the *sub judice* rule was, until recently, thought to be an offence of strict liability, which did not require any intention to prejudice court proceedings. However, in *Kelly v O'Neill* (1999) Keane J. expressed some doubt as to whether Irish law would still take this view, stating that the facts of that case:

> "raise the question as to whether the offence of criminal contempt had been committed at all, given the absence of any guilty mind or *mens rea* on the part of the respondents … While undoubtedly the generally accepted view of the law has hitherto been that the offence is absolute in its nature and does not require the establishment of *mens rea*, one certainly could not exclude the possibility that, in the absence of any modern Irish authority, the courts in this country might have come to the conclusion that *mens rea* was a necessary ingredient of the offence."

There is also debate as to whether *mens rea* is required for scandalising the court. It is an offence of strict liability in England, Australia, New Zealand and Canada, although South African law requires *mens rea*. In Ireland, there is still some confusion on this point. In *Re Kennedy and McCann* (1976) O'Higgins C.J. remarked (at p.387) that "The offence of contempt by scandalising the court is committed when, as here, a false publication is made which *intentionally or recklessly* imputes base or improper motives and conduct to the judge or judges in question" (emphasis added). Although this appears to require *mens rea*, the Law Reform Commission, in its *Consultation Paper on Contempt* (at p.63), has suggested that O'Higgins C.J. was referring to an *intent to impute improper motives* to the judiciary, not *an intent to interfere with the administration of justice*, so that a person would be guilty of contempt once they deliberately accused a judge of bias, even though they did not intend to interfere with the administration of justice.

The Law Reform Commission's interpretation has since been followed in *Re KAS (An Infant)* (1995). In that case, Budd J. held that *mens rea* is not required in respect of scandalising the court: so that lack of intention or knowledge is no excuse, though it may have a bearing on the punishment which the court will inflict.

9.2.4 Procedure

Criminal contempts of court can be prosecuted in the ordinary way by the DPP. Any person likely to be affected by a criminal contempt (such as an accused in a criminal trial) can also commence proceedings. In addition, the relevant court has power, of its own motion, to commence proceedings for criminal contempt. This last point makes contempt of court unusual in Irish law. In most cases, the court is passive and must wait for a case to be brought before it. In respect of criminal contempt, however, the court can take an active role and act as prosecutor if necessary: *Re the Youghal Election Petition* (1869). The reasoning behind this rule is (in part) that the doctrine of contempt of court exists to safeguard judicial independence, and judicial independence would be compromised if the court was dependent on some other party to commence contempt proceedings. In addition, it may be necessary for the court to deal with contempt urgently in the interests of justice, ruling out any delay to allow the DPP to consider whether to bring proceedings.

There are also some unusual features in respect of the trial of criminal contempts. Since a criminal contempt is a criminal offence, which may attract a substantial sentence, we might expect that it would carry a right to trial by jury under Art.38.5 of the Constitution. However, historically the courts have enjoyed a power to punish criminal contempts summarily—that is, without a jury. The reasons behind this rule include a need to deal urgently with certain forms of contempt, such as the disruption of an ongoing trial. In the case of contempt in the face of the court, there has also been a view that the court, having witnessed the contempt, did not need to engage in a full trial to determine the facts. Judicial independence has also been relevant, with judges expressing concern that a jury might perversely acquit a person who committed a criminal contempt, leaving the court without an effective means of safeguarding its independence.

These issues were addressed in *State (DPP) v Walsh* (1981) where the defendants (who were accused of scandalising the court) submitted that Art.38.5 required that they should be tried before a jury. This was, however, rejected by the Supreme Court. The court unanimously agreed that judicial independence, as provided for in the Constitution, required that the courts should be able to deal with criminal contempt of court summarily, at least where there were no disputed issues of fact. (As in this case, where the defendants admitted publishing the material in question.)

The members of the court differed, though, as to what would happen if issues of fact were disputed: for example, if a defendant denied that he was responsible for a publication. The majority took the view, *per* Henchy J., that in such a case the accused person would retain his constitutional right to trial by jury in respect of those issues of fact. The minority, *per* O'Higgins C.J., believed that while it might be *desirable* to try the factual issues before a jury, this was not *required*. Instead, this would be a matter for the discretion of the judge, and there might be circumstances where it would be undesirable to do this—for example, where the issue was whether a defendant had attempted to bribe or intimidate a jury. This discussion was, however, *obiter*, and did not form part of the reasoning in that case. Consequently, it is still unclear whether a defendant in these circumstances would enjoy a right to jury trial in respect of factual issues.

Further reading:

Walley, "Criminal Contempt of Court" Bar Review Vol. 5, Issue 6 (April, 2000) 295; Law Reform Commission, *Consultation Paper on Contempt of Court* (L.R.C. 1991); Law Reform Commission, *Report on Contempt of Court* (L.R.C. 1992).

10. PUBLIC ORDER OFFENCES AND INCITEMENT TO HATRED

10.1 Public order offences

10.1.1 Introduction

The law relating to public order offences is largely contained in the Criminal Justice (Public Order) Act 1994. That Act reformed the law in this area, abolishing the majority of common law public order offences and replacing these with statutory offences. In addition, it created extensive "crowd control" powers to be exercised by the Gardaí, controlling access to public events and enabling the seizure of alcohol, bottles, etc., found on persons going to public events. We will look briefly at the primary offences under this Act.

10.1.2 Offences of group violence

The most serious offences created by the 1994 Act are those which relate to violence by a number of people: that is, riot, violent disorder and affray. Each of these offences has in common the element of causing or potentially causing fear in others, and the offences are graduated in severity depending on the numbers involved. These offences will range in their application from large-scale public disorder (such as violent political protests) to small scale scuffles such as late night pub fights. Although we refer to these as public order offences, it is not a requirement that these offences should take place in public: in each case, the offence can also be committed in a private place.

10.1.3 Riot

The first of these offences is *riot* contrary to s.14 of the Act:

"Where -

(a) 12 or more persons who are present together at any place [*public or private*] ... use or threaten to use unlawful violence for a common purpose, and
(b) the conduct of those persons, taken together, is such as would cause a person of reasonable firmness present at that place to fear for his or another person's safety,

182

> then, each of the persons using unlawful violence for the
> common purpose shall be guilty of the offence of riot."

Section 14 goes on to provide that: the threats or uses of violence need not take place simultaneously or at the same place; the common purpose may be inferred from conduct; and no person of reasonable firmness need actually be present, or likely to be present.

The key elements of this offence are that at least 12 people must use or threaten to use violence; they must have a common purpose in doing so; the effect of their conduct is to put a hypothetical reasonable observer in fear for his safety, or the safety of some other person; and the particular defendant did in fact use unlawful violence.

An ordinary street brawl would not fall under this heading, as the fighters would lack the necessary common purpose. On the other hand, a violent demonstration for a political purpose would be capable of amounting to the offence of riot. A riot can be committed in any place, public or private—in this, the offence differs from other offences under the 1994 Act, which generally criminalises *public* conduct only.

It is important to note that for this offence to be committed by an individual, that individual must use unlawful violence. Suppose that 12 strikers agree to threaten violence outside a factory. Only one, however, goes further and actually uses violence. Only that person would be guilty of riot, since the others did not in fact *use* (as opposed to threaten) violence.

The maximum penalty for this offence is an unlimited fine and/ or imprisonment for up to ten years.

10.1.4 *Violent disorder*

Next is the offence of *violent disorder* contrary to s.15. This is essentially a scaled-down version of the offence of riot, and is committed where (a) a minimum of three persons present at any public or private place use or threaten to use violence; (b) the conduct of those persons, taken together, is such as would cause a hypothetical person of reasonable firmness, present at that place to fear for his or another person's safety; and (c) the particular defendant himself used or threatened to use violence.

In this last point, it differs from riot; the offence of riot is only committed by persons who *use*, rather than merely *threaten*, violence.

Violent disorder can, however, be committed by the mere threat of
violence also. We should also note that violent disorder differs from
riot in that there is no requirement that the group share a common
purpose. For example, an ordinary drunken fight could amount to
violent disorder, though not riot.

As with riot, this offence can occur in any place, public or
private. The maximum penalty for the offence is an unlimited fine
and/or imprisonment for up to ten years.

10.1.5 Affray

Finally, we have the offence of affray contrary to s.16:

"Where -

(a) two or more persons at any place [*public or
private*]... use or threaten to use violence towards
each other, and

(b) the violence so used or threatened by one of those
persons is unlawful, and

(c) the conduct of those persons, taken together, is such
as would cause a person of reasonable firmness
present at that place to fear for his or another person's
safety,

then, each such person who uses or threatens to use
unlawful violence shall be guilty of the offence of
affray."

Again, no person of reasonable firmness need actually be present.
As with the previous two offences, the offence can be committed in
any place, public or private.

Unlike riot and violent disorder, the violence involved for affray
must be violence towards each other. If this is not shown, then any
prosecution will fail. This point arose in *People (DPP) v Reid and
Kirwan* (2004). In this case, a number of people had been fighting
amongst themselves in the street. When gardaí attempted to arrest
the participants, they were in turn attacked. The first accused was
charged with affray: however, the evidence against him was not
that he had been involved in the initial fighting but that he had attacked
the gardaí when they were trying to make the arrests. On appeal,
his conviction was quashed on the basis that there was no evidence

of his using violence in the specific manner contemplated by the offence of affray. *Per* Hardiman J.:

> "Unlike the offences of riot or violent disorder, the actual or threatened use of violence for the purpose of the new offence of affray must be violence 'towards each other'. This point was raised at the trial but dismissed by the trial judge on the basis that it was unnecessary that each accused at the joint trial should have used violence towards the other co-accused. This is, of course, true but I think irrelevant to the fundamental issue in the case against the first accused. This is that there is no evidence of the first accused using violence towards any person except Garda Murray and Garda Dempsey. He was not charged with any assault on Garda Murray (or the garda who was with him) and was acquitted of the charge of assaulting Garda Dempsey. But there is no evidence whatever of him using, or threatening to use, unlawful violence towards any other person, and specifically towards any member of a group of two or more people. That being so, it follows that there was no prima facie case against the first accused on the charge of affray and that that count should have been withdrawn from the jury." (at para.14)

Interestingly, under s.16(2), the offence is not committed where threats are made by words alone: there must be some element of physical conduct, such as the shaking of a fist. Compare riot and violent disorder, which can be committed by threats made by words alone.

Only one person's violence needs to be unlawful for this offence to be committed. Suppose that A attacks B without provocation. B defends himself. A may be guilty of affray because of his unlawful violence, notwithstanding that B's violence is lawful self-defence. B should not be guilty of affray, as his violence is not unlawful: but there is a question mark over B's potential liability. In *People (DPP) v Reid and Kirwan* (2004), an argument was made that the section as drafted might catch B; however, the Court of Criminal Appeal declined to decide this point. Per Hardiman J.:

> "There is clearly a substantial issue, which does not require to be determined in this case, as to whether the section is

> broad enough to capture a person who is using violence, but not unlawfully so, against another who is using violence unlawfully, on the basis that the conduct of those persons taken together 'is such as would cause a person of reasonable firmness present at that place to fear for his or another person's safety'. If that is the correct construction of the section, then, obviously, it raises questions of a far reaching nature." (at para.27)

The maximum penalty for this offence is an unlimited fine and/or imprisonment for up to five years.

10.1.6 The notional bystander test

Riot, violent disorder and affray all require that a hypothetical person of reasonable firmness, if present at the scene, would fear for their own safety or the safety of another. This "notional bystander test" does not require that such a person was in fact present, or was in fact put in fear: these offences can be committed without an audience.

10.1.7 Offences in public places

Sections 4 to 9 of the 1994 Act create a number of offences specifically limited to public places. It should be noted that the term "public place" is given a very wide definition in s.3:

> "'public place' includes—
>
> (a) any highway,
> (b) any outdoor area to which at the material time members of the public have or are permitted to have access, whether as of right or as a trespasser or otherwise, and which is used for public recreational purposes,
> (c) any cemetery or churchyard,
> (d) any premises or other place to which at the material time members of the public have or are permitted to have access, whether as of right or by express or implied permission, or whether on payment or otherwise, and
> (e) any train, vessel or vehicle used for the carriage of persons for reward."

A licensed premises, for example, will be a public place for the purposes of the 1994 Act: see *Murphy v DPP* (2004).

10.1.8 Public intoxication

Under s.4, it is an offence for a person to be "present in any public place while intoxicated to such an extent as would give rise to a reasonable apprehension that he might endanger himself or any other person in his vicinity." The maximum penalty for this offence is a fine of €127

10.1.9 Disorderly conduct

Section 5(1) creates a broader offence of "disorderly conduct"

"It shall be an offence for any person in a public place to engage in offensive conduct—
(a) between the hours of 12 o'clock midnight and 7 o'clock in the morning next following, or
(b at any other time, after having been requested by a member of the Garda Síochána to desist."

"Offensive conduct" is in turn defined (by s.5(2)) as:

"unreasonable behaviour which, having regard to all the circumstances, is likely to cause serious offence or serious annoyance to any person who is, or might reasonably be expected to be, aware of such behaviour"

The maximum penalty for this offence is a fine of €634.86

10.1.10 Threatening, abusive or insulting behaviour in a public place

Section 6(1) provides:

"It shall be an offence for any person in a public place to use or engage in any threatening, abusive or insulting words or behaviour with intent to provoke a breach of the peace or being reckless as to whether a breach of the peace may be occasioned."

The maximum penalty for this offence is a fine of €634.86 and/or up to 3 months' imprisonment.

10.1.11 Distribution or display of threatening, abusive, insulting or obscene material

Section 7(1) provides:

> "It shall be an offence for any person in a public place to distribute or display any writing, sign or visible representation which is threatening, abusive, insulting or obscene with intent to provoke a breach of the peace or being reckless as to whether a breach of the peace may be occasioned."

The maximum penalty for this offence is a fine of €634.86 and/or up to 3 months' imprisonment.

It should be noted that under s.7, as with s.6, there must be either an intention to provoke a breach of the peace or recklessness in respect of same (but it is not necessary that a breach of the peace actually take place). In 1995, an anti-abortion protester was prosecuted under s.7 for displaying pictures of an aborted foetus, on the basis that these graphic pictures were "obscene". However, the prosecution was dismissed by the District Court, on the basis that there was no intention to provoke a breach of the peace, and a breach of the peace had not been likely. ("Case against anti abortion campaigner is dismissed" *The Irish Times*, December 13, 1995)

10.1.12 Constitutional concerns

Sections 5 to 7 have been criticised as excessively vague and as improper restrictions on freedom of expression. The Irish Council for Civil Liberties has said of the Act that:

> "The form of offence contemplated in section 6 and section 7 is wide open to discriminatory censorship of material and language which is morally, politically or socially and aesthetically unacceptable to the majority. Unfortunately, it is the Gardaí who are in charge of making fine distinctions and moral, political and social judgements in arbitrating, and executing this law. To cite recent examples, the display of placard photographs of foetus by pro-life campaigners could be deemed to be an obscene representation although problematic morally, politically and aesthetically. Similarly, the proffering for sale of 'The Satanic Verses', by Salman Rushdie certainly could be viewed as being insulting to the

Muslim minority and likely to provoke a breach of the peace
…The right to protest and express deeply unpopular views
in a dramatic way is offended by Section 7." (Irish Council
for Civil Liberties, *The Criminal Justice (Public Order)
Bill 1993 – A Commentary* (1993))

Similarly, Hogan and Whyte have noted that:

"Statutory provisions criminalising the use of abusive or
insulting language would appear, prima facie, to infringe
Article 40.6.1°.i and arguably may only withstand
constitutional scrutiny if they can be shown to be necessary
to prevent a breach of the peace. It may be, therefore, that
section 5 of the 1994 Act constitutes an excessive restriction
on freedom of expression inasmuch as it essentially subjects
that freedom to the listener's right not to be annoyed."
(*Kelly: The Irish Constitution* (4th ed., 2003), p.1741)

Hogan and Whyte have also suggested that:

"The inherent vagueness of [section 5] – what constitutes
'unreasonable behaviour' causing 'serious annoyance'? –
may give rise to constitutional difficulties under Article 38.1"
(at p.1785)

10.1.13 Failure to comply with Garda directions and loitering

Section 8 provides that a garda may direct a person, whom he
suspects with reasonable cause to be acting contrary to ss.4 to 7 (or
to be causing a wilful obstruction, contrary to s.9) to desist from so
doing and to leave the vicinity immediately.

Section 8 also replaces the offence of loitering with intent, which
was found to be unconstitutional in *King v Attorney General* (1981),
by allowing a garda to direct that a person desist and leave the vicinity
where that person is:

"without lawful authority or reasonable excuse … acting in
a manner which consists of loitering in a public place in
circumstances, which may include the company of other
persons, that give rise to a reasonable apprehension for the
safety of persons or the safety of property or for the
maintenance of the public peace."

The offence in this case is failure to comply with the direction, not the loitering itself.

In each case, the maximum penalty for failure to comply with a direction is a fine of up to €634.86 and/or imprisonment for up to 6 months.

In order to convict a person of an offence under s.8, Laffoy J. has held in *DPP (Sheehan) v Galligan* (1995) that it must be shown that the accused was warned (or was aware) that if he did not comply with the direction being given to him that he would be committing a criminal offence. However, it was also held that no particular form of words need be used in giving this warning. (See also *Bates v Brady* (2003) where a conviction under s.8(2) was quashed where the prosecution failed to give evidence of such a warning being given.)

10.1.14 *Entering a building with intent to commit a crime*

Section 11(1) creates an unusual offence of criminal trespass:

> "It shall be an offence for a person—
> (a) to enter any building or the curtilage of any building or any part of such building or curtilage as a trespasser, or
> (b) to be within the vicinity of any such building or curtilage or part of such building or curtilage for the purpose of trespassing thereon,
> In circumstances giving rise to the reasonable inference that such entry or presence was with intent to commit an offence or with intent to unlawfully interfere with any property situate therein."

This offence is remarkably wide: it applies not just to a person who actually enters a building (or its curtilage—that is, the grounds immediately surrounding the building) as a trespasser but also to a person found in the vicinity of a building for the purpose of trespassing, where there are "circumstances giving rise to a reasonable inference" that that person intended to commit a crime or unlawfully interfere with property. Proof of this offence may therefore involve piling supposition (that the defendant intended to trespass) on supposition (that the intended trespass was with the further intention to commit an offence). Charleton, McDermott and Bolger describe this offence as "akin to burglary" and suggest that it might be charged as a fallback in situations "where nothing is stolen or where the prosecution cannot prove an intent to steal." (*Criminal Law* (1999), p.768)

The maximum penalty for this offence is a fine of up to €1,269.74 or up to six months' imprisonment.

10.1.15 Trespass causing fear

Section 13 creates another unusual offence of criminal trespass:

> "It shall be an offence for a person, without reasonable excuse, to trespass on any building or the curtilage thereof in such a manner as causes or is likely to cause fear in another person."

It is not necessary to show that any person was in fact put in fear. The maximum penalty for this offence is a fine of €1,269.74 and/or imprisonment for up to 12 months.

Further reading:

National Crime Council, *Public Order Offences in Ireland* (2001)

10.2 Incitement to hatred

The Prohibition of Incitement to Hatred Act 1989 implemented Ireland's obligations under the UN Convention on Civil and Political Rights, which requires, *inter alia*, that advocacy of national, racial and religious hatred constituting incitement to discrimination, hostility or violence should be prohibited by law.

It does so by creating three main offences, each of which is phrased in terms of stirring up hatred. "Hatred" itself is defined in s.1 as meaning:

> "hatred against a group of persons in the State or elsewhere on account of their race, colour, nationality, religion, ethnic or national origins, membership of the travelling community or sexual orientation."

This definition focuses on the group and its distinguishing characteristics; it is not an offence to stir up hatred against an individual, *per se*, although it may be if the effect of doing so is also to stir up hatred against the group of which he is a member.

The first offence is that of *actions likely to stir up hatred* contrary to s.2 of the Act:

> "It shall be an offence for a person -
> (a) to publish or distribute written material,
> (b) to use words, behave or display written material -
> (i) in any place other than inside a private residence, or
> (ii) inside a private residence so that the words, behaviour or material are heard or seen by persons outside the residence, or
> (c) to distribute, show or play a recording of visual images or sounds,
>
> if the written material, words, behaviour, visual images or sounds, as the case may be, are threatening, abusive or insulting and are intended or, having regard to all the circumstances, are likely to stir up hatred."

This offence draws a distinction between public and private conduct: a person is free to stir up hatred within a private residence, so long as they do not do so by way of video or audio cassette. However, a private residence will be treated as being a public place where a public meeting is held there.

While there have been a number of attempted prosecutions, there has, it seems, been only one successful prosecution to date under this section. In 2002, a school bus driver was convicted in respect of racial abuse of a 12-year-old boy, a passenger on his bus:

> "The driver returned to the bus and said to the boy: 'What are you doing, you f***ing nigger? Sit down, you black bastard.' [The defendant] then asked the boy where he was from and told him to 'go back to Africa, where he came from' ... [T]he driver referred to a number of black people in a nearby car, saying: 'Them blacks in the car should be taken out and drowned'." ("School bus-driver fined for racist abuse of boy of 12", *The Irish Times*, September 12, 2002)

However, a similar 2001 case reached a different result. That case concerned a Dublin Bus driver who told a Gambian national, who was eating food on the bus:

> "In this country, we don't eat food on buses. What are you doing in this country? You should go back to where you came from."

The defendant went on to refer to the victim as a "nig nog". The defendant was convicted before the District Court, but was acquitted on appeal to the Circuit Court, Judge John Buckley ruling that: "however appalling his words were, they were not intended or likely to stir up hatred under the strict interpretation of the law." ("New incitement to hatred law sought", *The Irish Times*, March 14, 2001). It may be, therefore, that there is some confusion as to the type of language which will reach the level of "stirring up hatred", and mere racial abuse may not suffice.

Section 3 then creates an offence of *broadcasts likely to stir up hatred*:

> "If an item involving threatening, abusive or insulting images or sounds is broadcast, each of the persons [specified later] is guilty of an offence if he intends thereby to stir up hatred or, having regard to all the circumstances, hatred is likely to be stirred up thereby."

Those persons are then defined as the persons providing the broadcasting service, and persons producing the item concerned, and any person whose words or behaviour in the item are threatening, abusive or insulting. Detailed defences are then provided: for example, it is a defence to show that the offending clip could not practicably be removed, that the defendant was not aware that the offending clip would be broadcast, or that the offending clip would be broadcast in a context likely to stir up hatred, and so forth.

Finally, s.4 creates an offence of *preparation and possession of material likely to stir up hatred*:

> "It shall be an offence for a person -
> (a) to prepare or be in possession of any written material with a view to its being distributed, displayed, broadcast

> or otherwise published, in the State or elsewhere,
> whether by himself or another, or
> (b)   to make or be in possession of a recording of sounds
>   or visual images with a view to its being distributed,
>   shown, played, broadcast or otherwise published, in
>   the State or elsewhere, whether by himself or another,
>
> if the material or recording is threatening, abusive or insulting
> and is intended or, having regard to all the circumstances,
> including such distribution ... as the person has, or it may
> reasonably be inferred that he has, in view, is likely to stir
> up hatred."

This offence would address a situation where, for example, neo-Nazi groups were using Ireland as a base for preparing materials to be used abroad.

Defences are available to the above offences where the person charged did not intend to stir up hatred and was not aware of the content of the material in question, and had no reason to suspect that it was threatening, abusive or insulting, or was not aware that his words, behaviour or the material concerned might be threatening, abusive or insulting.

Further reading:

Keogh, "The Prohibition of Incitement to Hatred Act 1989 — A Paper Tiger?", 6 Bar Review 178 (December 2000).

11. DEFENCES SPECIFIC TO MURDER

11.1 Introduction

Defences can be divided into three categories. The first is made up of those defences which are *specific to murder* and which result in a conviction for a lesser offence than murder if successful. The second category consists of those defences which are available to every offence *except for murder*. The third and largest category consists of those defences which are *generally available*.

Two defences are specific to murder: provocation and excessive self-defence. This is not to say that these matters cannot be raised in other proceedings: if they are, then they will be mitigating factors in sentencing. However, only in the case of murder are these two defences available to enable a conviction to be brought in for a lesser offence than that which is charged. This is because of the particularly grave status of murder, creating a judicial reluctance to label as murderers those who act under the pressure of the moment, even though that would not amount to a defence in another, less serious, context. In addition, allowing these defences in the case of murder does not allow the accused to escape all liability for his actions; these defences merely reduce murder to manslaughter.

11.2 Provocation

This defence is well summarised in Charleton, *Offences Against the Person* (Round Hall Press, 1992), p.131:

> "Where the accused, in killing the victim, acts under the influence of provocation his crime will amount only to manslaughter, and not murder, notwithstanding that the accused intended to kill or cause serious injury. The test in Irish law is subjective. The provocation under which the accused was acting must be such that having regard to the particular accused's character, temperament and circumstances, it causes him to temporarily lose control of himself to the extent that he ceased to be master of himself when he killed the victim."

11.2.1 Subjective test

What do we mean by a subjective test in this area? The law early on adopted a test limiting the availability of provocation to situations in which a reasonable man would have lost his self-control. This makes sense; there is clearly some element of danger in allowing a particularly temperamental person to plead his hot-headedness as a defence in circumstances where a person of ordinary self-control would not have reacted to the particular provocation. However, a sequence of English cases took this objective approach to absurd lengths.

The high point of this approach was the case of *R. v Bedder* (1954). In that case, the defendant was an 18-year-old boy who was sexually impotent. He attempted to have intercourse with a prostitute; when he failed, she taunted him. A struggle followed, in which she slapped and punched him and kicked him in the crotch. He drew a knife and stabbed her twice. Clearly, the boy's impotence had been the reason for his extreme reaction; the taunt of impotence would not have been effective otherwise. However, the House of Lords held that the boy's impotence could not be taken into account in assessing the effect of the provocation on the boy. The reasonable man was not impotent, and would not have lost his self-control as a result of the taunt; and therefore the boy could not raise the defence of provocation.

The absurdity of this position was recognised in England in *R. v Camplin* (1978). This case involved a 15-year-old boy, who killed the deceased after (he alleged) the deceased had forcibly buggered him and then jeered at him. The trial judge refused to direct the jury to consider the effect of the provocation on a 15-year-old boy in the same position as the accused. On appeal, the House of Lords departed from *R. v Bedder* (1954), and held (at p.721), that, on a proper application of the test:

> "The jury had to consider whether a young man of about the same age as the accused but placed in the same position as that which befell the accused could, had he been a reasonable young man, have reacted as did the accused and could have done what the accused did."

This is a mixed subjective/objective test. It is subjective insofar as the jury are to consider the effect of the provocation on a person in the defendant's circumstances; but it is objective in that the jury are not to consider the effect of the provocation on the defendant himself, but on a reasonable person in his circumstances. The jury may not, therefore, take into account the fact that the accused had a quick temper or was particularly excitable or pugnacious; they should consider how a hypothetical reasonable 15-year-old would react if in all other respects placed in the shoes of the defendant.

At around the same time as *R. v Camplin*, the Irish decision of *People (DPP) v MacEoin* (1978) was reached, in which the Court of Criminal Appeal took a very different view of the law of provocation. We have already seen that Irish law favours subjective tests in, for example, the area of recklessness. This approach also holds true in the area of provocation. In *People (DPP) v MacEoin*, the accused and the deceased lived together in a flat. Both men were heavy drinkers, and on the day of the killing both had been drinking heavily. In the course of their drinking, the deceased began to behave aggressively towards the defendant, and eventually attacked the defendant with a hammer. The defendant wrestled it from him, and (as he put it) "simmered over and completely lost control", killing the deceased with several blows to the head.

The primary issue before the court was whether a person could rely on the defence of provocation where they intended to kill or cause serious injury. However, the court also dealt with the correct test to be applied in cases of provocation, and held that the objective test for provocation should be abandoned. Those factors which were excluded in *R. v Camplin*, such as the particularly hot temper of the defendant, are to be taken into account; the test in Ireland is not whether a hypothetical reasonable man in the defendant's shoes would have been provoked, but whether the defendant himself was provoked:

> "A hot-tempered man may react violently to an insult which a phlegmatic one would ignore." (At p.32, *per* Kenny J.)

11.2.2 What is provocation?

Given that the test is subjective, just what extent of loss of self-control will amount to a defence? The test applied in *People (DPP) v MacEoin* is as follows:

> "Provocation is some act or series of acts, done by the dead man to the accused which actually caused in the accused, a sudden and temporary loss of self-control, rendering the accused so subject to passion as to make him or her for the moment not master of his mind."

This test focuses on loss of self-control; and where a person has time to think and plan revenge, then there is sufficient mental control that the defence of provocation will not apply:

> "Circumstances which induce a desire for revenge are inconsistent with provocation, since the conscious formulation of a desire for revenge means that a person has had time to think, to reflect, and that would negative a sudden temporary loss of self-control, which is of the essence of provocation." (*R. v Duffy* (1949) *per* Devlin J.)

However, the fact that a delay has taken place does not conclusively indicate that there is no sudden loss of self-control, but is merely a factor making it less likely that a sudden loss of self-control has taken place. Similarly, it is not necessary that the acts of provocation should take place all at the same time: it is possible for cumulative acts of provocation to take place over an extended period. Both of these points are illustrated by *R. v R.* (1981). This was an Australian case in which the defendant was married to the deceased. He had, over a period of time, committed incest with all the daughters of the family. On the day of the killing he told the defendant what he had done; later that day, one of the daughters told her of another attempted rape by him. That night, a row took place; later, as the husband lay asleep in bed, the defendant went out, took an axe, and killed him. On appeal, it was held that the defence of provocation should have been left to the jury; the evidence could support a cold-blooded decision to kill, but it could equally be compatible with a delayed loss of self-control, particularly against the backdrop of what had gone before.

11.2.3 Proportionality of force used

People (DPP) v MacEoin appears to state that the force used should be reasonable having regard to the provocation to which the defendant was subject:

> "If the prosecution can prove beyond reasonable doubt that the force used was unreasonable and excessive having regard to the provocation, the defence of provocation fails." (At p.35.)

This is a remarkable requirement; having decided that the accused was provoked so as to lose self-control, the court goes on to require that he should exercise self-control in regard to the choice of weapon to be used. It is, of course, true that the extent of force used is evidence of whether the accused was truly provoked; it will be hard for a defendant to argue provocation in most cases where he responds to a minor insult by stabbing, while he may more easily argue provocation where he responds with a blow to the stomach. The more extreme response would tend to argue against provocation and in favour of premeditated intention waiting on an excuse.

It therefore appears from *People (DPP) v MacEoin* that there must be a balance between the provocation generated and the amount of force used. However, this view has since been rejected by the Irish courts, in two 1997 cases which reassess this aspect of the defence. The first is *People (DPP) v Mullane* (1997). In this case, the accused admitted killing his girlfriend who had taunted him about his lack of sexual prowess; the only question left to the jury was whether the defence of provocation was available. The trial judge put the applicable test of provocation to the jury, and went on to read out two paragraphs from the judgment in *People (DPP) v MacEoin* to the jury. The accused was found guilty. On appeal, it was argued that the judge had erred in simply quoting the passages from *People (DPP) v MacEoin*, since this might have given the jury the impression that an objective test applied in relation to the amount of force used, when the whole of the test was a subjective one.

The matter again came before the Court of Criminal Appeal in *People (DPP) v Noonan* (1998), where the trial judge had, in his directions to the jury, put a form of objective test for provocation before the jury, based on a combination of Irish and English case law. Although no objection was taken to this direction to the jury at the time, the court held that this was due to an oversight, and that in the interests of justice this point would be addressed. The court went on to hold that the jury may well have been left in confusion as to whether provocation was to be assessed on an objective or subjective basis, and on that ground the appeal was successful.

It appears from these two cases, therefore, that the Court of Criminal Appeal has explained away the passage in *People (DPP) v MacEoin* (1978) which seems to require an objective test in respect of the amount of force used, and has reaffirmed the principle of a purely subjective test for all aspects of provocation. (See, however, the recommendation of the Law Reform Commission, set out in

11.2.7, that provocation should be negatived if the conduct if the conduct of the accused is not proportionate to the alleged provocation).

This conclusion is confirmed by the decision of the Court of Criminal Appeal in *People (DPP) v Bambrick* (1999) which restates the law in relation to provocation. The defendant was a person who had had a very deprived and unhappy childhood and adolescence including physical and sexual abuse. He had a low intelligence level, and was virtually an alcoholic. On the night of the killing the appellant was drunk. The appellant and the victim came into each other's company and began to drink together. The appellant maintained that the victim then made suggestive, sexual remarks to him. The appellant claimed also that the victim made a physical, sexual advance towards him. The appellant claimed that this advance brought back memories of childhood abuse which he had suffered, and that as a result he lost all control of himself. At this point the appellant then pulled a wooden stake from the ground and killed the victim with it. The appellant put forward a defence of provocation.

In dealing with this defence, the trial judge directed the jury that to determine whether the defence of provocation is available it was necessary for them to decide on the appellant's state of mind. The trial judge directed the jury that if it was "likely" that the accused came into the category of being sensitive to a trigger mechanism which would cause him to lose all control, then he should be acquitted of murder. The trial judge also directed the jury that when a defence of provocation is raised, the jury should determine whether they would regard it as being reasonable that the provocation could "probably" have triggered off the uncontrollable reaction which the accused alleged.

The Court of Criminal Appeal found that this direction to the jury was incorrect. In the first place the court found that the trial judge had misdirected the jury on the question of intention. In particular, the trial judge had erred in linking provocation with intention. The impression given to the jury was that the defence of provocation was not available where the accused intended to kill or cause serious injury. However, this was not the law. Secondly, the trial judge had misdirected the jury with regard to the test to be used in determining if provocation had taken place. The test is not whether it was "likely" or "probable" that the provocation triggered off the alleged reaction, but rather whether it was reasonably possible that it could have done so, in which event a reasonable doubt would have been established. Finally, the Court of Criminal Appeal reiterated that the test in relation to provocation was a subjective one, and that that it was not necessary to show that the accused lacked an intention to kill or cause serious injury. This decision is, therefore, important in that it makes it clear that the defence of provocation is entirely distinct from an absence of intention to kill or cause serious injury.

Subsequent decisions in the area of provocation reiterate that the test for provocation is a *subjective* one. In *People (DPP) v Kelly* (2000), the Court of Criminal Appeal stated that "The problem with *MacEoin* is not with the decision itself but in the way the decision is worded. The difficulty with the wording has not been totally removed by the judgment in *Mullane*. For that reason we consider that a trial judge dealing with a plea of provocation in a murder trial should follow *MacEoin* but he may not find it necessary, or helpful to the jury, to quote from it." Barrington J. remarked that "the usefulness of the concept of excessive force is equivocal. On the one hand the jury, looking at provocation, might say: 'surely the accused was not provoked by that to use such excessive force against his victim.' On the other hand they might say: 'Surely this force was so excessive that the accused must have been totally out of control when he used it.'"

The court in *DPP v Boyle* (2000) acknowledged that *MacEoin* does not make it absolutely clear that the test for provocation is entirely subjective but emphasised that the subsequent case law does make it absolutely clear that the test is a subjective one. Similarly, in *People (DPP) v Heaney* (2000) the court stated that the test to be applied is purely subjective and that the intention of *MacEoin* was to introduce a purely subjective test and not a subjective test coupled with an element of objectivity.

Finally, Hardiman J.'s judgment in *People (DPP) v Davis* (2001) re-iterated the subjectivity of provocation in Irish law. He stated that the defence was in the nature of a concession to the acknowledged weaknesses of human nature, and in particular an acknowledgment, based on experience over centuries, that there were specific events calculated to rob a person of self-control. That concession was based on policy considerations which might change from time to time, and these considerations might dictate that the defence should be circumscribed or even denied in cases where it would promote moral outrage, for example cases of road rage. The test for provocation in

Ireland was characterised by Hardiman J. as "an extreme form of subjectivity ... to the exclusion of the standards of the reasonable man ... That standard, however, remains relevant on the question of credibility ... The totally subjective criteria for the defence of provocation has been criticised by a number of commentators who express concern that it places an exceptionally onerous burden on the prosecution ... The subjective test has been well-established in Irish law for more than twenty years and it is not appropriate for this court to discuss its merits or drawbacks."

It should be noted that the Law Reform Commission has proposed that the amount of force used should be proportionate to the gravity of the provocation. (See para.11.2.7 below).

11.2.4 Provocation and battered women

The application of a defence of provocation to battered women who kill their aggressors has proved controversial. The defence of provocation is based on the concept of a sudden loss of control and the law therefore requires the accused to have acted in the heat of the moment. The longer the delay between the provoking act and the accused's actions, the more likely a court is to view it as vengeance rather than provocation.

Battered women tend not to react immediately to provocation as they have learned that this is likely to give rise to increased violence from their spouses. (O'Donovan, "Defences for battered women who kill" (1991) 18 J. Law and Soc 219). They more usually suffer a "slow burn" of anger which eventually erupts and results in the killing of the abuser, often while he is asleep or drunk. The event which triggers the killing may appear relatively trivial but, when viewed in the context of a long history of domestic violence, can be seen as the last straw in a cycle of abuse.

The concept of "cumulative" provocation, whereby a court will look at the most recent provoking act not in isolation but in the context of long-term abuse, would seem to have been accepted in Ireland: *The People (DPP) v O'Donoghue* (1992), where the accused had obtained a barring order against her husband after a history of abuse. Having allowed him to return home, he again verbally abused her, whereupon she snapped and killed him with a hammer. She was convicted of manslaughter and given a suspended sentence.

However, there is still a requirement of a sudden loss of self-control under English law, although the position in Ireland is less clear. In *R. v Thornton (No.2)* (1996) and *R. v Ahluwalia* (1993), the defendants were battered women who waited for some time before reacting to provocation from their husbands. It was held that such a "cooling-off" period was inconsistent with a defence of provocation. However, in the latter case a less rigid approach was adopted whereby delay does not automatically rule out the defence but will be evidentially highly important as to whether provocation is made out. It could be argued that, in the light of *MacEoin*, Irish law does not require a battered woman to react in the heat of the moment. *MacEoin* illustrates a subjective approach to provocation, taking into consideration all the characteristics of the accused. In the case of a battered woman, evidence that a long history of abuse reduces the likelihood of such women killing in the heat of the moment might well be allowed. However, in *Davis*. Hardiman J. stated that there must be evidence of a "sudden and temporary loss of self-control, rendering the accused so subject to passion as to make him or her for the moment not master of his mind" and there must be some evidence that the loss of self-control was "total" and that the reaction came "suddenly and before there was time for the passion to cool". In *Kelly*, the court remarked that "there must be a sudden unforeseen onset of passion ..."

11.2.5 Self-induced provocation

An accused cannot rely on the defence of provocation where he has deliberately engineered a situation in which he can claim to have been enraged. This is so even if he was, in fact, sufficiently provoked at the time of the killing. Charleton draws an analogy with the defence of intoxication:

> "The situation is analogous to a person who drinks in order to get himself into a homicidal state; in that situation drunkenness is not a defence even though at the moment of the killing the accused may be so intoxicated as to be incapable of acting with intent." (Charleton, *Offences Against the Person* (Round Hall Press, 1992), p.149)

This principle extends to situations where the accused, although not engineering a situation in which he can claim that a killing was justified, nevertheless creates a situation where the conduct alleged to constitute provocation is a predictable outcome of his behaviour. In *R. v Edwards* (1973), for example, the accused was a blackmailer.

The victim, furious at the blackmail attempt, lunged at the defendant with a knife. The accused took the knife and killed the victim. Was the defence of provocation available? The Privy Council held that the accused could not rely on the "normal reactions" of a blackmailed person in those circumstances, but the jury should have been asked to decide whether the conduct of the victim went beyond those normal reactions. *Per* Lord Pearson:

> "No authority has been cited with regard to what may be called 'self-induced provocation'. On principle it seems reasonable to say that (1) a blackmailer cannot rely on the predictable results of his own blackmailing conduct as constituting provocation sufficient to reduce his killing of the victim from murder to manslaughter, and the predictable results may include a considerable degree of hostile reaction by the person sought to be blackmailed, for instance vituperative words or even some hostile reaction such as blows with a fist; (2) but if the hostile reaction by the person sought to be blackmailed goes to extreme lengths it might constitute sufficient provocation even for the blackmailer. (3) There would in many cases be a question of degree to be decided by the jury." (At p.658.)

11.2.6 *Provocation by a third party*

At common law provocation must come from the deceased. This would appear to be at odds with the underlying rationale of the defence as provocation was not developed to reflect condemnation of the conduct of the deceased but the sudden loss of self-control of the accused.

11.2.7 *Proposals for law reform*

The Law Reform Commission Consultation Paper, *Homicide: The Plea of Provocation*, published in 2003, set out the following draft formulation of a statutory provision to reform the law of provocation:

> "(1) Unlawful homicide that would otherwise be murder may be reduced to manslaughter if the person who caused the death did so under provocation.
> (2) Anything done or said may be provocation if – (i) it deprived the accused of the power of self-control and

thereby induced him or her to commit the act of homicide; and (ii) in the circumstances of the case it would have been of sufficient gravity to deprive an ordinary person of the power of self-control.

(3) (i) In determining whether anything done or said would have been of sufficient gravity to deprive an ordinary person of the power of self-control the jury or court, as the case may be, may take account of such characteristics of the accused as it may consider relevant. (ii) A jury or court, as the case may be, shall not take account of the accused's mental disorder, state of intoxication or temperament for the purposes of determining the power of self-control exhibited by the ordinary person.

(4) Anything done or said is deemed not to be provocation if – (i) it was incited by the accused; or (ii) it was done in the lawful exercise of a power conferred by law.

(5) Provocation is negatived if the conduct of the accused is not proportionate to the alleged provocative conduct or words.

(6) There is no rule of law that provocation is negatived if – (i) the act causing death did not occur immediately; or (ii) the act causing death was done with intention to kill or cause serious harm.

(7) This section shall apply in any case where the provocation was given by the person killed and in any case where the offender, under provocation given by one person, by accident or mistake killed another person."

Further reading:

McAuley, "Anticipating the Past: The Defence of Provocation in Irish Law" (1987) 50 M.L.R. 133; McAleese, "The Reasonable Man Provoked?" (1978) D.U.L.J. 53.

11.3 Excessive self-defence

Self-defence is a defence generally in the criminal law. Where a person uses force which is necessary to ward off an attack, and uses no more force than is necessary, then no crime is committed. (This defence has now been put on a statutory footing by s.18 of the Non-Fatal Offences Against the Person Act 1997.) However, what happens where a person acts in self-defence, but uses force which is more than is reasonably necessary?

In relation to most crimes, excessive self-defence is no defence, although it will of course be an important mitigating factor in passing sentence. This is also the position in England and Northern Ireland in relation to murder, as reiterated in *R. v Clegg* (1995). In that case, the defendant was a British soldier in Northern Ireland who was on duty at a vehicle checkpoint. A car drove through the checkpoint and then accelerated down the road. The defendant fired at the car as it went by, killing a passenger. He claimed that he fired at the car because he believed that the life of another soldier, on the other side of the road, was in danger. This defence was accepted with regard to three of the shots which he fired, but not the fourth, which was fired when the car had already passed and was fifty feet further down the road. This fourth shot had caused the death of the passenger, and he was convicted of murder with regard to this death. On appeal to the House of Lords, it was submitted that there should be a qualified defence available in those circumstances, which would reduce the offence from murder to manslaughter. This was rejected; it was well established that excessive self-defence was not available to reduce murder to manslaughter, and the House of Lords declined to change the law on this point. The court emphasised that the question of whether there should be a qualified defence of excessive self-defence was a matter for Parliament. In England, therefore, self-defence is an all or nothing affair; an accused is either guilty of murder or entirely innocent. There is no halfway house. This is also the position in Australia.

The position in Ireland in relation to murder is different. The Supreme Court dealt with this issue in *People (AG) v Dwyer* (1972), where the defendant had been involved in a fight outside a chip shop. He believed (he claimed) that the victim was armed with some item and that he feared for his life; as a result, he took a knife and stabbed and killed the victim. This was clearly not an objectively proportional response to any danger, and as such a plea of self-defence was not available. But could the defendant's subjective belief that the force was necessary reduce the crime to manslaughter?

The Supreme Court held that it could. Two judgments were given which adopted different reasons for this result. Walsh J. held that the effect of s.4 of the Criminal Justice Act 1964 (replacing "malice aforethought" with the modern *mens rea* for murder) was to make the mental element for murder entirely subjective. It followed that, if the defendant honestly believed that the force used was necessary, then he could not be guilty of murder:

> "Our statutory provision makes it clear that the intention is personal and that it is not to be measured solely by objective standards. In my opinion, therefore, when the evidence in a case discloses a question of self-defence and where it is sought by the prosecution to show that the accused used excessive force, that it to say more than would be regarded as objectively reasonable, the prosecution must establish that the accused knew that he was using more force than was reasonably necessary. Therefore, it follows that if the accused honestly believed that the force that he did use was necessary, then he is not guilty of murder. The onus, of course, is upon the prosecution to prove beyond reasonable doubt that he knew that the force was excessive or that he did not believe that it was necessary. If the prosecution does not do so, it has failed to establish the necessary malice." (At p.424.)

Butler J. took a different approach; if the accused honestly and primarily intended to defend himself, then he should not be held to have the necessary intention to kill or cause serious injury. Consequently, the moral culpability of the accused is reduced and the killing would amount to manslaughter only.

Notwithstanding the difference in approach between these two opinions, the overall result is clear: in Irish law excessive self-defence will operate as a partial defence, reducing murder to manslaughter. Excessive self-defence may in turn be defined as force used which is greater than that which is objectively necessary, but which the accused honestly believed to be necessary. Clearly, the accused will not be able to establish the necessary honest belief in situations where the victim presented no threat whatsoever. See, for example, *People (AG) v Commane* (1975) in which the victim was immobilised by a blow to the head with a whiskey bottle and subsequently strangled.

On those facts, excessive self-defence was held not to be available to go to the jury, since the killing had taken place after the victim had been rendered incapable of further aggression.

It should be noted that there is a debate as to whether this defence has survived the passing of the Non-Fatal Offences Against the Person Act 1997. Section 18 of the 1997 Act puts self-defence on a statutory footing, but is silent as to the case of excessive self-defence, while s.22(2) abolishes common law defences in relation to the use of force in self-defence. From this, it would seem that excessive self-defence is simply done away with by s.22(2). On the other hand, the report of the Law Reform Commission on which the 1997 Act was based (*Report on Non-Fatal Offences Against the Person (1994)*) did not deal with the question of excessive self-defence. In addition, excessive self-defence is limited to the crime of murder and is, therefore, entirely inappropriate to be dealt with in an Act limited in its scope to non-fatal offences. Finally, the decision in *People (AG) v Dwyer* (1972) is based largely on the statutory definition of the mental element of murder, which the 1997 Act does not alter. (See Bacik, "Non-Fatal Offences Against the Person Act, 1997" (1997) I.C.L.S.A. 26–19, 26–21.)

12. GENERAL DEFENCES

12.1 Duress

The defence of duress is, in some ways, the opposite of the defences of provocation and excessive self-defence. Those defences are only available to a charge of murder, while the defence of duress is available in respect of most crimes, and is only unavailable to a charge of murder. The defence applies in circumstances where a person is compelled to commit a crime by virtue of threats made against him (or perhaps another person); clearly, in these circumstances, the moral culpability of the accused is reduced to the extent that his will is overborne. However, there is no question of the accused not possessing the relevant *mens rea*. He fully intends to commit the offence but his ordinary resistance is overborne to such an extent that the law will not view him as morally responsible for his actions.

The leading Irish case is *People (AG) v Whelan* (1934). In that case, the accused was charged with receiving stolen property; his defence was that he acted under threats of extreme violence. The jury returned a verdict to the effect that he received the stolen goods, but did so under threat of immediate death or serious violence. The question presented to the Court of Criminal Appeal was whether, on foot of this verdict, the accused was guilty or innocent of the crime charged. The court treated this question as posing a simple issue: was there "such an absence of will as to absolve from guilt"? The prosecution contended that only actual physical force which left the accused no choice of will would absolve from guilt, while anything else would merely go to mitigation of punishment.

This position was, however, rejected by the court, which held that:

> "It seems to us that threats of immediate death or serious personal violence so great as to overbear the ordinary power of human resistance should be accepted as a justification for acts which would otherwise be criminal. The application of this general rule must, however, be subject to certain limitations. The commission of murder is a crime so heinous that murder should not be committed even for the price of life and in such a case the strongest duress would not be any justification." (*Per* Murnaghan J, at p 526.)

In addition, it is necessary to show that the threats in question were still in effect at the time that the crime was committed, and that the accused did not have an opportunity to extract himself from the effect of the threats:

> "Where the excuse of duress is applicable it must further be clearly shown that the overpowering of the will was operative at the time the crime was actually committed, and, if there were reasonable opportunity for the will to reassert itself, no justification can be found in antecedent threats." (*Per* Murnaghan J., at p.526.)

12.1.1 Immediacy of threats

People (AG) v Whelan requires that threats should be immediate. There are, it seems, two reasons for this. First, a threat of future violence will be treated as too remote to overbear the will of the accused in the here and now. Second, a threat of future violence leaves the recipient of the threats free to seek police protection. In light of these reasons, just how immediate must a threat be before it will ground a defence of duress?

This question was dealt with in *R. v Hudson and Taylor* (1971). The two accused were charged with perjury, having lied about the identification of a man charged with wounding. Their defence was duress: an associate of the man had threatened before the trial to cut them up, and at the trial they could see that associate sitting in the public gallery. Was this threat sufficiently immediate? And could they plead duress where it had been open to them to seek police protection before the threat would be carried out? It was held by the Court of Appeal on the first issue that it was a matter for the jury to decide if the threats were sufficiently immediate, remembering that:

> "the threats of [the associate] were likely to be no less compelling, because their execution could not be effected in the court room, if they could be carried out in the streets of Salford the same night." (*Per* Lord Widgery C.J., at p. 207.)

As regards the second issue, the availability of police protection, it was held that this would defeat a defence of duress where it was reasonably open to the accused to neutralise a threat:

> "it is always open to [the prosecution] to prove that the accused failed to avail himself of some opportunity which was reasonably open to him to render the threat ineffective, and that upon this being established the threat in question can no longer be relied upon by the defence. In deciding whether such an opportunity was reasonably open to the accused the jury should have regard to this age and circumstances, and to any risks to him which may be involved in the course of action relied upon." (*Per* Lord Widgery C.J., at p.207.)

This was, however, a question for the jury, and since the defence of duress had not been left to the jury, the convictions were quashed.

12.1.2 Objective or subjective test?

The test laid down by *People (AG) v Whelan* seems to be objective: an accused cannot avail of the defence unless the threats in question would have overborne "the ordinary power of human resistance" and not merely his personal power of resistance. The weak-willed accused will not, it seems, be able to plead duress. On principle, however, it seems to be right to impose an objective test in this area, notwithstanding that Irish criminal law usually leans towards subjective tests: as Charleton himself points out:

> "Duress ... involves a rational choice between two evils. The threat made to the accused must be of a grave order of magnitude to excuse the commission of a crime. The law might fail to fulfil its objective of ordering society if petty excuses for criminal action were allowed." (Charleton, *Criminal Law - Cases and Materials* (Butterworths, 1992), p.201.)

12.1.3 Application to murder

It is clear that duress does not apply to murder itself, and *People (AG) v Whelan* leaves open the question whether there are other, particularly grave offences to which it does not apply. It is unclear, however, whether the defence can apply to the various degrees of participation in the crime of murder. There is no authority from this jurisdiction on this point, and contradictory authority from the House of Lords. In *DPP for Northern Ireland v Lynch* (1975) (in which the House of Lords expressly approved *Whelan*), the appellant was charged with aiding and abetting the murder of a police constable by driving three armed men to and from a shooting. He pleaded duress, alleging that a well-known member of the IRA had threatened to kill him if he disobeyed. The trial judge ruled that duress was not a defence to a charge of murder. On appeal it was held that it was open to a person accused as a principal in the second degree to plead duress and a re-trial was ordered. This decision was overruled by the House of Lords some years later in *R. v Howe* (1987). It was held that the defence of duress is not available to a person charged with murder either as a principal in the first degree (the actual killer) or principal in the second degree (the aider and abettor).

12.1.4 *Membership of a violent organisation*

Suppose an accused voluntarily joins the IRA, commits a crime, and then claims that had he failed to do so, retribution would have been forthcoming. Can a defendant rely on "self-induced duress" in this way? The answer is no—the person who voluntarily puts himself in a position where duress will be applied is outside the scope of the defence. *R. v Fitzpatrick* (1977) was a case in which the accused was charged with murder, robbery and membership of a proscribed organisation. He was a member of the Official IRA, but testified that he had attempted to leave but was prevented from doing so by threats of violence to himself and his parents. The trial judge held that the defence of duress was not available on those facts. On appeal, it was contended that duress should be available to members of such organisations, at least where they had made sufficient efforts to disassociate themselves from the organisation. It was held by the Court of Criminal Appeal that duress was a defence having its roots in an absence of moral blameworthiness on the part of the accused and therefore the defence was not available where the accused knowingly and voluntarily joins such an organisation:

> "If a person behaves immorally by, for example, committing himself to an unlawful conspiracy, he ought not to be able

to take advantage of the pressure exercised on him by his fellow criminals in order to put on when it suits him the breastplate of righteousness." (*Per* Lowry L.C.J., at p.31)

For the same reason, it was held to be irrelevant that the accused had tried to leave the organisation.

However, it seems that the accused must have some knowledge of the violent nature of the organisation before he joins: "innocent" membership does not make the accused morally culpable so as to defeat the defence of duress. So, in *R. v Shepherd* (1987), the accused voluntarily joined an organised gang of shoplifters; when he sought to leave, his evidence was that he was threatened with violence. In these circumstances, it was held that the defence of duress should have been left to the jury: it was arguable that the defendant had failed to appreciate the risk of violence, and if that were the case, then the defendant would be entitled to rely on the defence of duress.

12.1.5 Duress and marital coercion

A curious rebuttable presumption existed at common law that a wife who committed a crime in the presence of her husband did so as a result of his coercion and so was immune from punishment, subject to an exception in the case of particularly serious crimes (Charleton, *Offences Against the Person* (Round Hall Press, 1992), p.165). The Supreme Court, however, in *State (DPP) v Walsh and Connelly* (1981), held that the presumption reflected a disparity in status between husband and wife which ran counter to the modern concept of equality, and that the presumption did not, therefore, survive the coming into force of the Constitution.

12.2 Necessity

The defence of necessity runs parallel to the defence of duress, and is often described as "duress of circumstances" The defence has the same underlying rationale, which is that a defendant ought not to be punished for breaking the law where he has no choice in the matter, whether as a result of threats (duress) or surrounding circumstances (necessity). The defence is also, therefore, subject to some of the same limitations. In particular, the defence of necessity is not available to a charge of murder.

In *R. v Dudley and Stephens* (1884), the two defendants and the deceased found themselves at sea, in an open boat, without food or water. After several days without food or water, the two defendants killed the deceased, a 17-year-old boy, and survived on his body and blood for four days, at which point they were rescued by a passing ship. Could they rely on the defence of necessity? The jury found that: if the defendants had not fed on the boy, that they would probably have died before the four days were out; that the boy was likely to have died first; that at the time of the killing there was no reasonable prospect of relief; but that there was no greater necessity for killing the boy than either of the two defendants. Even on these findings, the Queen's Bench Division held that necessity was not available as a defence:

> "To preserve one's life is generally speaking, a duty, but it may be the plainest and the highest duty to sacrifice it ... It is not correct, therefore, to say that there is any absolute and unqualified necessity to preserve one's life ... It is enough in a Christian country to remind ourselves of the Great Example which we profess to follow ... It is not needful to point out the awful danger of admitting the principle which has been contended for. Who is to be the judge of this sort of necessity? By what measure is the comparative value of lives to be measured? ... We are often compelled to set up standards we cannot reach ourselves, and to lay down rules which we could not ourselves satisfy. But a man has no right to declare temptation to be an excuse, though he might himself have yielded to it, nor allow compassion for the criminal to change or weaken in any manner the legal definition of the crime."

The accused were, therefore, sentenced to death, which was commuted to six months imprisonment.

The parameters of the defence of necessity have been set out by the Supreme Court of Victoria, in *R. v Loughnan* (1981). In that case, the defendant was charged with escape from prison; he admitted escaping, but claimed that he did so because he believed that he would be attacked and killed by other prisoners. The trial judge refused to allow the defence of necessity to go before the jury, and the defendant was convicted. On appeal, it was held that on the particular facts of the case, the defence did not have to go before the jury.

However, the court dealt with the wider issue of necessity and held as follows:

> "[T]here are three elements involved in the defence of necessity. First, the criminal act or acts must have been done only in order to avoid certain consequences which would otherwise have inflicted irreparable evil upon the accused or upon others whom he was bound to protect... The other two elements involved... can, for convenience be given the labels immediate peril and proportion... the accused must honestly believe on reasonable grounds that he was placed in a situation of immediate peril ... The element of proportion simply means that the acts done to avoid the imminent peril must not be out of proportion to the peril to be avoided. Put in another way, the test is: would a reasonable man in the position of the accused have considered that he had any alternative to doing what he did to avoid the peril? (*Per* Young C.J.) and
>
> The essential conditions, I consider, so far as presently relevant, are that: 1. The harm to be justified must have been committed under pressure either of physical forces or exerted by some human agency so that 'an urgent situation of imminent peril' has been created. 2. The accused must have acted with the intention of avoiding greater harm or so as to have made possible 'the preservation of at least an equal value' 3. There was open to the accused no alternative, other than that adopted by him, to avoid the greater harm or 'to conserve the value'." (*Per* Crockett J.).

If, therefore, the accused had genuinely escaped with the intention of avoiding a danger to his life, and there was no other alternative open to him, then the defence of duress would have been open to him.

Another example of the defence can be seen in *R. v Conway* (1988). In this case, the defendant was convicted of reckless driving. His defence was necessity or, as it was termed, duress of circumstances. Two young men in civilian clothes had come running towards the car, in which he had a passenger who had been the target of a shooting shortly before. The passenger shouted at the

216 of the Court of Appeal

defendant to drive off, and the defendant did so, believing that the two men were trying to kill the passenger. The car was then chased by the two men in an unmarked vehicle, at which point the driver drove in a reckless manner. The pursuers turned out to be police officers seeking to arrest the passenger. Could the driver plead necessity in those circumstances? It was held that he could. The Court of Appeal held that duress and necessity were different terms for aspects of the one underlying defence, and that the defence, whatever it is termed, should have been left to the jury. This of course illustrates the fact that the threat or danger involved need not be to the defendant himself, but may be to another person.

12.3 Lawful use of force/self-defences

We have already dealt with the defence of excessive self-defence in the context of murder. More generally, the use of force will be lawful in circumstances including self-defence, the defence of property, the carrying out of an arrest, or the prevention of a crime. The parameters of this defence are now set out in ss.18–22 of the Non-Fatal Offences Against the Person Act 1997, which implement the recommendations of the Law Reform Commission in their *Report on Non-Fatal Offences Against the Person* (L.R.C. 45–1994):

> "18(1) - The use of force by a person for any of the
>   following purposes, if only such as is reasonable in
>   the circumstances as he or she believes them to be,
>   does not constitute an offence -
> (a) to protect himself or herself or a member of the family
>   of that person or another from injury, assault or
>   detention caused by a criminal act";

This restates the Irish position that no special relation to the person threatened is required, which departs from the position in other jurisdictions that there must be "some special nexus or relationship between the person relying on the doctrine to justify what he did in defence of another and that other" (*Devlin v Armstrong* (1971), pp.35–36). In that case, the defendant was the activist Bernadette Devlin, charged with incitement to riot and other public order offences in the barricades in the Bogside. She had encouraged others to build the barricade, throw petrol bombs at the police, and so on. Her defence was that she was acting in legitimate self-defence and defence of others in the belief that the police, if they entered the Bogside, would commit crimes of assault and unlawful attacks on property. This defence was rejected on a number of grounds, including the ground that she could not act in self-defence of persons with whom she had no special nexus. Even though this ground would not be applicable in this jurisdiction, the other grounds would be, in particular the ground that the alleged danger was not sufficiently specific or imminent to justify the force used, which was, in any event, excessive to the alleged danger.

The position in this jurisdiction was set out in *People (AG) v Keatley* (1954). In that case, the defendant was charged with manslaughter, having struck and killed another in defence of his brother. The court held that it was not necessary to prove any special relationship between the defendant and the person being defended: the underlying principle of the defence is the right to prevent the commission of an unlawful act, and the question of any special relationship is irrelevant to that principle.

Section 18(1) also provides that the use of force by a person will be lawful:

(b) to protect himself or herself or (with the authority of that other) another from trespass to the person; or

(c) to protect his or her property from appropriation, destruction or damage caused by a criminal act or from trespass or infringement; or

(d) to protect property belonging to another from appropriation, destruction or damage caused by a criminal act or (with the authority of that other) from trespass or infringement; or

(e) to prevent crime or breach of the peace.

This does not authorise the use of excessive force to prevent *petty* crime. The force must still be "reasonable in the circumstances" and it is debatable whether the use of any force would be reasonable where the offence is trivial. Even where an offence is not trivial, the force used must still be proportionate to the gravity of the offence. Speeding motorists cannot be shot dead.

Section 18 goes on to provide that "crimes" and "criminal acts" include acts which would be criminal but for the fact that an accused would be able to raise a defence of infancy, duress, necessity, involuntariness, intoxication or insanity. In addition, whether an act

218 Criminal Law

falls within (a) to (e) of s.18(1) is to be judged by the circumstances as the accused believes them to be, *i.e.* a subjective approach. This has the consequence that a person cannot rely on a defence which was unknown to him at the time of the use of force. It follows that the use of force without apparent justification at the time, which in retrospect turns out to have been justified, is unlawful.

In addition, this section does not provide a defence for the use of force against a person known to be a Garda acting in the course of his duty unless immediately necessary to prevent physical harm to a person. This preserves the position at common law, which can be seen in the case of *R. v Fennell* (1970). In that case, the accused was convicted of assaulting a police officer who was attempting to arrest his son. His defence was that he believed, on reasonable grounds, that the arrest was unlawful. This was held not to be a defence in these circumstances.

A limitation on this defence is contained in s.18(7) which provides that:

> "The defence provided by this section does not apply to a person who causes conduct or a state of affairs with a view to using force to resist or terminate it: But the defence may apply although the occasion for the use of force arises only because the person does something he or she may lawfully do, knowing that such an occasion will arise."

A person may not engineer a situation in which he can use force, but may use force notwithstanding that he foresaw that his conduct might give rise to a need for force. This codifies the rule in *R. v Browne* (1973) that a person may not rely on self-defence where they have deliberately provoked an attack with a view to using force to resist. It also echoes the inability of a defendant to rely on self-induced provocation or intoxication. However, a person remains free to engage in lawful activities notwithstanding that unlawful violence from others may result, following *R. v Field* (1972). The Law Reform Commission states: "From the point of view of public order, the practical conclusion to be drawn from this is that where a danger arises that the lawful exercise of rights may result in a breach of the peace, the proper remedy is the presence of police in sufficient numbers to preserve the peace, and not the legal condemnation of those exercising their rights". (See *Report on Non-Fatal Offences Against the Person* (L.R.C. 45–1994), p.29.)

Another exception is provided where force is used to carry out an arrest. This is provided for by s.19(1), which states that:

> "The use of force by a person in effecting or assisting in a lawful arrest, if only such as is reasonable in the circumstances as he or she believes them to be, does not constitute an offence."

Section 19 goes on to provide that whether the arrest is to be treated as lawful is to be determined according to the circumstances, as the accused believes them to be, *i.e.* a subjective approach.

A definition of force is contained in s.20(1) of the Act which provides that:

> "For the purposes of sections 18-19 -
>
> (a) a person uses force in relation to another person or property not only when he or she applies force to, but also where he or she causes an impact on, the body of that person or that property;
> (b) a person shall be treated as using force in relation to another person if -
>> (i)   he or she threatens that person with its use, or
>> (ii) he or she detains that person without actually using it; and
> (c) a person shall be treated as using force in relation to property if he or she threatens a person with its use in relation to property."

This definition ensures that both direct and indirect assaults are treated as the use of force, as is the threatened use of force.

Section 20, subss.(3) and (4), also sets out certain criteria to be followed in deciding whether force used was in fact reasonable. These provide that:

> "(3) A threat of force may be reasonable although the actual use of force may not be.
> (4) The fact that a person had an opportunity to retreat before using force shall be taken into account, in conjunction with other relevant evidence, in determining whether the use of force was reasonable."

This restates the common law position, set out in *R. v McInnes* (1971) that there is no absolute duty to retreat, but whether the defendant had an opportunity to retreat is relevant to determining whether he acted reasonably. In that case, the accused was charged with murder arising out of a fight between greasers and skinheads, which ended in the stabbing of one of the skinheads. The trial judge directed the jury that there was a duty to retreat as far as possible before self-defence could be relied upon, but this direction was held to be incorrect by the Court of Appeal.

12.4 Other defences preserved

The 1997 Act, although it provides new statutory defences for the use of force, does not rule out the use of other defences which might be available also. This is clear by s.22(1), which provides that:

> "The provisions of this Act have effect subject to any enactment or rule of law providing a defence, or providing lawful authority, justification or excuse for an act or omission."

The Act does, however, do away with the common law defence of the lawful use of force, as made clear by s.22(2), which states:

> "(2) Notwithstanding subsection (1) any defence available under the common law in respect of the use of force within the meaning of sections 18-19 or an act immediately preparatory to the use of force, for the purposes mentioned in sections 18-19 is hereby abolished."

This subsection abolishes the common law defence of necessary force, and makes it clear that any such defence is now entirely contained in ss.18–19. It does not, however, affect the availability of any other defence. It should be noted that there is a possibility that this subsection does away with the defence of excessive self-defence in relation to murder. This point is discussed in Chapter 11 in relation to excessive self-defence.

The effect of this defence is that only reasonable force can be used. At the same time, however, the courts will not demand exact precision in the amount of force which is used. As Holmes J. put it in *Brown v US* (1921): "Detached reflection cannot be demanded in the presence of an uplifted knife." (at p.343.).

If a person mistakenly believes he is faced with a threat, then he will be judged according to his genuine judgment of the situation. This was the position at common law: *R. v Williams (Gladstone)* (1987), where the Court of Appeal held that the appellant was entitled to be judged according to his view of the circumstances, even though he had made a genuine error in believing that a youth was being assaulted when in fact he was being arrested for stealing. The 1997 Act preserves this position: ss.18(1), 18(5), 19(1) and 19(3).

12.5 Intoxication

The availability of intoxication as a defence has always been problematic. Moral disapproval of intoxication contributed to a reluctance to admit that it might mitigate guilt: Aristotle recommended that a person who committed a crime while drunk should be punished twice, once for committing the crime and once for being drunk. Moral disapproval aside, the large proportion of crimes which are committed as the result of intoxication leads to a justifiable judicial reluctance to admit intoxication as a defence lest the result should be unduly lenient. The fact that a person's inhibitions and assessment are lowered while drunk is not, therefore, in itself a defence; it may even be an aggravating factor, as in the case of road traffic offences. There is, it follows, no general defence of intoxication.

However, a so-called defence of intoxication does arise in situations where an offence requires *mens rea*, and the defendant claims that he lacked that mental element through the effects of intoxication. For example, murder requires an intention to kill or cause serious injury: if the accused is too drunk to form that intention, then a conviction for murder cannot be forthcoming.

12.5.1 Dutch courage

This defence is strictly limited in scope. In the first place, it does not apply in circumstances where a person took drink or drugs in order to give himself Dutch courage to carry out a crime. So, in *Attorney General for Northern Ireland v Gallagher* (1961), the accused was charged with the murder of his wife. The evidence showed that he, while sober, had made up his mind to kill his wife. He then downed a bottle of whisky, either for Dutch courage or to drown his conscience after the killing. While drunk, he killed his wife. His argument was simple: at the time of the killing, he was so drunk as to lack the intention to kill or cause serious injury. Although he had, earlier, intended to kill his wife, the *actus reus* and the *mens rea* did not coincide. This was, unsurprisingly, rejected by the House of Lords:

> "If a man, whilst sane and sober, forms an intention to kill and makes preparation for it, knowing it is a wrong thing to do, and then gets himself drunk so as to give himself Dutch courage to do the killing, and whilst drunk carries out his intention, he cannot rely on this self-induced drunkenness as a defence to a charge of murder, nor even as reducing it to manslaughter. He cannot say that he got himself into such a stupid state that he was incapable of an intent to kill... The wickedness of his mind before he got drunk is enough to condemn him, coupled with the act which he intended to do and did do." (*Per* Lord Denning at p.314.)

12.5.2 Basic/specific intent

The second major limitation to the availability of the defence is imposed by the distinction between specific and basic intent. This is an artificial distinction, best explained in terms of *intention to carry out an action* and *intention to achieve a result*. If a crime merely requires intention to perform a particular act, then it is a crime of basic intent. An example is the crime of assault, which simply requires an intention to inflict force on another without their consent. If, however, a crime requires an intention to achieve a particular result by that act, then the crime is one of specific intent. An example is the crime of murder, which requires both a particular act, and an intention as a result of that act to cause serious injury or death.

This distinction was elaborated in the context of intoxication by the House of Lords in *DPP v Majewski* (1976). In that case, the accused was charged with assault occasioning actual bodily harm and assault on a police officer in the course of his duty. He was a drug addict, and had taken a large quantity of drugs and alcohol before the offences. He claimed to have blanked out and not to know what he was doing, and there was some medical evidence to the effect that this was possible. The trial judge directed the jury not to treat intoxication as being in any way a defence to the charges. On appeal, this direction was upheld. The basic position was expressed as being that voluntary drunkenness is never an excuse, to which an exception existed only in the limited class of offences which require proof of a specific intent. Where a person becomes voluntarily drunk, then the *mens rea* required is in effect supplied by his conduct in becoming drunk:

> "A man who by voluntarily taking drink and drugs gets himself into an aggressive state in which he does not know what he is doing and then makes a vicious assault can hardly say with any plausibility that what he did was a pure accident which should render him immune from any criminal liability."
> (*Per* Lord Salmon at p.157.),

This approach has not met with universal approval. The distinction between basic intent and specific intent is admitted to be arbitrary, and for that reason the High Court of Australia has adopted a different approach in *R. v O'Connor* (1979–1980), holding that evidence of intoxication, however caused, was admissible to show absence of intent. The accused was observed stealing from a police car and subsequently stabbed a police man in his pursuit. He had taken a mixture of drugs and drink and claimed to have had no recollection of the incident. Evidence was given that the drug taken was hallucinatory and in association with alcohol could have rendered the accused incapable of reasoning or forming intent to steal or wound. The High Court rejected the basic intent/specific intent distinction. Barwick C.J. stated that "With great respect to those who have favoured this ... it is to my mind not only inappropriate but it obscures more than it reveals ... It seems to me completely inconsistent with the principles of the common law that a man should be conclusively presumed to have an intent which, in fact, he does not have ..." It was held that evidence of intoxication should have been allowed to go to the jury in order for the jury to decide whether it had deprived the defendant of the requisite *mens rea*.

The basic intent/specific intent dichotomy has also been rejected in New Zealand and South Africa.

12.5.3 Intoxication under Irish law

Until very recently, the law in Ireland was unclear. The Law Reform Commission, in its *Consultation Paper on Intoxication,* appeared to suggest that intoxication was never a defence under Irish law. However, a line of Irish case law supported the view that evidence of intoxication was relevant to the question of whether the accused had the relevant *mens rea*.

In *People (AG) v Manning* (1953) the question of intoxication was treated as being directly relevant to *mens rea*. The defendant was found guilty of murdering a nurse. Evidence was given that he had consumed alcohol on the evening in question. He replied to Garda questioning by saying "I will tell you all, drink was the cause of it." He argued that he had been unable to form the necessary intent for murder as a result. On appeal it was held that the following jury direction was correct: " ... drink is no defence if the only effect of the drink is the more readily to allow a man to give way to his passions ... The effect of drink has to go much further. It has to go so far as either to render him incapable of knowing what he is doing at all or, if he appreciated that, of knowing the consequences or probable consequences of his actions ..."

Another example of this approach was *People (DPP) v McBride* (1997). The defendant was tried for assault on his niece with a pickaxe handle. He made a statement to the Gardaí that he had been drinking prior to the incident—"my mind just went blank and I started hitting her with the handle." The trial judge directed the jury that intoxication is not a defence to a criminal charge. Counsel for the defence argued before the Court of Criminal Appeal that this direction was incorrect: intoxication as such is not a defence but it can be relevant on the question of whether the accused was capable of forming intent. The Court of Criminal Appeal directed a re-trial on other grounds and observed that there was no evidence that the accused was intoxicated at the time of the assault on his niece. The court did not comment adversely on the submission of defence counsel on the effect of intoxication.

It appeared from the above cases that the basic/specific distinction had no place in Irish law and that the sole question to be considered was whether the intoxication had negatived the requisite *mens*.

However, this interpretation is no longer accurate. The Irish courts have now clearly embraced the *Majewski* reasoning and, by default, divided all Irish offences into two separate categories of basic and specific intent.

The case to do so was the decision of the Court of Criminal Appeal in *DPP v John Reilly* (2004). The accused stayed the night at his cousin's house, where the group became intoxicated. The accused drank at lest one glass of poitín before calling it a night. He slept downstairs in the same room as his cousin's baby. During the night, the accused leapt to his feet, unsheathed a knife he always kept on his possession and stabbed the baby and killed him. The baby was found the next morning by his mother. The accused had no recollection of the killing and was extremely upset when he realised what had happened. McCracken J. expressly endorsed *Majewski* by citing the quote that: "If a man of his own volition takes the substance which causes him to cast off the restraints of reason and conscience, no wrong is done by holding him answerable criminally for any injury he may do while in that condition. His course of conduct in reducing himself by drugs and drink to that condition in my view supplies the evidence of *mens rea*, of guilty mind certainly sufficient for crimes of basic intent". The applicant's conviction for manslaughter was allowed to stand.

We have seen that the basic/specific intent dichotomy has been criticised extensively. It was also characterised by the Irish Law Reform Commission as "illogical." It also moves away from the subjective recklessness test which has been a feature of Irish criminal law for so long.

Despite the criticism of *Reilly*, it appears that it accurately reflects current judicial attitudes to intoxication and is likely to be upheld in future cases. The rationale behind the decision appears to be judicial enthusiasm for applying common-sense rules. The current climate of intolerance for binge-drinking and the recognition that Irish society does not deal well with alcohol may make it less likely that the decision will be overruled. In addition, it is submitted that the terrible facts of the case may have influenced the court in coming to a decision. Spencer, who characterises this recent endorsement of *Majewski* in Irish law as "a rule of … doubtful provenance and … dubious merit" is of the view that: "The *Majewski* rule is now embedded in our law and it will take an exorcism of supreme proportions to purge it from our legal system".

12.5.4 Intoxication by other drugs

The operation of the *DPP v Majewski* distinction can be seen in *R. v Lipman* (1970), which also demonstrates the application of the defence in the case of intoxication by drugs other than alcohol. In this case, the accused took LSD and, in the course of hallucinating that he was being attacked by snakes, killed his girlfriend. Charged with murder, he claimed that he had no knowledge of what he was doing and no intention to harm her. He was found guilty of manslaughter, and appealed. It was held by the Court of Appeal that where a killing results from an unlawful and dangerous act, that no specific intent is required for the crime of manslaughter: consequently, self-induced intoxication is no defence to a charge of manslaughter.

An interesting case on intoxication by drugs is *R. v Hardie* (1984). In this case, the accused was upset after the breakdown of his relationship with his girlfriend and took several valium pills to calm his nerves. In fact, he ended up starting a fire in her flat. Could he rely on the defence of intoxication? It was held that he could, as though he was involuntarily intoxicated. He did not know, nor should he have known, that valium in that quantity could produce aggressive effects. He reasonably believed that it would merely have a sedative effect. Had he known that it might produce aggression, then he would not have been able to rely on his self-induced intoxication, but since he did not, he was not morally blameworthy in simply taking the drug, and the issue of intoxication should have been left to the jury, who should have been directed to consider whether he was being reckless in taking the drug.

12.5.5 Involuntary intoxication

The parameters of the intoxication defence are set, consciously or otherwise, by judicial disapproval of those who voluntarily drink to excess or indulge in drugs. This disapproval obviously has no place in situations where a person is involuntarily intoxicated, and intoxication is, therefore, available as a defence in those situations, even to crimes of basic intent. This has been accepted since the case of *Pearson* in which Parke B. stated that "if a party be made drunk by the stratagem or fraud of another, he is not responsible" (at p.145). However, involuntary intoxication is given quite a narrow ambit. Where a person knows he is drinking alcohol, but is not aware of how strong it is, his intoxication is not involuntary: *R. v Allen* (1988).

In addition, the defence only applies where the involuntary intoxication is such as to negative intent. It does not apply where the accused, though intoxicated through no fault of his own, still has the capability to form an intention, although his inhibitions might be lowered. This can be seen in *R. v Kingston* (1994), in which the accused was a man with paedophiliac tendencies. Another man, in order to blackmail the accused, lured a boy to his flat and drugged him. He then (the defendant alleged) laced the defendant's drink. The defendant, involuntarily intoxicated, but aware of what he was doing, sexually abused the boy. The defence of intoxication was rejected, even on the assumption that without the spiked drink the accused would not have given way to his paedophiliac tendencies. The jury, the House of Lords held, had been properly directed that even a drugged intention was still an intention. The fact that the defendant's self-control had been lowered by deception was a factor which went to mitigation of penalty only.

12.5.6 Law Reform Commission

The Law Reform Commission was of the view that self-induced intoxication should never ground a defence to any criminal charge. It recommended that a distinct offence of committing a criminal act while intoxicated should be created. This would have the advantage of marking society's disapproval of intoxication while not artificially distorting the elements of criminal offences in order to ensure intoxication could not excuse behaviour that would otherwise be criminal.

The Commission characterised the basic/specific intent dichotomy as illogical and noted that it had been criticised by academics. The Commission emphasised that involuntary intoxication should always be a defence, and that a person's intoxication should be regarded as involuntary if the person took the intoxicant solely for a medicinal purpose and either was not aware that taking it would or might give rise to aggressive or uncontrollable behaviour or took it on medical advice and in accordance with any directions given by the person providing the advice.

Further reading:

O'Malley, "Intoxication and Criminal Responsibility" (1991) I.C.L.J. 86; McAuley, "The Intoxication Defence in Criminal Law" (1997) 32 Ir. Jur *(n.s.)* 243; Law Reform Commission, *Consultation Paper on Intoxication as a Defence to a Criminal Offence* (1995); Law Reform Commission, *Report on Intoxication* (1995); Dillon, "Intoxicated Automatism is no Defence: Majewski is law in Ireland" (2004) 14 (3) I.C.L.J. 7; Spence, "The intoxication 'defence' in Ireland" (2005) 15 (1) I.C.L.J. 3.

12.6 Mistake

Mistake, like intoxication, is not a general defence. Like intoxication, however, mistake may neutralise an element of the *mens rea* of the offence in question. This is subject to one obvious limitation: if the offence in question is one of strict liability, then any mistake will be of no effect, since there is no *mens rea* requirement to be defeated. An example of mistake as a defence can be seen in *R. v Morgan* (1976), where an honest though unreasonable belief in consent was held to be a defence to a charge of rape. Similarly, the shooting of a person mistaken for a deer will not amount to murder, nor will the taking of an article believed to be the accused's own amount to theft.

A mistake must go to an element relevant to the offence: if A thinks that he is killing B when in fact he is killing C, then the offence of murder is still committed. Mistake of law is not ordinarily a defence: so if I believe it is legal to kill a person who burgles my home, I may nevertheless be guilty of murder. However, mistake of law will be relevant in some cases. In theft, for example, an essential part of the offence is that the defendant should act without claim of right *made in good faith*. If a person holds a mistaken view of the law, leading him to the belief that he has a legitimate claim to a particular piece of property, then he will have a claim of right sufficient to defeat the charge of theft.

At common law, a mistake, in order to constitute a defence, had to be reasonable. In *R. v Tolson* (1889), the defendant believed on reasonable grounds that her husband was dead, having been lost at sea. She remarried, only to be charged with bigamy when her husband reappeared several years later. She was acquitted, but only on the ground that her belief was reasonable. (And, indeed, the minority would have held the offence to be one of strict liability.) However *R. v Morgan* expresses a more modern view, and makes it clear that in some circumstances an unreasonable mistake will amount to a defence. The Court of Appeal in *R. v Kimber* (1983) emphasised that *Morgan* was not limited to the case of rape, and a genuine though mistaken belief will generally excuse liability. The House of Lords endorsed the *Morgan* principle as a general principle in *B v DPP* (2000). Similarly, *People (DPP) v Murray* (1977) makes it clear that assessment of criminal responsibility in this jurisdiction is normally to be conducted on subjective standards. It follows that the defence of mistake is to be judged on subjective grounds.

There are, however, exceptions to this. If the *mens rea* of a crime is negligence, then clearly a negligent mistake will afford no defence. So, in the case of *R. v Foxford* (1974), the accused was a soldier on patrol in Northern Ireland who shot and killed a 12-year-old boy when firing at a gunman. His defence was that he had mistook the boy for the gunman, but it was held that since this mistake was in itself grossly negligent it could not afford a defence to a charge of manslaughter.

Whether a mistake was reasonable may be taken into account by a jury in deciding whether it was in fact made. This is set out by statute in the particular case of rape, in s.2(2) of the Criminal Law (Rape) Act 1981:

> "It is hereby declared that if at a trial for a rape offence the jury has to consider whether a man believed that a woman was consenting to sexual intercourse, the presence or absence of reasonable grounds for such a belief is a matter to which the jury is to have regard, in conjunction with any other relevant matters, in considering whether he so believed.".

However, this section merely restates the existing law, by which the reasonableness of a belief may be taken into account in deciding whether it was honestly held.

12.7 Consent

When will consent be a defence? This varies, as we have seen, from offence to offence, and from victim to victim. For example, consent is no defence to a charge of murder, while children under 15 and the mentally impaired are incapable of consenting to acts which would constitute sexual assaults, and a girl under 17 cannot consent to sexual intercourse. Equally, it appears from *R. v Brown* (1993) that consent will not be a defence to a charge of causing serious harm contrary to s.4 of the Non-Fatal Offences Against the Person Act 1997.

12.8 Infancy

> "Criminal law is essentially an adult business. Prisons are designed to punish and rehabilitate mature offenders. Children have no place within a system which may corrupt

them further or which may break an undeveloped spirit."
(Charleton, *Criminal Law - Cases and Materials*
(Butterworths, 1992), p.271.)

The criminal liability of children is governed at common law by the
doctrine of *doli incapax*. This has two parts. First, a child under the
age of seven years is conclusively presumed to be incapable of
committing a crime. While this is phrased in the form of a presumption,
it is important to note that it has the effect of a substantive rule of
law: a crime cannot be committed by a child under seven years.
Second, a child aged between seven and 14 years is presumed to be
incapable of committing a crime, but this presumption can be rebutted
if it can be shown that the child realised that what he was doing was
wrong, or, as some older cases put it, that the child had a "mischievous
discretion".

This is quite a high standard, and it is not enough to show that
the child knew that his conduct was merely naughty or mischievous.
The test was set out in the English decision of *R. v Gorrie* (1919)
and approved in *KM v DPP* (1994) where Morris J. accepted that it
must be shown that the child knew what he was doing was gravely
or seriously wrong. In that case, a child was charged with sexual
assaults on other children when he was aged 13. It was accepted
that his threats to kill the children if they told anyone what he had
done could establish that he knew his conduct was seriously wrong.

12.8.1 Infancy: the special case of rape

At common law, a conclusive presumption existed that a boy under
the age of 14 years could not commit rape. This presumption was
limited to cases of rape (or other offences involving intercourse)
and did not extend to any other forms of sexual offence. The
presumption was therefore an anomaly, and a boy under 14 could be
charged with indecent assault on facts which would otherwise
amount to rape. The presumption was removed by s.6 of the Criminal
Law (Rape) (Amendment) Act 1990, and a boy under the age of 14
can now be charged with rape, subject to the normal doctrine of
doli incapax.

12.8.2 Procedural matters

Where a person under the age of 21 is found guilty of a crime,
special rules apply to the institution to which that person may be

sent. These rules apply having regard to the age of the offender at the date of trial, not at the date on which the offence was committed.

A child offender under the age of 12 must be sent to industrial school if a custodial sentence is to be imposed. Offenders under the age of 15 may be sent to industrial school; and this upper age limit may be extended to the age of 17. A reformatory school is also available to offenders between the ages of 12 and 17. An offender may be detained here until the age of 19 or (in certain limited circumstances) 21.

Formally known as a borstal, St Patrick's Institution is available for offenders between the ages of 17 and 21. Persons over 17 years of age may be sent to prison. Below that age, persons may only be sent to prison where they are certified as being of such an unruly and depraved character that they cannot be detained elsewhere.

People (DPP) v W (1998) illustrated problems with this approach. The accused, a 16-year-old girl who pleaded guilty to murder before the Central Criminal Court, was sentenced to 7 years imprisonment. On appeal, the Court of Criminal Appeal found that no suitable detention facilities were available for the appellant (who was still aged 16); the only option available would be to detain her in the women's prison in Mountjoy (St Patrick's Institution only catering for males), which was clearly not a suitable environment. The court directed the remainder of her sentence be suspended.

The Children Act 2001 reforms the area of custodial sentences for young people but the relevant provisions have not yet been brought into force. The Act introduces a wider range of non-custodial options for young people. The custodial options will be detention in a children detention school (for children less than 16 years) or in a children detention centre (catering for children between 16 and 18 years). Imprisonment will not be available unless the young person has reached 18 years of age.

12.8.3 Reform

Problems with the criminal justice system as it relates to juveniles are readily apparent. At a basic level, the age at which a child faces criminal responsibility is strikingly low: compare Canada, another common law jurisdiction which has chosen the age of 12, or England, which applies an age of 10. It is interesting to note that the common law originally set the age of criminal responsibility at 12, during a time when childhood was not as protracted as it is today.

An interesting comparison can be made with the English position, which has been modified in stages by legislation. First, the age at which criminal responsibility begins was raised to 10: Children and Young Persons Act 1933, amended by the Children and Young Persons Act 1963. More recently, the Crime and Disorder Act 1998 abolishes the presumption of *doli incapax*. As a result, English law now takes the straightforward approach that children under the age of 10 are not criminally responsible, while those over that age are criminally responsible in the ordinary way.

The low age of responsibility in Irish law is to some extent mitigated by the presumption of *doli incapax*. However, this presumption presents difficulties of its own. The most significant of these is the paradox noted by Glanville Williams (*Criminal Law: The General Part* (1961), p.818) that the child whose moral standards are warped, so that he believes crimes to be right, is to be found innocent; as a result, the child most in need of help falls by definition outside the scope of the criminal law. The presumption also causes difficulty by reason of being a blunt instrument: it presents criminal responsibility in black and white terms, failing to recognise that in the case of a child there are varying degrees of awareness, maturity and thus responsibility.

The Irish position will be changed when s.52 of the Children Act 2001 is in force. This section provides that it shall be conclusively presumed that no child under the age of 12 is capable of committing an offence. There is a rebuttable presumption that a child who is not less than 12, but under 14, is incapable of committing an offence because the child did not have the capacity to know that the act or omission concerned was wrong. The result of s.52 is that the presumption of *doli incapax* for children under 14 has been put on a statutory footing.

Further reading:

O'Malley, *Sexual Offences - Law, Policy and Punishment* (Round Hall Sweet & Maxwell, (1996), pp.51–52; Charleton, *Criminal Law - Cases and Materials* (Butterworths, 1992), pp.271–275; Davis, "A Brief Outline of the Juvenile Justice System in Ireland" (July 1998) Bar Review, p.427; Hanly, "The Defence of Infancy", (1996) 6 I.C.L.J. 72; Hanly, "Child Offenders: The Changing Response of Irish Law" (1997) 19 D.U.L.J. 113.

12.9 Entrapment

Suppose that A approaches B with the suggestion that they commit a crime together. After some time, A persuades B of the merits of the plan. They carry out the crime, only to find the police waiting as they make their exit. It emerges that A is an undercover policeman who was acting with the intention of luring B into committing a crime. Has B committed a crime and, if so, does B have any defence?

Clearly, B has voluntarily carried out a particular act with the necessary intention. The fact that this intention was procured by another does not make a difference, so long as the intention was formed freely. (The situation would, of course, be different if there was any question of duress.)

The question therefore remains whether B has a defence in respect of the crime which otherwise he has committed.

12.9.1 Traditional approach to entrapment

The traditional answer was that entrapment was no defence, and this was the approach taken by the House of Lords in *R. v Sang* (1980). The defendant was charged with conspiracy to utter counterfeit US bank notes. He claimed that he had been induced to commit the offence by an informer acting on the instructions of the police, and that he would not have committed any crime but for the inducement. The House of Lords accepted earlier Court of Appeal authority, and held that:

> "it is now well settled that the defence called entrapment does not exist in English law... A man who intends to commit a crime and actually commits it is guilty of the offence whether or not he has been persuaded or induced to commit it, no matter by whom." (at p.443, *per* Lord Salmon.)

Of course, even under this view, an entrapment-type situation may be relevant as a mitigating factor when sentence is being passed, a point which was explicitly made in *R. v Sang*.

12.9.2 Recent English approach

The House of Lords substantially altered its attitude towards entrapment in *R. v Looseley; Attorney General's Reference (No. 3 of 2000)* (2002). It held that it was not acceptable that the State, through its agents, should lure its citizens into committing acts forbidden by law and then seek to prosecute them for doing so. Such conduct would be an abuse of process of the courts, while the conduct of the law enforcement agency may be so improper as to bring the administration of justice into disrepute. While entrapment is not a substantive defence, the House of Lords noted that the position had changed somewhat since the *Sang* decision by reason of the enactment of the Police and Criminal Evidence Act 1984. Section 78 of that Act gives a power to exclude prosecution evidence if, considering all the evidence, it is judged that the admission of the evidence would have such an adverse effect on the fairness of the proceedings that the court ought not to admit it. Lord Nicholls set out a useful test in an effort to delineate the boundaries of pro-active policing:

> " ... a useful guide is to consider whether the police did no more than present the defendant with an unexceptional opportunity to commit a crime. I emphasise the word unexceptional. The yardstick for the purpose of this test is, in general, whether the police conduct preceding the commission of the offence was no more than might have been expected from others in the circumstances."

12.9.3 United States' approach

Other jurisdictions have not taken the same view as is taken in England: for example, in the United States the courts have held that entrapment is a substantive defence which is available to an accused person who can show that he was not predisposed to commit a crime, but only did so as a result of the persuasion of agents of the State. This position was adopted in *Sherman v United States* (1958). In that case, the defendant was a drug addict who attended a drug treatment clinic. Another patient at that clinic was an undercover police agent. The agent repeatedly told the defendant that he needed a fix, and contrived opportunities to bump into the defendant and ask the defendant to supply him with drugs. The defendant refused on several occasions, but eventually agreed to buy heroin for the agent. When he did so, he was arrested.

On those facts, the Supreme Court held that a substantive defence of entrapment was open to the defendant. The court indicated that stealth and strategy were acceptable parts of police procedure, but only when they were directed towards the prevention and detection of crime: they ceased to be acceptable when they were directed towards the manufacture of crime. Accordingly, the Supreme Court held that the defence was available to a person who had no predisposition to commit the crime alleged, but did so only as a result of police persuasion.

12.9.4 Irish approach

What is the position in Ireland? It remains unclear how the Irish courts would adjudicate on a case where a substantive defence of entrapment was advanced. The case of *Dental Board v O'Callaghan* (1969) is still the leading Irish case on entrapment. The Dental Board, a regulatory body, suspected the defendant of practising as a dentist despite being unqualified to do so. To obtain evidence, it sent an inspector to have the defendant carry out work which was reserved for dentists, which he did. An issue arose as to whether, in the circumstances, the evidence obtained by an *agent provocateur* was admissible. The High Court (Butler J.) held that it was, and approved of English authority to the effect that the methods used by the police in obtaining evidence should not be grounds on which a conviction could be quashed, although the element of entrapment could be taken into account in determining sentence.

On the other hand, the more recent case of *Quinlivan v Conroy* (1998) seems to suggest the contrary. In that case, the extradition of the applicant was sought, on foot of a number of charges, including charges arising out of an escape from prison. The applicant alleged that this escape was facilitated by a prison guard who was acting as an *agent provocateur* in order to gather evidence on the applicant and his associates. The applicant made the case that, in those circumstances, extradition should not be granted since, under Irish law, no offence would have been committed. (That is, that in such circumstances a defence of entrapment would be available in Irish law.) Although the Supreme Court did not explicitly rule on this point, it did seem to have some sympathy for the argument that a state which had facilitated the commission of a crime should be debarred from seeking the extradition of a person in relation to that crime (*per* O'Flaherty J., at p.8 of transcript). Such an argument would, of course, tend to favour the concept of entrapment as a substantive defence.

We have, therefore, seen several possible ways of dealing with the entrapment problem. One, exemplified by the US approach, is to allow entrapment as a substantive defence to a criminal charge. Another is to refuse to allow entrapment as a substantive defence, but to take it into account as a factor mitigating any punishment which may be imposed. A further possibility is that the courts could take the view that evidence obtained by way of entrapment was unfairly obtained, and refuse to admit that evidence; or the courts could rule that prosecutions founded on entrapment-type situations amount to an abuse of the process of the courts (which latter approach would be similar to that adopted by the Supreme Court in *State (Trimbole) v Governor of Mountjoy Prison* (1985), where the court held that the wrongful arrest of a person amounted to a deliberate and conscious breach of his constitutional rights so as to make any subsequent proceedings consequent on that arrest an abuse of the process of the court). The Canadian position is that proceedings in entrapment-type situations can be stayed as being an abuse of process. Whether proceedings will be stayed depends primarily on the outrageousness of police conduct. The prior disposition of the accused towards committing the crime may also be taken into account.

A case on entrapment was stated to the High Court at the beginning of 2005. It concerned the use of minors by Health Boards to prosecute shop owners for selling cigarettes to underage customers. The case has not yet been decided, and it is to be hoped that the High Court may take the opportunity to clarify the Irish approach to entrapment.

12.9.5 Influence of the E.C.H.R.

To some extent, Irish law has been overtaken by developments at European level. A decision of the European Court of Human Rights has determined that the European Convention on Human Rights requires member states to control the use of *agents provocateurs* and in particular requires member states to limit the use of evidence obtained in such circumstances.

This decision is *Texeira de Castro v Portugal* (1997). In that case, the applicant had been convicted before the national courts of drug trafficking. His name had been supplied to undercover officers by another individual, and the officers, accompanied by that individual, went to his house and indicated that they wished to buy a considerable amount of heroin. The applicant agreed to sell it to them, and shortly afterwards procured it and brought it to the officers. At that point he was arrested. Before the national courts his argument relating to the use of entrapment was rejected: in particular, the national courts found that the use of *agents provocateurs* was not forbidden under domestic law so long as the use was justified by the seriousness of the offence being investigated.

Before the court, the applicant submitted that his rights under Art.6.1 of the Convention had been infringed. That section provides, so far as relevant, that "In the determination of ... any criminal charge against him, everyone is entitled to a fair ... hearing". He submitted that this provision had been infringed in circumstances where, he alleged, he had no previous convictions and would not have committed the offence but for the use of the *agents provocateurs*. In addition, he complained that the activities of the police had been unsupervised by the courts. The respondent made the case that the special circumstances of drug sales, and in particular the secrecy and victimless nature of the crime, made it necessary to use investigative techniques of this kind, which were customary in a number of jurisdictions.

The court took the view that on the facts of this particular case the rights of the applicant under Art.6.1 had been infringed, in that the activities of the undercover agents had prejudiced the fairness of the applicant's trial. The activities of the agents had been unsupervised by the courts: no preliminary investigation had been opened. The authorities had no reason to suspect the applicant, who had no criminal record and who was at the outset unknown to the police officers. The drugs which the applicant ultimately supplied were not held by him; instead he obtained them from a third party. The inference which the court drew from these facts was that the applicant was not predisposed to commit such an offence; rather, the police officers, instead of investigating in a passive manner, themselves incited the commission of the crime alleged. Accordingly, the court held that:

> "In the light of all these considerations, the Court concludes that the two police officers' actions went beyond those of undercover agents because they instigated the offence and there is nothing to suggest that without their intervention it would have been committed. That intervention and its use

in the impugned criminal proceedings meant that, right from
the outset, the applicant was definitively deprived of a fair
trial. Consequently, there has been a violation of Article
6.1." (para.39.)

The implications of this decision for Irish practice are not yet clear.
It will be necessary for the courts to shape domestic law so as to
comply with the requirements of *Texeira de Castro v Portugal*, or
for legislation to be introduced to the same effect. Perhaps it is most
likely that the courts will develop the concept of abuse of process,
outlined in *State (Trimbole) v Governor of Mountjoy Prison*, to
include situations in which the E.C.H.R. would require that a
prosecution not be instituted. However, should the law remain as it
appears to be from *Dental Board v O'Callaghan*, then it is clear
that an accused person convicted in such circumstances would have
a remedy under the European Convention of Human Rights.

Further Reading:

Spencer & Veale-Martin, "Fashioning an Irish entrapment doctrine
based on international experience" (2005) 15(2) I.C.L.J. 2.

12.10 Automatism

The defence of automatism is available in circumstances where an
accused was, at the material time, physically unable to control his
actions. As defined by Ritchie J. for the Supreme Court of Canada:

"Automatism is a term used to describe unconscious,
involuntary behaviour, the state of a person who, though
capable of action, is not conscious of what he is doing. It
means an unconscious, involuntary act, where the mind does
not go with what is being done." (*R v Rabey* (1980) 15
C.R. (3d) 225 at p.232.)

It is closely intertwined with the defence of insanity, but differs from
that defence in two important ways. First, once the foundations for
the defence have been laid, it is for the prosecution to disprove the
defence, not for the accused to prove it. Second, an acquittal on the
ground of automatism is a complete acquittal, unlike an acquittal on
the ground of insanity, after which the accused will be held in the
Central Mental Hospital until he can demonstrate that he has
recovered.

The defence is available only where the accused had no control over his body, as in the case of the sleepwalker, or the driver attacked by a swarm of bees who veers off the road and kills a pedestrian. It is not available in circumstances where the accused had control over his body, but chose to act in a particular way. If a driver sees a swarm of bees ahead, chooses to swerve to avoid them, and kills a pedestrian, his defence (if any) would be necessity. Similarly, the defence is not available where the accused had control over his body, but that control was lessened due to anger, intoxication, disease of the mind, and so forth. An important point is that where conduct is involuntary, but results from the self-induced intoxication of the accused, then the accused must rely on the defence of intoxication rather than the defence of automatism: *R. v Lipman* (1970).

In addition, it seems that the defence is available only where the automatism is a transient state caused by *some external factor*, and is not available where the automatism is caused by a factor internal to the accused. It appears that in cases of an internal factor, the courts take the view that the possibility of recurrence of violence justifies the accused being detained rather than completely acquitted. In *Bratty v Attorney General for Northern Ireland* (1963), Lord Denning remarked that any mental disorder which has manifested itself in violence and is prone to recur is a disease of the mind.

In *Bratty,* the accused strangled an 18-year-old girl. He stated that at the time he had "a terrible feeling" and that "a sort of blackness" came over him; but he was able to give some account of what had happened. The defences of automatism due to psychomotor epilepsy and insanity were run at trial, and the trial judge left the defence of insanity to the jury, but refused to so leave the defence of automatism. On appeal, the House of Lords held that the trial judge had been correct. The court drew a distinction between insane and non-insane automatism, and held that where the cause alleged for the unconscious act was a disease of the mind (such as psychomotor epilepsy) then the only verdict which could be returned by the jury was one of insane automatism: in other words, the automatism would be characterised as a species of insanity and dealt with by way of the defence of insanity and not the defence of automatism. It was also held that the onus of proving voluntariness in cases of automatism is on the prosecution, once the foundations are laid by the defendant, and that the prosecution must prove voluntariness beyond a reasonable doubt.

This can also be seen in *R. v Rabey* (1980). In that case, the defendant was a student who was smitten with another student. The day before the attack, he found a letter she had written complaining about him and expressing an interest in someone else. On the day of the attack, he took a rock from the geology laboratory, met the victim (by chance, it seemed) struck her with the rock and attempted to choke her. The defence of automatism was successfully pleaded at trial, on the basis that the accused was in a complete dissociative state. However, on appeal it was held that this defence could not be sustained: any malfunctioning of the mind or mental disorder which has its source primarily in some matter internal to the defendant is a disease of the mind within the meaning of the defence of insanity, and cannot form the basis of the defence of automatism.

This principle has been applied in the case of sleepwalking. In *R. v Burgess* (1991), the defendant was watching videos with a neighbour. When she fell asleep, he hit her over the head with a bottle and the video recorder, and then grabbed her by the throat. When she screamed, he "came round", appeared to be concerned, and called an ambulance for her. He was charged with wounding with intent, to which his defence was that he was sleepwalking at the time. At trial, this was found to amount to a defence of insanity, and the defendant was ordered to be detained in a secure hospital. On appeal, the defendant contended that the defence was in fact one of automatism. The Court of Appeal held that the automatism could not be said to be due to an external factor such as a blow on the head: it was caused by an internal factor. The automatism was also liable to recur, though recurrence in the form of serious violence was unlikely. It followed as a matter of law that, although the automatism was far removed from insanity in a colloquial or psychiatric sense, it amounted to a defence of insanity in legal terms:

> "[T]his was an abnormality or disorder, albeit transitory, due to an internal factor, whether functional or organic, which had manifested itself in violence. It was a disorder or abnormality which might recur, though the possibility of it recurring in the form of serious violence was unlikely. Therefore, since this was a legal problem to be decided on legal principles, it seems to us on those principles the answer was as the judge found it to be." (at p.776.).

This apparently logical distinction, between internal and external factors, breaks down in the case of defendants who suffer from diabetes and who commit crimes while suffering either from high or low blood sugar levels (hyperglycaemia and hypoglycaemia respectively). Are states of automatism resulting from such conditions to be treated as resulting from internal factors (the diabetes) or external factors (failure to take insulin, etc.)? In *R. v Quick* (1973), the defendant's automatism resulting from hypoglycaemia was held to result from an external factor (self-administered insulin injections). In *R. v Hennessy* (1989), however, the defendant's automatism resulting from hyperglycaemia due to his failure to take insulin was held to result from an internal factor (the underlying disease of diabetes). *R. v Quick* (1973) was distinguished, on the ground that the hypoglycaemia resulted from injections of insulin, not from the underlying diabetes. This is, however, a distinction without a difference.

R. v Hennessy raised the issue of whether automatism resulting from stress and similar situations was to be treated as resulting from internal or external factors. The defendant was arrested in the process of driving a stolen car. One aspect of his defence has already been dealt with: that he was suffering from hyperglycaemia. Another aspect of the defence was that automatism could also have been triggered by his depression and by his marital and employment problems. This aspect of the defence was also rejected by the Court of Appeal. If automatism had been triggered by these factors, then it would still have been caused by internal factors so as to make the defence of insanity applicable:

> "In our judgment, stress, anxiety and depression can no doubt be the result of the operation of external factors, but they are not, it seems to us, in themselves separately or together external factors of the kind capable in law of causing or contributing to a state of automatism. They constitute a state of mind which is prone to recur. They lack the feature of novelty or accident..." (Lord Lane C.J., at p.14.).

It is not necessarily fatal to the defence that the automatism was self-induced. If, for example, a diabetic fails to eat following an insulin injection and, as a result, commits a crime while in a hypoglycaemic state, then the defence of automatism can be pleaded unless it can be proved that in failing to eat he acted sufficiently recklessly. In *R.*

v Bailey (1983), the accused suffered from diabetes. His girlfriend left him, and he subsequently attacked the man for whom she had left him, having shortly before drank a sugar and water solution. His defence was that the resulting hypoglycaemia, owing to his failure to take food and having drunk the solution, had produced a state of automatism. The trial judge directed the jury not to consider this defence since the state was self-induced. On appeal, this direction was held to be incorrect: self-induced automatism (other than by intoxication: *R. v Lipman* (1970)) could provide a defence, unless the conduct of the defendant in inducing automatism had been sufficiently reckless to establish the *mens rea* for the offence.

Finally, in respect of automatism, the case of *O'Brien v Parker* (1997) should be noted. This was a decision of the High Court in a civil matter, where the plaintiff sued in respect of personal injuries suffered in a road traffic accident. The defendant claimed that at the time of the accident he was suffering an epileptic fit by reason of temporal lobe epilepsy, so that he could not have been said to be negligent. The defendant had no history of epilepsy, but claimed that he had, immediately before the accident, experienced heightened sensitivity to light and smells and an "altered state of consciousness", and that the next thing he remembered was the accident itself.

In the High Court, Lavan J. (at p.176) held that automatism could amount to a defence in a civil context to a claim based on negligence. However, for that to be the case, it would have to be shown that there was "a total destruction of voluntary control on the defendant's part. Impaired, reduced, or partial control is not sufficient to maintain the defence." In this case, therefore, the defendant had not made out the defence, since he had testified that he was capable of making the decision to continue driving, notwithstanding that his ability to make such a decision was impaired.

Similar criteria apply in a criminal context: the loss of control must be total for a defence of automatism to be available.

12.11 Insanity

12.11.1 Introduction and procedural aspects

The defence of insanity is distinct from the defence of automatism. It does not apply where the defendant's body is acting without conscious control, but instead applies where the defendant is conscious of his actions but his mental state is in some way impaired The burden of proving insanity lies on the accused, contrary to the normal rule that the prosecution bear the responsibility of disproving any defence raised: *People (DPP) v O'Mahony* (1985), at p.522 *per* Finlay C.J.:

> "If it were established, as a matter of probability, that due to an abnormality of mind consisting of a psychiatric condition the appellant had been unable to control himself and to desist from carrying out the acts of violence leading to the death of the deceased, he would have been entitled to a finding of not guilty by reason of insanity.".

The accused, therefore, must prove his insanity, but only on the balance of probabilities, not beyond a reasonable doubt. It is, however, also open to the prosecution to prove insanity in an appropriate case: *Bratty v Attorney General for Northern Ireland* (1963).

The effect of a finding of insanity is that the accused is innocent of the crime charged, but is to be held in the Central Mental Hospital until recovered: Criminal Lunatics Act 1800; Lunacy (Ireland) Act 1821 and the Trial of Lunatics Act 1883. This is so even where the disorder which constitutes insanity in law is not such a disorder as would make it appropriate for a person to be detained. If Irish law follows English decisions to the effect that diabetic hyperglycaemia is a disease of the mind within the meaning of the defence of insanity, then it is possible that a person who commits a crime while in such a state will be detained in the Central Mental Hospital, notwithstanding the fact that they have been found innocent of the crime charged and notwithstanding the fact that they pose no danger to themselves or anyone else.

The decision as to whether a person found not guilty by reason of insanity has recovered is one for the Executive: *DPP v Gallagher* (1991). That case departed from previous case law which had held that the decision to release such a person was a judicial act forming part of the administration of justice. Instead, the role of the court was said to be to order the detention of a person found not guilty by reason of insanity:

> "until the executive, armed with both the knowledge and the resources to deal with the problem, decides on the future disposition of the person." (*Per* McCarthy J., at p.344.)

However, *DPP v Gallagher* (1991), made it clear that the Executive, in deciding whether a person should continue to be kept in custody, must consider only whether he is suffering from any mental disorder warranting his continued detention in the public and private interests, and must do so in accordance with fair and constitutional procedures. The decision of the executive will be subject to judicial review if necessary.

12.11.2 Fitness to plead

Another procedural aspect related to insanity is that of *fitness to plead*. This is distinct from insanity *per se*, and relates not to whether a defendant understood what he was doing at the time of the crime, but to whether that defendant is capable of understanding the proceedings at his trial. The law takes the view that it is unjust to try a person who is incapable of understanding the trial and therefore incapable of adequately defending himself, and for that reason a person who is unfit to plead will be detained in the same way as a person found not guilty by reason of insanity.

It is important to note that fitness to plead is entirely distinct from insanity at the time of the alleged offence. The criminal who is insane at the time of his crime may have recovered to the point where he is capable of understanding his trial; and the criminal who is entirely sane at the time of his crime may, pending trial, suffer some illness or injury which leaves him incapable of standing trial.

The test of fitness to plead is set out in the case of *R. v Robertson* (1968), and looks to whether the accused is able to: understand the charges against him; understand the nature and effect of a plea of guilty or not guilty; challenge a member of the jury to which he might object; instruct counsel; and understand the evidence which is given. If the accused is unable to do one or more of these things, then he will be found unfit to plead. The decision as to whether a person is fit to plead is made by the jury. Where the prosecution raise the issue, then they must prove unfitness to plead beyond a reasonable doubt; where the defence does so, it must prove unfitness to plead on the balance of probabilities.

12.11.3 Insanity under English law

In England, it has been held that the defence of insanity is exclusively encapsulated in the M'Naghten Rules of 1843. Where a defendant does not bring himself within those rules, a defence of insanity cannot succeed.

The M'Naghten Rules were formulated in 1843 in response to the *M'Naghten* case, in which the defendant shot Edward Drummond, the private secretary to the Prime Minister, Sir Robert Peel, mistaking him for the Prime Minister. His defence was that he believed himself to be persecuted by the Tory party, and that consequently his life was in danger. The verdict reached in his case, not guilty by reason of insanity, produced public disquiet, leading the House of Lords to summon the judges before it to answer a series of questions on the law of insanity.

To fall within the M'Naghten rules, the following elements are necessary.

The accused must establish that he suffered from *a defect of reason from disease of the mind.* Disease of the mind does not mean mental illness or brain damage, but includes, as we saw, conditions resulting from diabetes, epilepsy, and so on. In *R. v Kemp* (1957), therefore, a defendant was found to be suffering from a disease of the mind where he made a senseless attack on his wife with a hammer, which was triggered by arteriosclerosis causing a blood congestion in the brain. He argued that this should be treated as automatism rather than falling within the M'Naghten rules, as the condition had not lead to any degeneration of the brain but merely cut off the blood supply in the same way as concussion might. However, this argument was rejected, notwithstanding that this was a transitory and curable physical interference with the workings of the brain. Similarly, *Ellis v DPP* (1990) involved a defendant who was charged with murder of a man who, he alleged, was blackmailing him. He relied on the defence of automatism, on the basis that he was in an epileptic state at the time of the killing. The trial judge refused to leave the issue of automatism to the jury but did leave the issue of insanity, and the accused was found not guilty by reason of insanity.

There must have been a *causal link* between the defect of reason and the act: If I believe that the Vatican is bugging my phone and I go shoplifting, then there is clearly no such causal link. It is not enough that the defect of reason and the crime should coincide in point of time; there must also be a causal relationship between the two.

Where the defect of reason takes the form of an *insane delusion*, then the delusion, if it relates to existing facts, must be one which would mean that the act committed was not a crime. If I shoot a person, believing him to be a tree, then the act would not be a crime if the delusion were true. But if I shoot a person, believing him to be Bill Clinton, then this act would be a crime even if the delusion were true, and the defence will not apply.

The accused must establish either that he *did not know the nature and quality of his act, or that he did so know but did not know that the act was wrongful.* The nature and quality of the act refers to its physical nature only, not its moral nature (*R. v Codère* (1916)). So, not understanding the nature and quality of an act would encompass situations of shooting a person thinking he was a tree. A defendant knows that an act is wrongful if he knows it is illegal, or, notwithstanding that he does not know it is illegal, he knows it is an act which he ought not to do. It is irrelevant that the defendant thinks that a particular act is morally right if he knows it is legally wrong. So, in *R. v Windle* (1952), the defendant, who was mentally ill, believed he was acting in a moral way by killing his wife by poisoning, supposing that he was putting her out of her unhappiness. He knew what he was doing was legally wrong, but believed, due to mental illness, that it was morally right. However, it was held that the defence of insanity could not, on those facts, be put before the jury: once the defendant knew what he was doing was illegal, then he could not avail of the M'Naghten Rules, and there was no wider defence of insanity open to him.

To summarise: to come within the M'Naghten Rules a defendant must show that at the time the act was committed, he or she was suffering from a defect of reason arising from a disease of the mind such that he or she did not know the nature and quality of his or her actions or, if he or she did know, he or she did not know that they were wrong, *i.e* contrary to the law.

12.11.4 Insanity under Irish Law

The Irish position is entirely different, and it has been held by the Supreme Court, in *Doyle v Wicklow County Council* (1974), that the M'Naghten Rules are not the beginning and end of the insanity defence:

> "In my opinion, the M'Naghten Rules do not provide the sole and exclusive test for determining the sanity or insanity of an accused. The questions put to the judges were limited to the effect of insane delusions and I would agree with the

opinion expressed by the Court of Criminal Appeal in
Attorney General v O'Brien (1936) that the opinions given
by the judges must be read with the same specific limitation."
(*Per* Griffin J.)

The M'Naghten Rules are, therefore, only one component of the
defence of insanity in this jurisdiction. They do, however, form the
primary test.

The defence of insanity in Irish law is tangled in that there is no
one test which is conclusive of whether a defendant pleading insanity
will or will not be held criminally responsible for his actions. It is
important to note how this differs from the English position. Irish
law encompasses a defence of irresistible impulse which is available
to certain defendants who cannot bring themselves within the narrow
M'Naghten Rules. Irresistible impulse is discussed below. It is
important to note that irresistible impulse is not a separate defence
to insanity, but it describes behaviour that is characterised as insanity
under Irish law.

12.11.5 Irresistible Impulse

The M'Naghten rules are quite restrictive. In particular, they do not
allow any scope for the defence of volitional insanity. This is a
particular form of mental defect covering situations where an accused
knows that conduct is wrong (and therefore falls outside the
parameters of the M'Naghten rules) but nevertheless has a
diminished capacity to act or refrain from acting based on that
knowledge. An example of such a situation would be the case where
a person claimed to have had an irresistible impulse to commit a
specific crime. The defence of irresistible impulse was never accepted
under the M'Naghten rules; indeed, as one judge stated:

"If you cannot resist an impulse in any other way, we will
hang a rope in front of your eyes, and perhaps that will
help." (*Per* Riddell J., in *R. v Creighton* (1909)).

The defence of irresistible impulse has never been a feature of
English law and has also been rejected in Australia. However, it is
now clear that Irish law recognises a defence of volitional insanity.
This was foreshadowed by *AG v O'Brien* (1936). In that case, the
defendant sought to raise the defence of irresistible impulse, but the
trial judge refused to leave the defence to the jury on the ground that

it was unknown to the law. On appeal, the Court of Criminal Appeal held that the facts of the case were not sufficient to justify leaving the defence to the jury. The defendant had never suggested that he was labouring under or driven by an impulse of any kind, and such a contention would have been quite inconsistent with his denial of all knowledge of the events in which he acted, as he had alleged, an unconscious part. The court went on, however, to hold that the M'Naghten rules were not intended to be exclusive, and left open for later the decision whether Irish law recognised the defence of irresistible impulse.

Later cases saw trial judges adopt a wider test of insanity. Particularly significant was the case of *People (AG) v Hayes* (1967), in which the defendant was charged with murdering his wife. He had, over a long period, built up an irrational sense of grievance against his wife, and sought redress for imaginary complaints by killing his wife, as he claimed, to clear the name of their children. Although this defence would probably not have fallen within the scope of the M'Naghten rules, Henchy J. directed the jury in terms which were wider than the M'Naghten rules, saying that "if the jury was satisfied that at the time of the attack the accused man's mind was so affected by illness that he was unable to restrain himself, a verdict of guilty but insane should be returned".

Further, Henchy J. gave a detailed judgment regarding the scope of the defence, stating that:

> "The [M'Naghten] rules do not take into account the capacity of a man on the basis of his knowledge to act or to refrain from acting and I believe it to be correct psychiatric science to accept that certain serious mental diseases, such as paranoia or schizophrenia, in certain cases enable a man to understand the morality or immorality of his act or the legality or illegality of it, or the nature and quality of it, but nevertheless prevent him from exercising a free volition as to whether he should or should not do that act."

This approach was then confirmed by the Supreme Court, in *Doyle v Wicklow County Council* (1974). This was a claim for compensation brought by the owner of an abattoir burnt down by an 18-year-old boy. The claim would succeed only if what was done by the boy was a crime, which made it necessary to consider whether the defence of insanity would have been available to the boy. The facts showed that the boy was suffering from some form of mental disorder which led him to believe that setting fire to the abattoir was a justifiable and moral act, based on his love of animals. The boy knew, however, that the act was nevertheless a criminal one. Griffin J. adopted what had been said by Henchy J. in *People (AG) v Hayes* as being a correct statement of the law, and held that the defence of volitional insanity would have been open to the boy.

The decision in *People (DPP) v Courtney* (1994) provides an example of the defence of irresistible impulse (albeit an unsuccessful example). In that case, the accused was charged with murder. He had been a passenger in a car driven by the deceased, who had picked him up while looking for directions. She had, he said, taunted him, at which he "blew a fuse and went mad" He punched her several times, then took the car and drove into the mountains. When she regained consciousness, he hit her with a rock, killing her. He took her clothes off her body, then drove back into the city and abandoned the car.

The defence was that the accused had acted in a panic, without any control of himself, and the accused tendered psychiatric evidence to the effect that he was suffering from post-traumatic stress disorder stemming from his tours of duty as a soldier in Lebanon. Based on this evidence, the trial judge left two questions to the jury: was the accused acting under the influence of an irresistible impulse caused by a defect of reason due to mental illness, which debarred him from refraining from killing the victim; and had it been proved beyond a reasonable doubt that the accused intended to kill or cause serious harm to the victim. The trial judge went on to direct the jury that, depending on their answers to these questions, they could find the accused to be: guilty of murder; not guilty by reason of insanity; or guilty of manslaughter (if it had not been proved beyond a reasonable doubt that the accused intended to kill or cause serious injury). The jury found the accused to be guilty of murder.

On appeal, the Court of Criminal Appeal upheld the conviction of the applicant. It approved the reference by Henchy J. in *Hayes* to irresistible impulse as being a correct statement of the law.

This defence has not been elaborated upon to any great extent, but the *obiter* comments of Finlay C.J. in *People (DPP) v O'Mahony* (1986) are interesting. In that case, the defendant appealed his conviction for murder on the grounds that the defence of diminished responsibility existed at common law and should have been left to the jury. The Supreme Court rejected the argument that diminished responsibility was part of Irish law, but Finlay C.J. noted that:

> "Having regard to the definition of insanity laid down by this Court in *Doyle v Wicklow County Council* (1974) ... it is quite clear that the appellant in *R v Byrne* (1960) ... a sexual psychopath who suffered from violent perverted sexual desires which he found it difficult or impossible to control [but did not suffer any other mental illness] if tried in accordance with the law of this country on the same facts, would have been properly found to be not guilty by reason of insanity." (at pp.248–249.).

It appears from these comments, therefore, that in Irish law a person might be able to rely on insanity even in circumstances where they might have some control over their actions, provided that their control was significantly diminished by mental illness. This may also encompass cases where, for example, the accused's ability to make decisions is significantly impaired, as in the example of a father who believes that he and his family would be better off dead, and therefore kills the other members of his family. In these circumstances, it is not the defendant's control over his actions which is in issue, but rather his ability to make decisions concerning his actions. The underlying logic of *Doyle v Wicklow County Council* (1974) would suggest that this would also amount to the defence of insanity.

12.11.6 Diminished responsibility

The above comments suggest that a defence similar to diminished responsibility might already be available in Irish law. A defence of diminished responsibility was introduced into English law by s.2 of the Homicide Act 1957. The defence is confined to cases of murder and reduces the charge to one of manslaughter. For the defence of diminished responsibility to be made out, the defendant must have been labouring under mental impairment such that his ability to control his actions and make decisions is defective. This does not necessarily mean that he acted with an irresistible impulse. The impulse may well have been easily resisted but the defendant lacked the insight into his actions to do so.

12.11.7 Reform of insanity

Insanity is an all or nothing defence: there is, in this jurisdiction, no defence of diminished responsibility such as there is in England for a defendant who suffered from such "an abnormality of mind ... as substantially impaired his mental responsibility for his acts or omissions". This point has been confirmed by the Court of Criminal Appeal in *People (DPP) v Reddan* (1995) and by the Supreme Court in *People (DPP) v O'Mahony* (1996). This English defence is confined to murder, in much the same way as the defences of provocation and excessive self-defence.

Because of the lack of an intermediate verdict, juries are faced with a stark choice between guilty and not guilty by reason of insanity; and juries have proved reluctant to bring in the latter verdict ever since the defendant Gallagher successfully pleaded insanity at trial and shortly afterwards mounted a legal campaign to secure his release on the ground that he was now sane.

The Criminal Law (Insanity) Bill 2002, which has not yet been enacted, radically reforms and simplifies the Irish law of insanity.

Section 4 proposes that a special verdict of not guilty by reason of insanity should be returned by a jury where the jury finds that the accused person committed the act alleged and, having heard evidence relating to the mental condition of the accused given by a consultant psychiatrist, finds that:

> "(a) the accused person was suffering at the time from a mental disorder, and (b) the mental disorder was such that the accused person ought not to be held responsible for the act alleged by reason of the fact that he or she – (i) did not know the nature and quality of the act, or (ii) did not know that what he or she was doing was wrong, or (iii) was unable to refrain from committing the act."

This section would put irresistible impulse on a statutory footing.

The term "mental disorder" is defined as mental illness, severe dementia or significant intellectual disability where: (a) because of the illness, disability or dementia, there is a serious likelihood of the person concerned causing immediate and serious harm to himself or herself or to other persons; or (b) (i) because of the severity of the illness, disability or dementia, the judgment of the person concerned is so impaired that failure to admit the person to an approved centre would be likely to lead to a serious deterioration in his or her condition or would prevent the administration of appropriate treatment that could be given only by such admission, and (ii) the reception, detention and treatment of the person concerned in an approved centre would be likely to benefit or alleviate the condition of that person to a material extent. This will guard against a situation developing, like under English law, where behaviour resulting from epilepsy or diabetes may sometimes come within the category of insanity.

"Mental illness" means a state of mind of a person which affects the person's thinking, perceiving, emotion or judgment and which seriously impairs the mental function of the person to the extent that he or she requires care or medical treatment in his or her own interest or in the interest of other persons.

"Severe dementia" means deterioration of the brain of a person which significantly impairs the intellectual function of the person, thereby affecting thought, comprehension and memory and which includes severe psychiatric or behavioural symptoms such as physical aggression.

"Significant intellectual disability" is defined as a state of mind or arrested or incomplete development of mind of a person which includes significant impairment of intelligence and social functioning and abnormally aggressive or seriously irresponsible conduct on the part of the person.

Section 5 of the Bill introduces the concept of Diminished Responsibility into Irish law for the first time. It provides that

> "Where a person is tried for murder and the jury or, as the case may be, the Special Criminal Court finds that the person – (a) committed the act alleged, (b) was at the time suffering from a mental disorder, and (c) the mental disorder was not such as to justify finding him or her not guilty by reason of insanity, but was such as to diminish substantially his or her responsibility for the act, the jury or court, as the case may be, shall find the person not guilty of that offence but guilty of manslaughter on the ground of diminished responsibility."

Further Reading:

McAuley, *Insanity, Psychiatry and Criminal Responsibility* (Dublin, Round Hall Press, 1993); Boland, "Diminished Responsibility as a Defence in Irish Law" (1995) 5 I.C.L.J. 173 and (1996) 6 I.C.L.J. 19; Mills, Simon "Criminal Law (Insanity) Bill 2002: Putting the Sanity back into Insanity?" (2003) 8(3) Bar Review 101.

12.12 Unconstitutionality

Article 38.1 of the Constitution states that no person shall be tried on any criminal charge save in due course of law. While standards of procedural fairness must be adhered to by the police and prosecution, an accused can also rely on constitutional provisions in a substantive manner to render a criminal provision unconstitutional. This happens only rarely, however, as there is a presumption that legislation is constitutional, and the accused must have exhausted all other arguments before relying on unconstitutionality.

The constitutional right to privacy has been relied on several times to render criminally proscribed conduct legal. For example, it was successful in *McGee v AG* (1974), where it was held that s.17 of the Criminal Law (Amendment) Act 1935 (prohibiting distribution of contraceptives) violated the guarantee of marital privacy protected by Art.40.3.1. More recently, the constitutional rights to life and privacy were relied on in *Re a Ward of Court* (1996) to permit medical treatment to be withdrawn from a woman who had been in a persistent vegeatative state for over 20 years, conduct which mights otherwise have been criminal.

It is clear that legislation creating an offence may be struck down where it creates an offence which is insufficiently clear and precise. The definition of the offence must be certain to enable an accused to prepare a defence; vagueness may prove to be a fatal constitutional defect. So, for example, in *King v AG* (1981), various offences of loitering under the Vagrancy Act 1824 were struck down as being unconstitutionally vague.

13. INCHOATE OFFENCES

Inchoate offences are offences where the harmful objective intended may not be eventually realised. An attempt is made to commit a crime, but it may not be successful. A encourages B to commit a crime but B may not go on to do so. An agreement is made to commit a crime, but it may not eventually be carried out. In each of these situations, although the objective may not be achieved, the action may nevertheless give rise to criminal liability. Although inchoate offences are often described as incomplete offences, it should be noted that they are complete offences in themselves.

13.1 Attempt

Offenders should not escape punishment simply because they have not been successful in their endeavours to commit a crime. The incompetent criminal cannot be granted immunity because of his bungling. The law of attempt recognises this, and deems to be criminal those acts which are intimately connected with an offence which is desired to be committed, although the attempt to commit the completed offence failed. Consequently, where there is an attempt to commit an indictable offence, the attempter may be fined and/or imprisoned as if he had successfully committed the offence. In practice, of course, the penalty for an attempt will be significantly less than the penalty for the completed offence, reflecting the fact that no harm actually resulted.

13.1.1 Mens rea

The prosecution must prove intention on the part of the defendant for an attempt, even if recklessness is sufficient for the completed offence. Charleton has put forward a justification of this "on the basis that the requirement for a more blameworthy state of mind than the completed offence is balanced by the fact that the accused need not have done so much, or indeed any, harm in order to be convicted" (Charleton, *Criminal Law*, p.263.). In *R. v Mohan* (1975), the Court of Appeal explained the logic of such a rule. This case concerned a charge of attempting by wanton driving to cause bodily harm to a police constable. The trial judge directed that recklessness as to whether bodily harm was caused would suffice but this was rejected on appeal. While recognising that an attempt to commit a crime may well be a grave offence which is as morally culpable as the completed offence, James L.J. stated that it is preparatory to the commission of the crime and therefore is a step removed from the attempted offence. He held that it would be wrong to strain to bring conduct which was outside the well-established boundaries of the offence within the offence of attempt.

In the case of offences requiring a specific result, it is necessary to show an intention to bring about that specific result. This can be seen by considering the case of murder. The *mens rea* for murder is an intention to kill or cause serious injury; but if A attempts to cause serious injury to B, A is not guilty of attempted murder. Instead, A must have intended to bring about the specific result of death and only an attempt intending to kill will amount to attempted murder: *People (DPP) v Douglas and Hayes* (1985). An attempt intending to cause serious injury amounts only to the *mens rea* of assault with intent to commit serious injury.

However, although an accused must intend the result in an offence requiring a specific result, it should be noted that he need not have intention as to all the circumstances of an offence. In situations of attempted rape, for example, although the accused must have intention to have sexual intercourse he need only be reckless as to whether the victim consents: *R. v Khan* (1990). This position has caused academic controversy. In the United Kingdom, the Law Commission was originally of the view that a distinction between consequences and circumstances would be unworkable and recommended that intention should be required as to all elements of the offence. The Commission subsequently took the opposite position and recommended that recklessness as to a circumstance should suffice where it suffices for the offence itself.

13.1.2 Actus reus

The position at common law was explained in *R. v Eagleton* (1855). In that case, the accused supplied bread to the poor in return for vouchers distributed by the Poor Law Authority. On presenting the vouchers to the authority, he would be paid a certain sum for each loaf. After he had presented the vouchers, and after his account had been credited, but before the money was paid over to him, it was found that the loaves he supplied had been below the agreed weight. If the money had been given to him, he would have been guilty of obtaining by false pretences; was he guilty of any offence on the facts proven?

He was held to be guilty of an attempt to obtain by false pretences. *Per* Parke. B:

> "[T]he mere intention to commit a [crime] is not criminal. Some act is required; and we do not think that all acts towards committing a [crime] are [themselves criminal]. Acts remotely leading towards the commission of the offence are not to be considered as attempts to commit it, but acts immediately connected with it are; and if in this case, after the credit with the relieving officer for the fraudulent overcharge, any further step on the part of the defendant had been necessary to obtain payment, as the making out of a further account, or producing the vouchers to the Board, we should have thought that the obtaining credit in account with the relieving officer would not have been sufficiently proximate to the obtaining the money. But on the statement in this case, no other act on the part of the defendant would have been required. It was the last act depending on himself towards the payment of the money and therefore it ought to be considered as an attempt."

This short passage establishes a number of distinct principles which apply throughout the law of attempt. Intent is not enough. It must be coupled with conduct. Whether an act is criminal depends on whether it is accompanied by the relevant intent and whether it is sufficiently proximate to the completed offence.

The law of attempt in England and Wales is governed by the Criminal Attempts Act 1981. The Act does not state a test of proximity but requires that the act be "more than merely preparatory to the commission of the offence".

(1) Proximity—"last act theory"

There must be proximity between the act committed and the crime which was intended. If A buys a box of matches with the intention to burn down a house, is A at that point guilty of attempted criminal damage or arson? He is clearly not as his conduct is too far removed from the completed crime.

However, determining how proximate conduct must be to a completed crime has proven to be difficult. A number of different theories exist on this topic. One is the "last act theory", which asks: did the defendant commit the final act before the completion of the

offence? This has some merit but produces strange results, so that I
have not attempted arson merely by splashing petrol all over a building
and lighting a match, since I have not yet committed the last act of
throwing the match onto the floor. But it is clear from *R. v Eagleton*
(1855) that if a person does commit the "last act" then this is in itself
sufficient to ground a charge of attempt.

The "last act" theory depends on whether the defendant has
done an act which is more than merely preparatory to the commission
of the offence. This is a matter of fact for the jury to decide. In *R. v
Robinson* (1915), the defendant was charged with attempting to
obtain money by false pretences. He was a jeweller who had staged
a burglary in his shop in order to make an insurance claim. A passing
policeman heard him shouting from inside the shop and found him
bound and gagged beside an empty safe. The ruse was uncovered
before the defendant had a chance to inform his insurers of the
robbery. It was held that the defendant had merely prepared for the
commission of an offence and had not taken a step in its commission
as there had been no communication with the insurance company.

Similarly, in *R. v Ilyas* (1983), the Court of Appeal held that an
appellant had not done every act necessary for him to do to achieve
a result. He reported to the police that his car had been stolen and
telephoned his insurers to obtain a claim form but had never actually
filled out the claim. It was held that his acts were merely preparatory
and remote from the contemplated offence.

The House of Lords considered the theory in *DPP v Stonehouse*
(1977). The appellant had insured his life for a large sum with five
different insurance companies. He faked his death by drowning while
in Miami in order that his wife, who was not a party to the deception
and believed he was dead, could claim on the insurance policies.
The news was rapidly conveyed to England by the media as the
appellant was a well-known public figure, but his wife did not claim
on any policy. Five weeks later he was discovered in Australia. His
conviction for attempting by deception to enable another to obtain
property was upheld by the House of Lords. He had done all the
acts within his power to commit the offence and all that was left for
him to do was not to be discovered. Lord Diplock stated (at p.917)
that: "Acts that are merely preparatory to the commission of the
offence, such as, in the instant case, the taking out of the insurance
policies, are not sufficiently proximate to constitute an attempt. They
do not indicate a fixed irrevocable intention to go on to commit the

complete offence unless involuntarily prevented from doing so ... In other words the offender must have crossed the Rubicon and burnt his boats."

The last act theory was again addressed in *R. v Jones* (1990). The appellant was charged with attempted murder. He got into a car driven by his ex-girlfriend's new boyfriend and pointed a loaded sawn-off shotgun at him. The relevant English legislation on attempts sets out the test as "if with intent to commit an offence a person did an act which was more than merely preparatory to the commission of the offence, he was guilty of attempting to commit the offence." There was evidence that the safety catch of the gun was on at the time of the attack and there was no evidence that the appellant's finger had been on the trigger. It was argued that the full offence of murder could not have been committed unless the appellant had performed at least three more acts: releasing the safety catch; putting his finger on the trigger; pulling the trigger. The Court of Appeal held that, although his actions in obtaining the shotgun, shortening it and going to the victim's car were merely preparatory, his actions in getting into the car, taking out the loaded shotgun and pointing it at the victim with the intention of killing him provided sufficient evidence for the jury to consider whether those acts were more than merely preparatory.

R. v Campbell (1991) was a case of attempted robbery. Police had information that a post office would be robbed and put the premises under surveillance. The appellant was seen lurking in the vicinity. He rode a motorcycle along the road and walked around. He wore a crash helmet and gloves. Shortly before noon, he put on sunglasses and put his right hand in his pocket which appeared to contain something heavy. He stopped about 30 yards in front of the post office and took off his glasses. He looked around before turning away. Half an hour later, he walked back to the post office and was arrested. An imitation gun, sunglasses and a threatening note were found in his possession. He admitted that he had been considering robbing the post office but claimed to have decided not to carry out the robbery and had been arrested before he could return to his motorcycle to leave. The court emphasised that an accused must do an act which was more than an act of preparation to commit the offence. In the present case a number of acts remained undone, and the accused's acts were indicative of mere preparation. The court noted that it would be unwise to try to lay down hard and fast rules as to when, in varying circumstances, an attempt has begun. The matter has to be decided on a case-by-case basis.

(2) Proximity—"theory of probable desistance"

Another theory, popular in the United States, is that of probable desistance: Would the particular conduct have resulted, in the ordinary course of things, in the completed crime if there had been no outside interference? Or would the offender probably have desisted from his conduct? This also, however, produces strange results. The man who gets on a train to go to Cork to kill another is engaging in conduct which, in the ordinary course of events would result in the completed crime; but if the train breaks down, can it be said that he is guilty of attempted murder?

(3) Proximity—Irish approach

The Irish cases appear to take a pragmatic approach to proximity. In *People (AG) v England* (1947), the defendant was charged with attempting to procure the commission of an act of gross indecency with another man. He was friendly with a young man and one day talked to him about sex, and invited him to go to a nearby "secluded spot"; when the young man agreed, he offered him ten shillings. Could this amount to an attempt? It was held that it could not, since it did not "directly approximate to the commission of an offence". It was, instead, mere preparation for the commission of an offence, which is not in itself criminal.

The appellant in *People (AG) v Thornton* (1952) was convicted of unlawfully attempting to procure a poison, known as ergot, knowing that it was intended to be unlawfully used or employed to procure the miscarriage of a girl. Evidence was given of a conversation alleged to have taken place between the appellant and a doctor, in the course of which the appellant asked: "Wasn't there some drug named ergot?" This remark took place on the third occasion on which the appellant had visited the doctor. On the first occasion he asked whether anything be done about the girl's case and the doctor said he could not interfere in any way. At the second meeting he asked for a prescription for medication to interfere with the pregnancy and the doctor replied that no self-respecting Catholic doctor would have anything to do with that business. On appeal, it was held that the conviction must be quashed. On a charge based on an alleged attempt to commit a crime, the jury should be informed by the trial judge that a mere desire to commit the crime, or a desire followed by an intention to do so, is not sufficient to constitute an attempt. An attempt consists of an act done by the accused with a specific intent to commit a particular crime. It must go beyond mere preparation and must be a direct movement towards the commission, after the preparations have been made. Some act is required, and if it only remotely leads to the commission of the offence and is not immediately connected therewith it cannot be considered as an attempt to commit an offence.

People (AG) v Sullivan (1964) is another example. The defendant was a midwife who was paid a salary plus an additional allowance for each woman treated over a basic number of 25. She prepared and handed in claim forms in respect of fictitious patients. The evidence did not disclose whether these related to patients 1 to 25 or subsequent patients. The completed crime, if money had been handed over, would have been obtaining by false pretences. Since the fraud was detected before money was handed over, the issue became whether she was guilty of an attempt to obtain by false pretences. She submitted that her conduct, assuming the forms related only to patients 1 to 25, could not amount to an attempt, since, even had the forms been processed in the ordinary way, she would not have received any money until patient number 26 was reached, which might not happen. Instead, she submitted that her conduct was mere preparation for the crime which would be committed when she handed in a completed form for patient 26 and subsequent patients.

This argument was, however, rejected by the High Court and on appeal the Supreme Court. It was not necessary that there was a possibility of the successful completion of the offence, and what she had done went beyond mere preparation once she had handed in the false forms. Nor was it relevant that she might have changed her mind even after handing in the false forms and desisted from committing the completed offence. The Supreme Court, applying the test of proximity, found that each false claim put in was, as a matter of law, sufficiently proximate to constitute an attempt to obtain by false pretences.

13.1.3 Impossibility

What happens where a defendant attempts to do something which is not a crime or which is impossible? There are three main types of impossibility—legal impossibility, physical impossibility and impossibility due to inadequate method.

Legal impossibility is where a defendant attempts to do something, believing it to be illegal, when it is not. In this situation there is no attempt. The motive of the defendant cannot criminalise an activity that is innocent in the eyes of the law. In *Haughton v Smith* (1975), it was held by the House of Lords that a person could not be guilty of attempting to handle stolen goods where the goods were not in fact stolen (since they had passed into police custody on being intercepted by the police). Similarly, in *R. v Taaffe* (1984), the defendant imported cannabis into the UK believing it to be currency. Since importation of currency was not a crime, then despite his intention to carry out what he thought to be a criminal act he could not be guilty of an attempt.

The alternative Australian position may also be noted. In the case of *Britten v Alpogut* (1987) the facts were quite similar to *R. v Taaffe* (1984). Here, however, the defendant believed he was smuggling cannabis when in fact he was smuggling a substance the importation of which was not an offence. Could he be guilty of an attempt to import cannabis? Clearly, under *R. v Taaffe,* the defence of impossibility would have been open to him, but it was held that under Australian law he could not plead this defence:

> "If the evil intent of the actor can make a sufficiently proximate though objectively innocent act criminal, so as to amount to an attempt, it would seem irrelevant to have to go on to see whether the attempt could or would have succeeded. At common law, if the intent was to commit a recognised and not an imagined crime, and the act done was not merely preparatory but sufficiently proximate, than at that stage an attempt to commit the recognised crime has been committed, and it seems to me that it is not necessary to go further ..." (*Per* Murphy J.)

Physical impossibility is also a defence. Suppose a defendant stabs, intending to kill, a person who appears to be asleep but is in fact dead. Such a defendant could not be guilty of attempted murder.

However, the situation is more complicated where there is impossibility due to inadequate method. Impossibility is not a defence in circumstances where the objective would be a crime, if achieved, but the defendant fails to achieve that objective because the means chosen are inadequate. It is an attempt to obtain by false pretences notwithstanding that the false pretence never had a chance of success; it is an attempt to murder to place into a victim's tea poison which is in fact ineffective.

13.1.4 Abandonment

There does not appear to be any defence of abandonment, since abandonment has no logical relevance to attempts. Once the proximate act has been carried out, then abandoning the enterprise will not absolve the defendant from culpability. Similarly, if the activity is abandoned before any proximity is reached, then there is no inchoate offence. In Canada, abandonment may be used as evidence that the defendant did not intend to complete the crime attempted. In the United States, however, voluntary desistance not procured from an external source may amount to a defence to an attempt.

13.2 Incitement

We will see in chapter 14 that if A incites B to commit a crime, and B does so, then A is liable to be punished as if he himself committed the crime. This result follows from s.7(1) of the Criminal Law Act 1997, in the case of indictable offences, and from s.22 of the Petty Sessions (Ireland) Act 1851, in respect of summary offences.

Now suppose that A incites B to commit the same crime, but B for whatever reason fails to do so. In these circumstances, neither the 1851 Act nor the 1997 Act are applicable since both require as a prerequisite that a crime should have been committed. However, A's conduct will amount to the common law offence of incitement to commit a crime (sometimes known as solicitation), since this common law does not depend on whether B does in fact proceed to commit the crime.

This crime must be distinguished from attempt in this way: it is not necessary to show that the incitement is in any way proximate to the completed crime. The law takes the view that the incitement is sufficiently dangerous in itself to merit punishment, regardless of how close it comes to success.

This crime is punishable at discretion: that is to say, there is no upper limit on the penalty which the court can impose. This leads to the strange result that the punishment for incitement could, in theory, be greater than the maximum punishment for the completed offence.

13.2.1 What constitutes incitement?

Being a common law offence, there is no hard and fast definition of incitement in this context. One prominent textbook states that incitement is committed where a person "counsels, procures or commands" another to commit a crime (Williams, *Textbook of Criminal Law* (1978), p.384), a definition which is in its essentials co-extensive with "counselling or procuring" under the 1851 Act or the 1997 Act. Authorities under those Acts are, therefore, also relevant in this context, and *vice versa*. In *R. v Fitzmaurice* (1983), it was held that the necessary *actus reus* was satisfied by a "suggestion, proposal or request ... accompanied by an implied promise of reward". It should be noted, however, that incitement can occur by threatening as well as persuasive behaviour.

(1) Irish approach

The leading Irish authority on what constitutes incitement is *People (AG) v Capaldi* (1949). In that case, the defendant was a man charged with inciting a doctor to commit the crime of bringing about an abortion. Referring to a girl whom he had brought to the doctor, he asked whether the doctor would "do something for her" in relation to her pregnancy. The doctor replied "do you realise what you are asking me to do, you are asking me to perform an illegal operation" to which the defendant said "Yes. Would you perform; there is ample money to meet your fees". The doctor refused, and the defendant was ultimately charged with incitement.

It was argued for the defendant that this did not amount to incitement, but rather to the mere expression of a desire; and further, that an incitement must include some element of "overcoming the reluctant mind". The Court of Criminal Appeal accepted that incitement must include some element over and above the mere expression of a desire; however, on the evidence, it was clear that the defendant had made a positive request to bring about an abortion, which could not realistically be characterised as the mere expression of a desire. The court rejected the argument that incitement must involve an effort to overcome the reluctant mind: rather, a person may commit incitement by doing something if "but for it, it would not have occurred to the party incited to commit the crime, whether he had any particular reluctance to commit it or not" (*Per* Black J., at p.97).

It is not necessary that the incitement should be directed to any particular person; instead, it may be "thrown out" for any person to act upon. This can be seen from, for example, *Invicta Plastics Ltd. v Clare* (1976), where a company advertising "radar detectors" for motorists was convicted of inciting readers of the advertisement to use unlicensed wireless apparatus.

This decision is interesting in another way, since it shows that incitement may extend to a situation where A encourages B to do something which is itself legal (buying a radar detector) but knowing that it is practically certain that B will as a result do something illegal (using it). In this situation, A must be taken to have intended that B commit the illegal act.

The incitor's liability is limited to the act incited. If A incites B to rob a woman and B not only robs her but proceeds to kill her in the process, then A can only be found guilty of inciting the robbery, since B has gone further than the offence contemplated by A.

It must be noted that the act incited must itself be criminal before the crime of incitement is committed. Suppose that A incites B, a child who is *doli incapax*, to kill C. If B does so, then A is guilty as principal, as we have seen elsewhere. But if B does not, can A be charged with inciting B to murder C? The answer is no: since B would have committed no crime by killing C, then A cannot be said to have incited B to *commit a crime*. This rule is illustrated by *R. v Whitehouse* (1977), where it was held that a father could not be convicted of inciting his daughter under the age of 16 to commit incest with him. This was because she would commit no crime if she did so, as the legislation recognised that a daughter under 16 would be a victim rather than a perpetrator.

Similarly, if the incitor realises that the incitee has no *mens rea* then there is no incitement, since he is not inciting a criminal offence.

Impossibility may be a defence to incitement. It will depend upon the nature of the incitement. If the object is a very general one, for example to commit a burglary, then impossibility is not a defence. If, however, the object is to burgle a specific building and that building is no longer in existence at the time of the incitement, then impossibility may be a defence. In *R. v Fitzmaurice* (1983), the appellant's father wished to obtain a reward from a security firm by informing the police that there was a plan to rob a security van. He asked the appellant to find someone to carry out the robbery. The appellant approached B, who recruited two further men to help him.

It transpired that B and the two men had been the victims of the father's trick to obtain the reward. The appellant, who had believed that the robbery plan was genuine, was convicted of unlawfully inciting B and the other men to rob. An appeal against conviction, on the ground that the appellant could not be convicted of incitement to commit a crime that was impossible to commit, was dismissed. The Court of Appeal held that the correct approach was to decide in every case what was the course of conduct which was incited. Here, the case against the appellant was based on his recruitment of the three men at a time when he believed that there was to be a robbery. The offence which was incited was not in itself an impossible offence to carry out.

13.2.2 Prohibition of Incitement to Hatred Act 1989

This is a statutory form of incitement. It is an offence to publish, distribute or broadcast threatening abusive or insulting material that is likely or intended to incite hatred. Preparation and possession of material likely to stir up hatred is also prohibited, and the Gardaí are given powers of search and seizure in relation to such material. This Act is discussed further in chapter 10.

13.3 Conspiracy

At common law, it is an indictable offence for two or more persons to agree to do an unlawful act or even, in some circumstances, to perform an act which is in itself lawful. The offence of conspiracy is complete once the agreement has been concluded: it is not necessary that the conspirators should thereafter commit the agreed crime. As with incitement, it is unnecessary to show any proximity between the conspiracy and the completed crime: the conspiracy itself is punishable regardless of how close it came to fruition.

The offence, as with incitement, is punishable at discretion, and again we have the anomaly that conspiracy to commit a crime may carry a punishment more severe than that applicable to the completed crime.

13.3.1 What agreements amount to conspiracy?

The scope of the offence of conspiracy is exceedingly wide, and consequently "[a]ny agreement manifested by words or conduct to commit the wrong constitutes a conspiracy" (Williams, *Textbook of Criminal Law* (1978) p.351).

The agreement must be a concluded one: discussions as to whether a crime should be committed will not suffice. *R. v Mills* (1963) illustrates this point. In that case, the defendant was charged with conspiring with a woman to procure an abortion. She had telephoned him seeking an abortion, and he had told her to come to his flat bringing payment. On reaching the flat, they talked about the proposed abortion. She asked whether there would be a risk involved, and he asked whether her pregnancy was too far advanced for the operation to be performed. At this point, the police entered the flat.

It was argued for the defence that there was no concluded agreement, but this argument was rejected by the Court of Appeal, which held that there was a concluded agreement at the stage of the telephone conversation. Although the agreement was certainly subject to reservations or conditions, those reservations did not take away from its nature as a concluded agreement. As the court pointed out, every agreement is subject to conditions, express or implied, and to accept the defence argument would have the result that no one could ever be convicted of conspiracy.

It follows, therefore, that an agreement to commit a crime if a particular condition is satisfied is sufficient to amount to a conspiracy: if A agrees with B to kill C if C decides to give evidence in a trial, this conditional agreement will ground a charge of conspiracy.

Where a number of persons are alleged to be parties to a conspiracy, it is not necessary to show that each was aware of the existence of the others, so long as each is a party to the same conspiracy. Suppose that A recruits B, C, D and E to bomb a building, and that B, C, D and E have never met and are unaware of each other's identities. Notwithstanding this, each is party to the same conspiracy: that is, the conspiracy to bomb the building. This is sometimes described as a cartwheel conspiracy, with A at the hub and the rest at each spoke. Equally, one can have a chain conspiracy, where A recruits B, B recruits C, and so on.

Each person involved in the conspiracy must realise the criminal objective of the plan but it is not necessary that each knows the precise details. Cussen J., in *Orton* (1922), stated that each party should have a conscious understanding of a common design. It is not unusual, particularly in a cartwheel conspiracy, for the person at the "hub" to deliberately keep information from each of the "spokes" and this will not lead to the acquittal of any of the parties unless it is shown that the lack of information lead to the reasonable belief that the objective was not a crime. Similarly, each party must realise that they are part of a plan, even if they are unaware as to the precise method of execution of the plan or the number of people involved. The law is merely concerned to distinguish a conspiracy from a situation where a number of individuals coincidentally work towards the same goal. There must be a co-ordination of action towards a common purpose.

Oldridge (2000) illustrates that if a conspiracy is already formed when a person joins it he will still be guilty of conspiracy. The defendant allegedly participated in an elaborate scheme to defraud three banks. It was alleged that his role was during the "lulling phase" following the commencement of the scheme and consisted of providing assurances to the banks to induce them to forebear from suing. The Supreme Court held that his role in lulling the banks into a false sense of security was an essential feature of the alleged fraudulent scheme and that he played a vital part in continuing the conspiracy to defraud the banks.

Whether a conditional intention is sufficient intention for conspiracy was addressed by the Court of Appeal in *O'Hadhmaill* (1996). Evidence was adduced that the appellant intended to become involved in an IRA bombing campaign if the peace process failed. The Court of Appeal held that this was sufficient intention to result in a conviction for conspiracy to cause an explosion.

13.3.2 Purpose of the agreement

(1) Criminal acts

It is clear that the crime of conspiracy is committed where the purpose of the agreement is to commit a criminal act, or where the purpose of the agreement is itself lawful, but it is agreed to use criminal means to bring it about.

(2) Civil wrongs

It seems that agreements to commit *civil wrongs* (torts, breaches of contract, breaches of fiduciary duties, and so forth) may or may not amount to criminal conspiracies, depending on the precise nature of the wrong. The rationale for this rule was expressed as follows in *R. v Parnell* (1881) (at p.520):

"It is obvious that a wrongful violation of another man's

right committed by many assumes a far more formidable and offensive character than when committed by a single individual ... The law has therefore, and it seems to us wisely and justly, established that a combination of persons to commit a wrongful act with a view to injure another shall be an offence though the act if done by one would amount to no more than a civil wrong."

In this case, the accused, Charles Stuart Parnell, was charged with conspiracy to prevent tenants paying their rents. The judges set out three categories of conspiracy: where the end to be attained is in itself a crime; where the object is lawful, but the means to be resorted to are unlawful; and where the object is to do injury to a third party or to a class, though if the wrong were effected by a single individual it would be a civil wrong but not a crime.

(3) Tort

The leading case is *DPP v Kamara* (1974), where a number of students were charged with conspiracy to commit the tort of trespass by agreeing to occupy the London premises of the High Commissioner of Sierra Leone. Did this amount to a criminal conspiracy?

The House of Lords took the view that it did, and that an agreement to commit a tort could ground a conspiracy, but only where the execution of the tort was intended to involve either (a) some invasion of the public domain (as in this case, by the occupation of a foreign embassy) or (b) the infliction of more than merely nominal damage on the victim (as where premises were occupied to the exclusion of the owner). The same test was put somewhat differently in a concurring opinion of Lord Cross, who stated that whether an agreement to commit a tort amounted to conspiracy depended on whether the public had a sufficient interest: that is, whether the execution of the conspiracy would have sufficiently harmful consequences to justify penal sanctions.

(4) Breach of contract

Charleton (*Criminal Law Cases and Materials* (1992), p.119) states simply "There are no recent examples of the successful use of breach of contract as the unlawful element in criminal conspiracy."

(5) Acts which are neither criminal nor civil wrongs

It is clear that Irish law in some circumstances regards as criminal an agreement by two or more people to do certain things, notwithstanding that those things, performed by one person, would amount neither to a criminal offence or a civil wrong. This is a somewhat murky area of the law of conspiracy with very little case law to offer guidance. The only recent Irish authority on point is *AG (SPUC) v Open Door Counselling*, which applied the English case of *Shaw v DPP* (1962) to find that there existed at common law a crime of conspiracy to corrupt public morals and that the activities of the defendants, in providing non-directive counselling in relation to abortion, could amount to such a crime, notwithstanding that the counselling was not otherwise unlawful and that the agreement was therefore to assist in the commission of a lawful act. The High Court judgment, however, was appealed and this issue was not dealt with by the Supreme Court.

Whether Irish law might be extended further in this direction is unclear. In the Australian case of *R. v Cahill* (1978) it has been held that an agreement to bring about "sham" marriages for immigration purposes could not be said to be so offensive to public morality as to justify a charge of conspiracy to bring about an unlawful object. Street C.J. warned of the dangers in criminalising conduct based on the uncertain and ephemeral concept of public morality.

13.3.3 Conspiracy and impossibility

Suppose A and B agree to do something which it emerges is in fact impossible to do. Are A and B guilty of conspiracy? The answer to this question will depend upon the nature of the agreement. If it is an agreement to do a particular act, which is in fact impossible, then no crime is committed. The House of Lords dealt with impossibility and conspiracy in *DPP v Nock* (1978). The accused were charged with conspiracy to manufacture cocaine using ingredients which they believed were the raw materials for cocaine. However, the ingredients were actually incapable of producing cocaine and their conviction was quashed. However, if it is an agreement to carry out a more general purpose, then it remains an offence notwithstanding that a particular means of carrying out the purpose is impossible.

13.3.4 Abandonment

It is unclear whether abandonment of a conspiracy is a defence or merely a mitigating factor. Conspiracy is a completed offence once two or more persons agree to work together towards a common objective. It would therefore seem to be illogical that a subsequent withdrawal from the arrangement is a defence.

Martin Wasik, ("Abandoning Criminal Intent" (1980) Crim. L.R. 785) argues that abandonment of inchoate crimes should only be relevant in mitigation of sentence. Glanville Williams has argued, in favour of excusing such a defendant, that his previous intention is capable of being interpreted as only half-formed or provisional and therefore insufficient to amount to *mens rea*. It could also be argued that abandonment of a conspiracy is evidence that the defendant should be regarded as no longer dangerous. A third argument, based on public policy, is that the law should provide an inducement to people to abandon crimes and therefore prevent the commission of harm.

14. DEGREES OF COMPLICITY IN CRIME

14.1 Complicity in crime

Suppose that A sets out to kill his wife. B, knowing of A's intention, provides him with a gun. A carries out the killing. A is clearly guilty of murder; but what responsibility does B bear for the crime? At first glance, the answer is none. B's actions may be criminal; but they do not amount to the *actus reus* of the crime of murder, nor does B have the necessary *mens rea*. But this result is intuitively unappealing: it is plainly wrong that a person should escape criminal liability where they deliberately assisted in the commission of a crime.

Indeed, a person other than the actual offender may bear a greater degree of responsibility in some circumstances, as where A is the mastermind, and persuades B, a stupid youth, to inflict the wound. As Glanville Williams puts it: "Lady Macbeth was worse than Macbeth." (*Textbook of Criminal Law* (1978), p.287)

For this reason, the law recognises that a person who does not himself carry out the *actus reus* of a particular crime may nevertheless be convicted of that crime in some circumstances. This is the concept of secondary liability. Such a person can be charged, tried and punished as if he himself committed the crime. We will use the term "accessory" to describe such a person (although this terminology is no longer used in the legislation) and the term "principal" will be used to describe the primary perpetrator (this term does remain in the legislation).

14.1.1 Innocent Agency

However, before we consider the position of accessories, we need to distinguish the situation where a crime is carried out through an "innocent agent". Suppose, for example, that A gives a gun to a six-year-old child, B, telling B to shoot C. B does so, and C dies as a result. In this situation, we cannot say that A is liable *as an accessory* to B's crime, as B has committed no offence (B lacks criminal capacity because of his age).

Instead, the law has evolved a concept of *innocent agency* to deal with this type of situation. Where A deliberately acts through an intermediary B, who carries out the *actus reus* of a crime but lacks criminal responsibility, A will be guilty as a principal rather than an accessory. Consequently, the charge to be brought against A will not be that A incited the commission of an offence by B, but rather that A committed the offence of murder himself, albeit via a third party.

A good example is *R. v Michael* (1840). In that case the defendant wished to kill her child. She procured poison and gave it to her nurse, telling the nurse that it was medicine for the child. The nurse decided not to use the "medicine", leaving it on a shelf. Another child, however, came across the "medicine" and administered it to the baby, killing him. The defendant was found guilty, the court accepting that both the nurse and the child could be described as innocent agents.

Similarly, in *R. v Cogan* (1975) it was held that if A procured B to have sexual intercourse with his wife, in circumstances where the wife appeared to consent but did not, then A would be liable for the crime of rape as a principal offender, notwithstanding that B would lack the *mens rea* for rape (since B would not be aware of the lack of consent). (On a side note, it was also held that A could not rely on the then-recognised marital rape exemption: any presumed consent on the part of the wife was consent to intercourse with her husband only.)

Another example is *R. v Stringer and Banks* (1992). In this case, the defendant was a manager who directed employees to pay invoices which (unknown to them) were fraudulent. Charged with theft, he argued that he himself had not appropriated property, but that this was done by the acts of the employees in arranging payment. The court held, however, that since the employees were unaware of the fraud they acted as innocent agents, with the result that the manager was guilty as a principal.

14.1.2 Background

Prior to 1997, the area of complicity in crime was governed in part by common law, and in part by the Accessories and Abettors Act 1861. Four categories of participants in crime were recognised by the law:

1. Principal in the first degree—the person who actually carried out the crime.
2. Principal in the second degree—a person who was present at the time of commission of a felony or misdemeanour and aided or abetted its commission.
3. Accessory before the fact—a person who gave

        assistance before a felony or misdemeanour was committed.
4.   Accessory after the fact—a person who, knowing that a felony had been committed, assisted the criminal in evading apprehension, trial or punishment.

You will see from this classification that liability as an accessory depended on whether the crime alleged was a felony or a misdemeanour—in particular, it was not possible to be an accessory after the fact to a misdemeanour.

The Criminal Law Act 1997 does away with many of the technicalities which were inherent in the old law, and the law relating to secondary liability is now contained in ss.7 and 8 of that Act.

14.1.3 *Assistance and Encouragement of Offences*

Section 7(1) deals with *assistance and encouragement of offences*. It states:

> "Any person who *aids, abets, counsels or procures* the commission of an indictable offence shall be liable to be indicted, tried and punished as a principal offender." (Emphasis added.)

The first point which we must make is that s.7 *requires that an offence must in fact be committed*: if I assist in the preparation for an offence or incite its commission, but no offence ultimately takes place, then this section does not apply. Suppose, for example, that A encourages B to rob a bank. B purchases a gun and a getaway car. B later changes his mind and gives up on the bank job. A is not liable for robbery under s.7 since no robbery in fact took place.

The distinction between offences of participation and inchoate (or incomplete) offences should be noted at this point. With inchoate offences such as incitement, attempt and conspiracy (which are discussed further in the chapter on Inchoate Offences), a defendant can be convicted even though the full offence is not completed. The inchoate offence does not depend upon the commission of the primary offence as it constitutes an offence in itself. In contrast, offences of secondary liability depend on the primary crime being committed. In the above example, B is not guilty of an offence under s.7(1) but would be guilty of the inchoate offence of incitement.

We should also note that while s.7(1) is limited to *indictable offences*, precisely the same principles apply to *summary offences* by virtue of s.22 of the Petty Sessions (Ireland) Act 1851. Consequently, the following discussion applies equally to indictable and summary offences.

14.2 *"Aids, abets, counsels or procures"*

These terms are carried over from the 1861 Act and relate to distinct types of participation in crime. Unfortunately, these are not words in common use and it can be difficult to determine their exact meanings. Indeed, judges have differed as to how these words should be interpreted. In some cases it has been suggested that each of these four words has a different meaning. This point was made by Lord Widgery C.J. in *Attorney General's Reference (No. 1 of 1975)* (1975) (at p.686), where he held that:

> "the probability is that there is a difference between each of those four words and the other three, because, if there were no such difference, then Parliament would be wasting time in using four words when two or three would do."

On the other hand, cases such as *Attorney General v Able* (1984) have suggested that these words should be regarded as merely synonyms for helping, and in that case Woolf J. suggested (at p.809) that rather than analyse each word separately: "it is preferable to consider the phrase 'aids, abets, counsels or procures' as a whole." Nevertheless, historically most commentators, and the bulk of the case law, have looked at each word separately, and we will follow this approach here.

(1) Aiding

A person aids an offence where they knowingly help or assist in its commission—for example by supplying the poison, the gun or the getaway car. Even the mere provision of information can suffice—as in *Attorney General v Able* (1984), where the assistance consisted of the supply of a pamphlet describing how to commit suicide. There is no requirement that the person be present at the scene of the crime: as in *People (DPP) v O'Reilly* (1991), where it was held that the defendant could be found guilty of aiding a post office burglary, despite the fact that he merely provided a getaway vehicle and was at no stage physically on or near the post office premises.

In fact, a person can be guilty of aiding an offence even though they might never meet the offender, a fact also illustrated by *Attorney General v Able* (1984), where the pamphlet was distributed widely.

It is not necessary that the assistance was essential for the crime—it is not a defence, for example, for A to say that B would have found a gun elsewhere even if A had not supplied it. However, it must be shown that the defendant did in fact assist the commission of the crime. Suppose, for example, A supplies B with a gun, knowing that B intends to commit a burglary. B, however, ultimately decides not to bring the gun and carries a knife instead. In that situation, A would not be guilty of assisting the burglary.

(2) Abetting

This term has proved difficult to define. One leading academic (Herring, *Criminal Law: Text, Cases and Materials* (2004), p.821) has stated simply: "To be honest no one knows what abetting means". The best definition appears to be that to abet is "to incite, instigate or encourage the commission of a crime". (Charleton, McDermott and Bolger, *Criminal Law* (1999), p.198, citing Smith and Hogan, *Criminal Law* (8th ed., 1996), p.129). However, as we will see shortly, this definition will overlap substantially with the definitions of counselling and procuring.

(3) Counselling

By counselling, we mean to encourage, incite or instigate a criminal offence. So if A persuades or encourages B to commit a crime, A can himself be punished in respect of that crime. Again, however, we must remember that the crime must be completed. If A suggests that B rob a bank and B declines, A is not guilty as an accessory, but may be guilty of the inchoate offence of incitement.

It is not necessary to show that the encouragement *caused* the crime to be committed. Suppose that A suggests that B kill C, and B replies that he was going to do so anyway. In that case, (assuming that B follows through) A would be guilty of counselling the murder even though there was no causal link between his intervention and the killing. Similarly, if A discovers B raping C and shouts encouragement to B, this would amount to counselling the rape, notwithstanding that it was already underway when A arrived.

Any act of encouragement, however slight, may suffice. In *R. v Giannetto* (1997), the defendant was charged with the murder of his wife. The prosecution alleged that either he killed her himself, or he encouraged someone else to do so. In relation to encouragement, the jury sought guidance from the judge, asking:

> "How much of an involvement in the murder does the defendant need to have in order to convict for murder, i.e. planning, paying for, knew of & didn't prevent."

In response, the trial judge gave the following direction (which was upheld on appeal):

> "Supposing somebody came up to [him] and said, 'I am going to kill your wife', if he played any part, either in encouragement, as little as patting him on the back, nodding, saying, 'Oh goody', that would be sufficient to involve him in the murder, to make him guilty, because he is encouraging the murder."

(4) Procuring

The leading case on procuring is *Attorney General's Reference (No. 1 of 1975)* (1975), where to procure was defined as "to produce by endeavour" so that the defendant in some way caused the principal to commit the offence. In that case, A "spiked" B's drink by adding alcohol, unbeknownst to B, knowing that B was about to drive home. B did so, was stopped and was found to be over the limit. A was charged on the basis that he had procured B's offence. A argued, however, that he could not be convicted as a secondary party to B's offence where there was no encouragement or "meeting of minds" between them. The court replied, however, that A could be guilty of procuring, holding *per* Lord Widgery that (at 779–780):

> "To procure means to produce by endeavour. You procure a thing by setting out to see that it happens and taking the appropriate steps to produce that happening. We think that there are plenty of instances in which a person may be said to procure the commission of a crime by another even though there is no sort of conspiracy between the two, even though there is no attempt at agreement or discussion as to the form which the offence should take …

Giving the words their ordinary meaning in English, and

asking oneself whether in those circumstances the offence has been procured, we are in no doubt that the answer is that it has. It has been procured because, unknown to the driver and without his collaboration, he has been put in a position in which in fact he has committed an offence which he never would have committed otherwise."

14.2.1 What degree of participation is required for aiding, abetting, counselling or procuring?

R. v Giannetto (1997) made the point that even a trivial act of encouragement could be sufficient to trigger secondary liability. However, a failure to act will not generally be sufficient. In particular, a person does not assist in or incite the commission of an offence merely by being present at the scene and failing to intervene. There is no general duty in Irish law to intervene to prevent the commission of an offence. An exception, where failure to act does give rise to secondary liability, is where the defendant is under a specific legal duty to act. Such situations are dealt with in the earlier chapter on the *actus reus*.

One of the earliest cases on this point is *R. v Coney* (1882). In that case the defendants had gathered to watch an illegal prize fight. They were charged with aiding and abetting a battery. However, it was held that proof of their mere presence was not enough: they could not be guilty of aiding and abetting unless the prosecution could prove that they took some active part in the proceedings, such as shouting encouragement.

Coney has since been applied in *R. v Clarkson* (1971). In that case a young woman was brutally raped by a number of soldiers in a British army base in Germany. Two other soldiers heard her screams and came into the room to watch. They remained there and watched while she was raped again, although they did not actively assist. They were charged with aiding and abetting the rape. However, since they had not taken any active part, the prosecution case was that their mere presence encouraged those who were committing the rape. The court accepted that the rapists may have been encouraged by their presence. However, the court went on to hold that it was not enough that their presence did in fact encourage the rape—the prosecution must also show that they also *intended* to encourage the rape.

A similar conclusion was reached in *Dunlop and Sylvester v R.* (1980), where the charges against two defendants included a charge that they stood by and watched a rape being committed, therefore aiding and abetting the commission of the crime. This was held to be an incorrect statement of the law by the Canadian Supreme Court, which applied *Clarkson* to hold that mere presence at the scene of a crime is not enough to ground culpability: there must be something in the way of encouragement of the offender, or something which facilitates the commission of the offence. Mere presence and passive acquiescence is not enough—there must be actual assistance or encouragement coupled with an intention to assist or encourage.

In Ireland, *People (AG) v Ryan* (1966) makes the same point. Here, the defendant was one of a group of five who attacked another group after a dance. There had been a verbal exchange between the groups earlier, after which the attackers proceeded to arm themselves with car tools. They then confronted the other group, and the ringleader (Coffey) struck and killed one victim and seriously injured another. Coffey was convicted of murder. Ryan, although he did not directly take part in the attack, was charged as an accessory and was convicted of manslaughter. He appealed, alleging that the trial judge had misdirected the jury in relation to the level of involvement necessary to trigger liability. In particular, he claimed that the trial judge gave the impression to the jury that mere "standing around" in Coffey's presence while Coffey attacked was enough to incriminate Ryan in the killing.

The Court of Criminal Appeal, however, rejected the appeal. Although mere presence or "standing around" on its own was not enough to implicate Ryan, the trial judge had made it clear that Ryan could be convicted if by his presence he was "knowingly giving [Coffey] encouragement at the time he used the weapons". The Court of Criminal Appeal approved of this direction, explaining that:

> "If Coffey was enabled to accost these people by reason of the presence of a superior number in his gang, of whom [Ryan] was one, then mere presence, if it was knowingly to lend him support in his enterprise, could implicate the applicant and others in the crime."

More recently, in *People (DPP) v Rose* (2002), the Court of Criminal Appeal had to consider the extent of participation required in a situation where the defendant took no physical part in an attack, but was present throughout and was alleged to have encouraged the other attackers. In this case, there was an argument between the victim and two men (Roche and Sage) about money. A fight broke out when the men tried to take the money, leaving the victim unconscious. The defendant, Rose, was present for the fight. It was then suggested that the victim would be driven to hospital, and he was put into the car together with the two men and the defendant. In the car, however, Roche started to punch and kick the victim and to demand his bank card and his PIN code. At this point, the defendant told Roche to "search his pockets". Instead of being driven to hospital, the car was driven to a small dirt road, and the victim was taken out and beaten by Roche with a crowbar. While the beating was taking place, the defendant said "mind the blood lads". Roche continued to beat the victim, killing him.

The defendant was convicted of murder and assault with intent to rob based on her statements during the attack. On appeal, the Court of Criminal Appeal accepted that she could not be convicted for "mere callousness" or if she was merely a spectator, even if she did not express any words or take any steps to prevent what was happening. Consequently, the words she used during the attack were of vital importance, as they were the only basis for imposing liability. In respect of the charge of assault with intent to rob, the court held that she was properly convicted. Although she argued that the words "search his pockets" were not intended to encourage robbery (on the basis that she was merely doing her best to stop the violence and that searching the pockets would have that effect), this was a matter for the jury and they had rejected this interpretation.

However, in respect of the murder charge, the court held that the conviction could not stand. There was no evidence of any participation or assistance by her prior to the car stopping. The only basis on which she could become a participant were her words during the beating when she said "mind the blood lads". However, the court found that these words were ambiguous and could have been intended as a "plea to go easy", intended to prevent more serious injuries (rather than, as the prosecution alleged, a warning that blood stains would lead to easy detection). As such, it hadn't been established that she intended by her comments to encourage the attack, and her conviction on the murder charge was overturned.

14.2.2 What mens rea is required for aiding, abetting, counselling or procuring?

In order for secondary liability to be established, we must show both *intention* and *knowledge*. We must show that the accessory intended to assist or encourage the principal, and we must also show that the accessory knew the nature of the offence being carried out by the principal.

(1) Intention

In relation to intention, we have already seen from *R. v Clarkson* (1971) that it is not sufficient that the accessory did in fact encourage or assist the principal—we must go further and show that there was an intention to encourage or assist. However, we must not confuse *intention to assist* with an *intention or desire to see the crime completed.* For example, suppose that A sells B a gun, knowing that A plans to use it to kill his wife. A, however, is indifferent to whether B succeeds. In this case, we can say that A intends to assist B, notwithstanding that A might not intend or desire the death of the wife. (See the decision in *National Coal Board v Gamble* (1959), where Devlin J. said that such a person could be liable even though he was "interested only in the cash profit to be made out of the sale".)

(2) Knowledge

The extent of knowledge required is a difficult matter. Must the accessory be aware of the precise crime which the principal will carry out? If not, what degree of knowledge will suffice?

Consider the facts of *R. v Bainbridge* (1960). In that case, the defendant supplied another with oxygen-cutting equipment, which was ultimately used to break into a bank. The defendant, charged as an accessory, admitted knowing that the equipment would be used for some illegal purpose, but claimed to have no idea that it would be used to break into a bank, much less that particular bank. The English Court of Criminal Appeal held that it would not be enough to show that he knew that some illegal venture was planned. Instead, it would have to be shown that he knew the *type* of crime which was planned. So the defendant could be convicted if he knew that the principal intended to break and enter, and steal. However, the court went on to hold that knowledge of the details of the crime was not necessary—for example, the defendant could be convicted even though he did not know which particular bank was targeted.

The decision in *DPP for Northern Ireland v Maxwell* (1978) took a similarly wide view. The defendant was a member of the UVF who drove four other members to a bar owned by a Catholic. One of the passengers then threw a pipe bomb into the bar. The defendant admitting knowing that some form of "job" was planned against the bar, but argued that since he did not know its exact nature he could not be guilty of aiding and abetting the crime actually committed. This argument was, unsurprisingly, rejected. The House of Lords held that the accused knew he was facilitating a military attack of some kind, whether it was a robbery, shooting or bomb attack. He knew that the principal was about to carry out one or more of a number of possible crimes, and he intentionally lent his assistance in order that one of those crimes should be committed. He was, therefore, liable for the crime which was in fact committed by the principal, so long as that crime was in his contemplation as being a *possible* result.

Another Irish case is *DPP v Madden* (1977), where four men were convicted of the murder of a particular victim, although the prosecution had not been able to establish who fired the fatal shot. The case made against them was therefore that each aided and abetted the killing, in various ways. The Court of Criminal Appeal stated the law as follows:

> "[M]otives and desires are irrelevant, and ... mere evidence of common association is insufficient. The kernel of the matter is the establishing of *an activity on the part of the accused* from which his intentions may be inferred and the effect of which is to assist the principal in the commission of the crime proved to have been committed by the principal, or the commission of a crime *of a similar nature* known to the accused to be the intention of the principal when assisting him." (O'Higgins C.J., at p.341, emphasis added).

Consequently, one appellant was held to have been properly convicted where, knowing that a car was required for the commission of a serious crime of violence against one of a number of people, he took

active steps to provide that car. Even though he might not have
known that an individual would be killed, he knew that a crime *of a
similar nature* was contemplated.

People (DPP) v Egan (1989) goes even further. In this case,
the accused was charged with robbery and receiving stolen goods.
He had received a telephone call stating that he should make his
workshop available to store a van, that he should be available at a
particular time and that "a small stroke" was to take place. The
"small stroke" proved to be the robbery of a manufacturing jewellers,
and at the appointed hour a van full of armed and masked men
showed up with sackloads of jewellery, which he stored for them.

The accused was convicted of robbery, on the basis that he had
aided and abetted the commission of the robbery. He argued,
however, that he would never have helped if he knew that an armed
robbery was planned, and as such he didn't have sufficient
knowledge of the crime for secondary liability.

His conviction was upheld by the Court of Criminal Appeal,
which approved of *Maxwell* and *Madden*. The court accepted (as
we have already seen) that a person could aid and abet the
commission of a crime without being present at the crime scene. It
was not a bar to his conviction that he did not know the *exact nature*
of the crime to be committed so long as he knew the *general nature*
of the intended crime. On these grounds, the accused was guilty of
robbery, since he knew that a crime was about to be committed and
that it involved the theft of goods, notwithstanding that the theft could
be carried out in a variety of ways. *Egan* has, however, been criticised
on the basis that robbery is not a crime of the same general type as
theft—the element of violence makes it a much more serious crime,
and it can be argued that the defendant should not have been convicted
unless it was shown that he was aware that violence might be used.

14.2.3 *Victims as Accomplices?*

Where a statute is designed to protect a certain class of person, then
such a person will not be guilty of aiding and abetting the commission
of that crime notwithstanding that they do in fact encourage or
facilitate the commission of that crime. Otherwise, the victims of a
crime could be charged with its commission. If, for example, a young
girl consents to sexual intercourse with her father, then she has
undoubtedly facilitated the commission of incest by him; but she is
not therefore liable as an accessory, for the reason that the law in

question was designed for her protection: *R. v Whitehouse* (1977). Similarly, in *R. v Tyrell* (1894) it was held that the defendant, a girl under the age of 16, could not be convicted of abetting unlawful sexual intercourse with herself, as the Act creating the offence was passed for the protection of girls in her position.

14.2.4 Procedure

Section 7 provides where a person aids, abets, counsels or procures the commission of a crime they shall be "shall be liable to be indicted, tried and punished as a principal offender". This means that they can be tried as if they themselves committed the crime. For example, A provides a gun to B knowing that B intends to use it to kill C, and B does so. A can be charged with, convicted of and punished for murder as if he were the principal notwithstanding that A did not pull the trigger. It follows that the maximum punishment for an accessory to a crime will be the same as that for the principal.

We have already seen that a person can only be punished as an accessory once the primary offence has been committed. Consequently, it will be necessary to prove that the offence took place. It is not necessary, however, to show that a person has already been convicted as the principal offender. If, for example, A is accused of aiding B to commit a robbery, it is not necessary to show that B has been convicted in respect of the robbery. A can be prosecuted notwithstanding that B has yet to be tried, or even if B has been acquitted.

An interesting problem arises from the procedure whereby the accessory is tried as if they were the principal offender. In some cases, it is possible that the accessory might not be qualified to commit the crime as a principal. For example, before rape became a gender-neutral offence it could only be committed by a man. Would this mean that a woman who assisted in a rape could not be convicted of rape? The courts have held that a person may be guilty as an accomplice even though they could not be guilty as a principal offender: see *R. v Ram* (1893), where it was held that a woman could be guilty of aiding and abetting a rape committed by someone else.

14.3 The doctrine of common design/joint enterprise

Closely related to secondary liability is the doctrine of common design, also known as the doctrine of joint enterprise. This doctrine is concisely summarised in *R. v Anderson and Morris* (1966):

> "Where two persons embark on a joint enterprise each is liable for the acts done in pursuance of that joint enterprise and that includes liability for unusual consequences if they arise from the execution of the joint enterprise but ... if one of the adventurers goes beyond what has been tacitly agreed as part of the common enterprise his co-adventurer is not liable for the consequences of the unauthorised act."

Suppose, for example, that A and B agree to rob a bank together. A sits outside in the getaway car while B goes into the bank. They plan to carry guns and to shoot if necessary. In the course of the robbery, B shoots a security guard. Under the doctrine of joint enterprise, A will be liable for B's actions if they arose as part of the agreed plan of action.

On the other hand, if B "goes beyond what has been tacitly agreed" then A will not be liable for his actions. Suppose that A and B set out to burgle an apparently empty house. When confronted by the householder, B produces a knife (of which A was unaware) and stabs the householder, killing him. A will not be liable for B's actions: if A did not agree to the use of force and was not aware of the possibility that it might be used, B's actions are outside the scope of any common design or joint enterprise.

This doctrine, although very similar to secondary liability, seems to be somewhat different in its nature. The difference has been explained by the English Court of Appeal in *R. v Stewart and Schofield* (1995) as follows:

> "The allegation that a defendant took part in the execution of a crime as a joint enterprise is not the same as an allegation that he aided, abetted, counselled or procured the commission of that crime. A person who is a mere aider or abettor etc. is truly a secondary party to the commission of whatever crime it is that the principal has committed although he may be charged as a principal. If the principal has committed the crime of murder, the liability of the secondary party can only be a liability for aiding and abetting

murder. In contrast, where the allegation is joint enterprise, the allegation is that one defendant participated in the criminal act of another. This is a different principle. It renders each of the parties to a joint enterprise criminally liable for the acts done in the course of carrying out that joint enterprise."

Applying this distinction we see that in a case of secondary participation, A assists B to commit a crime. A is not a principal, but may be treated as though he were. On the other hand, in a case of joint enterprise, A and B set out to commit a crime together. In this case both A and B are principals and each is liable for the acts carried out by the other in the course of the crime.

Separating the two concepts can, however, present problems. Hanly points out that:

> "[I]f X, Y and Z jointly agree to rob a bank, the doctrine of common design arises, but if X hires Y and Z to help him rob a bank, secondary liability should arise. However, in both cases, an observer would simply conclude that three men robbed a bank, and making a distinction between the two cases would be difficult." (*An Introduction to Irish Criminal Law* (Gill and Macmillan, 1999), p.91).

In addition, the Irish courts have tended to use the two concepts interchangeably. For example, in *People (AG) v Ryan* (1966), the Court of Criminal Appeal referred to providing "aid or encouragement" and being part of a "common design" without drawing any distinction between the two. Similarly, in *People (DPP) v Rose* (2002), the Court of Criminal Appeal appears to equate the two concepts, stating that:

> "The case against the applicant was that she was part of a joint enterprise or venture with two men and that her participation in the crimes was sufficient to render her equally guilty as a principal offender in accordance with section 7 of the Criminal Law Act, 1997."

As a result, it is still "not certain whether the doctrine should be perceived as forming part of the law of participation or whether it encompasses a separate form of liability." (McAuley and McCutcheon, *Criminal Liability: A Grammar* (2000), p.481)

14.3.1 When will a crime be part of a joint enterprise or common design?

We have already noted that *R. v Anderson and Morris* (1966) refers to an "agreement" between the parties as to the scope of the crime, so that a person will be liable for acts committed by other parties if they are within that scope. However, the term "agreement" might be misleading, as there is no need for an explicit agreement between the parties. As *R. v Anderson and Morris* (1966) notes, it is enough if there is a "tacit agreement", and this is something which can be inferred from the nature of the crime.

In that case, the two accused, A and M, went together in search of another man (W) who was said to have tried to strangle A's wife. On finding him, A produced a knife and stabbed W to death. M looked on but appeared to play no part in the fight. On being questioned, M admitted that he had set out with A to beat W, but said that he did not know that A had a knife and did not intend that W would be stabbed. There was no reliable evidence against M to show that he knew of the knife.

At trial, the jury were directed that they could find M guilty of manslaughter if there was a common intention to attack the victim, and if M took some part in the fight, even if the use of the knife was entirely outside the contemplation of M and there was no intention on M's part to kill or cause serious bodily harm.

This direction was held to be improper by the English Court of Criminal Appeal, which held that this form of imputed intention was unacceptable. Instead, the court held that M would not be liable for A's actions since they fell outside the common design or tacit agreement between the parties. (On the other hand, had M known that A had a knife, but proceeded regardless, then it could have been inferred that there was a common design or tacit agreement to use the knife.)

The decision in *R. v Anderson and Morris* focuses on an agreement between the parties as to the scope of the crime, so that A is liable for a crime carried out by B if he has agreed to that crime being committed (even though he might not have intended or desired that it be committed). In addition, however, it seems that a person may be liable for a crime committed by another if they foresaw the possibility of that crime being committed in the course of their joint activity, even they might not have agreed to that crime being committed.

This can be seen from *Chan Wing-Siu v R.* (1985), in which three gang members went to a flat armed with knives intending to rob a victim. In the course of the robbery, the victim received stab wounds from which he died. Each of the three was charged with the murder of the deceased. The defence case was that the use of the knives had not been intended: that they had been brought along simply to frighten the victim, and that their use (in response to apparent self-defence by the deceased) was not foreseen.

The direction to the jury, which was upheld on appeal, was that each defendant would be guilty of murder if that defendant had *foreseen* the infliction of serious bodily harm (or death) *as a possibility* arising out of the joint enterprise, notwithstanding that that defendant did not *intend* that result. Therefore, it need not be shown that the use of the weapon (or whatever conduct is alleged) was foreseen as being *more likely than not*: it is enough for the prosecution to show that the use of the weapon was foreseen by the accused as *being a real possibility, or a genuine risk.*

One consequence of this approach is that foresight on the part of the accessory is sufficient *mens rea, i.e.* the accessory need not intend the ultimate result provided he is aware the ultimate result is a possibility. This can be seen from *R. v Powell* (1997). In that case, the House of Lords explicitly held that *foresight* rather than *intention* is the basis for liability of parties to a killing carried out in the course of a joint enterprise, notwithstanding the anomaly which this creates, given that foresight is not sufficient *mens rea* in the case of the actual perpetrator.

In that case, the argument put forward on behalf of the applicant was that any common intention was limited to intimidating the others, and that the companion had gone beyond the ambit of the common design. This argument was, however, rejected by the Court of Criminal Appeal, which held that it was a matter for the jury to determine whether there had been a common intention to injure; and there had been ample evidence before the jury to justify such a finding. In particular, the applicant knew that his companion was armed with a lethal weapon, and could *foresee* that the weapon might be used as it ultimately was.

Turning to the Irish case law, we see that it is often difficult to determine whether a particular act falls within a common design. For example, in *People (DPP) v Murray* (1977) the defendants, who were husband and wife, took part in an armed bank robbery.

They were pursued by an off-duty Garda, and, to prevent the capture of the husband, the wife shot and killed the Garda. Both were convicted of capital murder. On appeal, however, the Supreme Court held that while there was clearly a common design to kill or cause serious injury if necessary, there was no evidence that they had agreed on the use of violence *against the police* and thus there was no common design in respect of *capital* murder.

On the other hand, two subsequent cases found that there was a common design in respect of capital murder on very similar facts. In *People (DPP) v Pringle* (1981) and *People (DPP) v Eccles* (1986), the defendants took part in armed robberies which went wrong, and in both cases members of the Garda Síochána were shot dead. In each of those cases, the Court of Criminal Appeal found that there was a common design in respect of capital murder, since in each case there was evidence of a common intention to overcome any resistance by the Gardaí, using firearms if necessary. While these cases appear very similar to *People (DPP) v Murray* (1977), McAuley and McCutcheon note that an important distinction may have been the evidence of prior discussion and planning:

> "[I]n *Murray,* the lack of evidence relating to the agreement led to the majority of [the] Supreme Court being unwilling to conclude that the agreement extended as far as capital murder. By way of contrast, in *Eccles,* there was considerable evidence of the discussions and planning which preceded the raid and that facilitated the conclusion that there was agreement to commit capital murder if necessary." (at p.485)

The most recent Irish decision on common design is *People (DPP) v Doohan* (2002). In this case, the defendant had taken offence at the manner in which his father had been treated by the victim, one Mr Madden. He set out to find somebody to avenge the perceived insult, and ultimately hired a man (Heron) for £1,500 to give Madden "a bit of a battering". The defendant claimed that his intention was that this was to be "only a whacking with the legs done in but no shooting", and told Heron that he was to "stay away from the head". Heron, however, ultimately killed Madden by using a shotgun to fire two shots to the leg.

Charged with murder, the defendant argued that any joint enterprise was limited to a punishment beating, and that Heron had gone further than agreed by using a shotgun. The court rejected this argument, holding that *R. v Anderson and Morris* was a correct statement of the law, and that the use of a gun did not depart from the common design:

> "There was ample evidence that the common design was to cause serious injury to Mr. Madden. The method of causing serious injury was left to the discretion of Mr. Heron. The court is satisfied that there was ample evidence upon which to determine that the participants in the common design intended to cause serious injury to Mr. Madden, and this is sufficient mens rea for murder ... In all the circumstances, while on the evidence the discharge of the gun was not expressly agreed, it was open to a jury properly directed to find that its use was not beyond what had been tacitly agreed. Consequently the actions of Mr. Heron were not such as to go beyond what had been agreed, and so the applicant is liable for the consequences."

14.4 Withdrawal from complicity

It is possible for an accessory to withdraw from complicity in a crime: they may call off the arrangement before the crime is completed. Where they do so, they will no longer be liable for actions committed after they have terminated their involvement. However, whether particular conduct amounts to a withdrawal is a question of fact in each case. In *R. v Whitehouse* (1940), it was held that there should be some communication of the withdrawal to the other participants, while in *R. v Jensen and Ward* (1980), it was held that an effective withdrawal requires either such communication, or some positive step, such as calling the police.

This issue was considered in detail in *R. v Becerra* (1976) where the appellant broke into a house with two others, to steal from it. They were surprised by an occupant; the appellant shouted "let's go" and climbed out of a window, while one of his partners took a knife and stabbed and killed the occupant. The appellant had known that the knife was being carried; his defence was not that what happened was outside his contemplation, but rather that he had withdrawn from the joint enterprise before the killing took place. This contention was rejected by the Court of Appeal, which held that withdrawal requires "something more than a mere change of intention and physical change of place": instead, there must be some timely communication with the other parties, to the effect that if they proceed, they do so without the aid and assistance of the person who is withdrawing.

14.5 Assistance after a crime has been committed

Prior to 1997 there were several different offences which could be committed by a person who assisted only after a crime took place. In the case of felonies, a person might have been guilty as an accessory after the fact or might have been guilty of misprision of a felony (*i.e.* concealing a felony which they knew to have been committed). There were also separate offences of compounding a felony and compounding a misdemeanour (*i.e.* agreeing to conceal an offence in return for a reward). The 1997 Act abolishes these offences and replaces them with two general offences.

The first is contained in s.7(2), which creates an offence of impeding the arrest or prosecution of a person who has committed an arrestable offence:

> "Where a person has committed an arrestable offence, any other person who, knowing or believing him to be guilty of the offence or of some other arrestable offence, does without reasonable excuse any act with intent to impede his or her apprehension or prosecution shall be guilty of an offence."

This would cover, for example, knowingly harbouring an offender or the destruction of evidence. Punishment is governed by s.7(4) and will vary from up to three years' imprisonment to a maximum of 10 years' imprisonment depending on the gravity of the offence being concealed. For example, if the primary offence carries a maximum penalty of life imprisonment, then a person guilty under s.7(2) will face a maximum penalty of 10 years' imprisonment.

Section 8(1) then creates a separate offence of *concealing offences for a reward*:

> "Where a person has committed an arrestable offence, any other person who, knowing or believing that the offence or some other arrestable offence has been committed and that he or she has information which might be of material assistance in securing the prosecution or conviction of an

offender for it, accepts or agrees to accept for not disclosing that information any consideration other than the making good of loss or injury caused by the offence, or the making of reasonable compensation for that loss or injury, shall be guilty of an offence and shall be liable on conviction on indictment to imprisonment for a term not exceeding three years."

This is intended to deal with the situation where witnesses are "bought off" and corresponds to the old offences of compounding a felony or misdemeanour. The crime is committed where a person knows or believes that an arrestable offence has been committed, knows or believes that they have information which would assist in the detection or prosecution of that crime and agrees not to disclose that information in return for some consideration. There is an exception where the consideration is limited to restitution for the actual injury suffered. Suppose, for example, that A burgles B's house. B discovers that A was responsible and agrees not to notify the police provided that he is paid compensation for the goods stolen. B will not have committed an offence under s.8 provided that the amount agreed is limited to reasonable compensation.

Note the different scope of each category of offences. Section 7(1) (aiding, abetting, etc.) applies to *indictable* offences, while s.7(2) (impeding arrest or prosecution) and s.8(1) (concealing offences for a reward) apply only to the more serious *arrestable* offences. Section 7(1) applies to assistance in an offence, either or before or after the fact, while s.7(2) and s.8(1) are offences which can only be committed after the primary offence.

14.6 Is there a duty to report crimes?

Prior to 1997 there was a duty to report felonies. Where a person knew that a felony had been committed by another and had a reasonable opportunity to report that crime but failed to do so, the offence of *misprision of a felony* was committed unless there was some good reason (such as a confidential lawyer/client relationship) for that failure. It was not necessary that there should be active concealment (such as destruction of evidence); a mere failure to bring the crime to the attention of the authorities was enough. *Per* Lord Denning in *Sykes v DPP* (1962) (at p.563):

"[T]he essential ingredients of misprision of felony are:

1. Knowledge. The accused man must know that a felony
   has been committed by someone else ... He need not
   know the difference between felony and
   misdemeanour - many a lawyer has to look in the books
   for the purpose - but he must at least know that a
   serious offence has been committed ...
2. Concealment. The accused man must have 'concealed
   or kept secret' his knowledge. He need not have done
   anything active: but it is his duty by law to disclose to
   proper authority all material facts known to him relative
   to the offence ... If he fails or refuses to perform this
   duty when there is a reasonable opportunity available
   to him to do so, then he is guilty of misprision."

After the 1997 Act, however, the offence of misprision of a felony
was abolished and with it the general duty to report offences. The
1997 Act did not create a corresponding duty: the s.7(2) offence of
impeding arrest or prosecution applies only to positive acts of
concealment and will not cover mere silence, while the s.8 offence
of concealment applies only where a person conceals an offence in
return for some reward.

However, after the 1998 Omagh bombing, the Offences Against
the State (Amendment) Act 1998 reintroduced a general duty to
report in slightly different form. Section 9(1) of that Act provides:

"A person shall be guilty of an offence if he or she has
information which he or she knows or believes might be of
material assistance in

(a) preventing the commission by any other person of a
    serious offence, or
(b) securing the apprehension, prosecution or conviction
    of any other person for a serious offence,
and fails without reasonable excuse to disclose that
    information as soon as it is practicable to a member
    of the Garda Síochána."

Consequently, there is now a general duty under s.9 to disclose
information in respect of serious offences to the police: it is a crime,
carrying a maximum penalty of five years' imprisonment, to fail to

disclose information which a person knows or believes might assist in preventing or prosecuting a serious offence.

Somewhat confusingly, the definition of "serious offence" under s.9 differs from the definition of "serious offence" which we have already encountered in relation to the Bail Act 1997. While a "serious offence" under the Bail Act is one which is punishable by five or more years' imprisonment, a "serious offence" for the purposes of s.9 is one which is punishable by five or more years' imprisonment and also involves one of the following aggravating elements:

> "loss of human life, serious personal injury (other than injury that constitutes an offence of a sexual nature), false imprisonment or serious loss of or damage to property or a serious risk of any such loss, injury, imprisonment or damage."

This narrower definition reflects the 1998 Act's focus on terrorist violence, rather than serious crime generally.

In effect, the 1998 Act creates an offence which is very similar to the old offence of misprision of a felony, with the differences that there is now a duty to report in respect of "serious offences" rather than felonies, and there is now a duty to disclose information *before* an offence is committed. (It was not clear whether misprision of a felony ever extended to knowledge of a contemplated offence: see the comments of Lord Denning in *Sykes v DPP* (1962) at p.564–565.)

Quite apart from this general duty to disclose, it must be remembered that there are also some specific duties to report offences in particular situations. For example, under s.57 of the Criminal Justice Act 1994 financial institutions such as banks are required to report suspect money laundering to the police: failure to do so is itself an offence.

Further Reading:

Lanham, "Accomplices and Withdrawal" (1981) 97 Law Quarterly Review; Ni Raifeartaigh, "The Mental Element of Accessories to Murder" [1994] 4 I.C.L.J. 31; Smith, "Criminal Liability of Accessories: Law and Law Reform" (1997) 113 L.Q.R. 453.

15. CRIMINAL LIABILITY OF CORPORATIONS

15.1 Introduction

Corporations are legal persons and may, therefore, be found guilty of crimes. However, there are obvious difficulties in applying the ordinary principles of criminal law to corporations. The most significant of these difficulties comes from the fact that the principle of *mens rea* breaks down when it is applied to a body which can have no intention of its own. Other difficulties include the fact that the legal capacity of corporations does not mirror that of natural persons: for example, a corporation cannot marry, and therefore cannot be guilty of bigamy. From a practical point of view, corporations cannot be imprisoned, creating problems where the only penalty for an offence is imprisonment (as with the offence of murder). How are these difficulties to be resolved?

15.2 Development of the principle of corporate liability

The common law originally did not recognise criminal liability of corporations. This appears to have stemmed from practical difficulties: corporations could not appear in person (and there was no right to representation under the common law). In addition, felonies were punishable by death: a sanction which had no meaning in the case of a corporation. These practical points lost their force when the right to representation was granted and when fines were introduced as a penalty, thus leaving the way clear for the development of corporate criminal responsibility.

The spotlight is increasingly being put on the criminal behaviour of corporations. The Zeebrugge ferry disaster and more recent English rail crashes have increased public awareness of the harm corporations can do and how ill-equipped the traditional concepts of the criminal law can be to deal with it. It is widely perceived that health and safety legislation is a poor tool to use against corporations, especially when lives are lost. No Irish corporation has yet been charged with manslaughter in circumstances of negligent management resulting in death. A conviction of manslaughter would carry a far greater stigma than penalties under health and safety legislation.

15.3 What acts can be attributed to the corporation?

Is the corporation to be held liable for every criminal act of an employee? If not, how can it be determined which acts should be ascribed to it? No legislation deals with this question, and as a result the courts have, on a case by case basis, developed certain principles to determine when the corporation should be criminally liable.

15.3.1 Controlling mind theory/identification doctrine

The early cases in this area originated in the UK in the 1940s and took the view that a corporation could be identified with its principals, *i.e.* that the acts of the main individuals within the company could be treated as the acts of the company itself. *DPP v Kent* (1944) and *R. v ICR Haulage Ltd* (1944) both held that the acts of managers within a company could be treated as being the acts of the company itself.

These cases were said to adopt the controlling mind theory: to determine whether the company would be liable, one had to ask whether the act was committed by a person who could be said to be substantially in control of the company's operations. Thus, the act of a mere employee with little discretion would not suffice: one would have to show that the act was carried out by a person such as a senior manager with the ability to direct the operations of the company.

This test has since been elaborated upon. A leading English case is *Tesco Supermarkets v Nattrass* (1972), where the House of Lords considered whether a supermarket chain could incur criminal liability based on the acts of a regional supermarket manager. The House of Lords concluded that the branch manager was not sufficiently senior to equate to the directing mind and will of the company, and the prosecution failed.

Lord Diplock explained (at p.199) that:

"What natural persons are to be treated in law as being the company for the purpose of acts done in the course of its business, including the taking of precautions and the exercise of due diligence to avoid the commission of a criminal offence, is to be found by identifying those natural persons who by the memorandum and articles of association or as a result of action taken by the directors or by the company in general meeting pursuant to the articles, are entrusted with the exercise of the powers of the company."

This test is a restrictive one: it requires that any wrongdoing exist at a senior level within the company, effectively excluding liability for criminal offences committed at a lower level. Having said that, it must be remembered that if senior officers are aware of and connive in activities at a lower level this will suffice.

The restrictive nature of the test can be seen from the Canadian case of *R. v Safety-Kleen Canada Inc.* (1997). Here the defendant company ran a fleet of waste-oil collection trucks. One of its drivers was found, contrary to Canadian environmental legislation, to have knowingly given false information in a return made to a provincial officer. The driver was the only representative of the company in a wide area and carried out a variety of roles: he was, in effect, the only point of contact for customers in the area, and was responsible for administration in the area. However, the employee did not have any managerial or supervisory function and had no power to make policy. The court found no evidence that the truck driver had authority to make corporate decisions which went beyond those arising out of the transfer and transportation of waste. On this basis, the Ontario Court of Appeal felt that the criminal acts of the employee could not be imputed to the company, notwithstanding the wide discretion which he enjoyed in carrying out his duties.

The inadequacy of the identification approach in certain situations was highlighted in *DPP v P&O Ferries (Dover) Ltd.* (1991). This prosecution arose from the sinking of the ferry, Herald of Free Enterprise, just outside the port of Zeebrugge. The tragedy was caused by the assistant bosun's failure to ensure that the bow doors had been closed, and the company was charged with corporate manslaughter. The Central Criminal Court held there was no conceptual difficulty in charging a corporation with manslaughter. Turner J. noted, at p.84, that "where a corporation, through the controlling mind of one of its agents, does an act which fulfills the prerequisites of the crime of manslaughter, it is properly indictable for the crime of manslaughter". However, the prosecution ultimately failed as it was not possible to identify the assistant bosun with the company and he was the only person possessing the sufficient *mens rea* of recklessness.

Attorney-General's Reference (No. 2 of 1999) (2000) concerned another prosecution for corporate manslaughter. Here the defendant was a train operator, and the allegation was that gross negligence had caused a train crash as a result of which seven passengers were killed. The crash was caused by a combination of factors: the train driver had not seen warning signals along the track; two automatic warning systems were not operative; the company did not insist on two drivers manning each train. The trial judge ruled that where a defendant was a corporation it could only be convicted where a human being, with whom the corporation could be identified, had the requisite *mens rea*. The Court of Appeal agreed that a corporation's liability for manslaughter was based on the identification theory. Unless the actions of a grossly negligent individual could be attributed to the company, it could not be convicted of manslaughter. Rose L.J. emphasised, at p.815, that no authority since *Tesco* had supported the demise of the identification doctrine.

> "In each, the decision was dependent on the purposive construction that the particular statute imposed, subject to a defence of reasonable practicability, liability on a company for conducting its undertaking in a manner exposing employees or the public to health and safety risk. In each case it was held that there was an identified employee whose conduct was held to be that of the company. In each case it was held that the concept of directing mind and will had no application when construing the statute. But it was not suggested or implied that the concept of identification is dead or moribund in relation to common law offences."

15.3.2 Organisational theory

The controlling mind theory, convenient though it may be for particular cases, has obvious limitations. One of these is evident when we consider sins of omission rather than commission. Where a company fails to do something then it may not be possible to point the finger of blame at any one individual. The fault may lie with the systems in place within the company, so that the company, rather than any one individual, is at fault. Another fault is that the controlling mind theory allows companies to escape liability for wrongs committed by more junior employees. The theory works best in the context of a small company and is far less suited to larger corporations with more complex management structures. Yet another disadvantage of the controlling mind theory is that it encourages proceedings to focus, not on the commission of the crime itself, but on the defendant's internal management hierarchy. These faults have led in some more recent case law to a theory of organisational liability, under which the courts will look to the structures and decision-making processes within the defendant corporation.

An example of this can be seen in *R. v British Steel plc* (1995), where the defendant corporation was charged with health and safety offences, such offences being offences of strict liability (subject to a defence of reasonable care having been taken). A worker was killed because of the collapse of a steel platform during an operation that should have been recognised as inherently dangerous. The argument the defence put forward was that the senior management had taken all reasonable care in the circumstances, and that any fault lay with independent contractors. This defence was not, however, accepted by the Court of Appeal. It took the view that where strict liability had been imposed, it would be seriously undermined if the company were to escape liability on the basis that the "directing mind" was not at fault. In reaching this decision, the court was greatly influenced by the fact that practical difficulties had arisen at the trial of corporate offences, with the bulk of trial time being taken on whether or not particular employees were part of senior management.

Similarly, in *Director General of Fair Trading v Pioneer Concrete (UK) (Ltd)* (1995), the House of Lords held that a company could be liable where employees acted in breach of court injunctions, notwithstanding that they did so contrary to express instructions and without the knowledge of senior management, on the basis that any other position would effectively give companies immunity from action.

It would appear from these two cases, in particular, that English law is moving towards a wider test of corporate responsibility. However, it should be noted, as Rose L.J. in *Attorney-General's Reference (No. 2 of 1999)* remarked, that both cases dealt with very specific statutory contexts; it remains to be seen whether a similar approach would be taken in respect of other offences.

15.4 Restrictions on corporate liability

15.4.1 Corporation the victim

A number of restrictions limit corporate liability. The first is straightforward and readily understandable: a corporation will not be criminally liable for the acts of an employee where those acts are directed towards defrauding the corporation, *i.e.* where the corporation is itself the victim. This point was made in *Canadian Dredge & Dock Co. v R.* (1985), where the Supreme Court of Canada accepted that where a manager set out to "intentionally defraud" a corporation, then it became "unrealistic in the extreme" to identify the manager with the corporation. However, that case also illustrates the difficulties in establishing the defence. The defendant companies had colluded to bid at rigged prices in respect of public procurement contracts. The employees in question had benefited from this arrangement, receiving kickbacks for doing so. The defendant companies therefore claimed that they had been defrauded by the collusion, and so could not be held responsible for it. This argument was rejected by the court, which noted that the companies had received benefits from the collusion: the employees were acting partly for their own benefit, but also partly for the benefit of the companies. The companies were not, therefore, true victims of the conduct in question.

15.4.2 Corporation incapable of committing particular crime

It remains the case that a corporation cannot commit certain crimes by reason of its nature: bigamy and perjury being the obvious examples. Equally, a company cannot be convicted of a crime for which the only punishment is imprisonment, such as murder. It is, however, unclear whether a company could be charged with, for example, counselling or procuring the commission of perjury, for which it could be tried as a principal.

15.4.3 Employees acting contrary to instructions

As we have seen, *Director General of Fair Trading v Pioneer Concrete (UK) (Ltd)* (1995) held that the existence of instructions against a particular course of conduct did not amount to a defence. A similar view has been taken in Canada, in *Canadian Dredge & Dock Co. v R.* (1985), where the court expressly held that instructions preventing the conduct in question were irrelevant to the question of guilt. Note, however, that such instructions, or a detailed policy in relation to the conduct, may be an important factor mitigating the penalty to be imposed.

15.5 Punishment of companies

The only sanction which can generally be imposed on a company guilty of a crime is a fine. (Statute does provide for other forms of enforcement in particular cases, see for example the Safety, Health and Welfare at Work Act 1989 which provides for enforcement notices in relation to unsafe workplaces.) These fines will often be derisory in relation to the profits of the company, particularly where the crime is one prosecuted in the District Court. In such cases, the real punishment of the company may come from other sources: unwelcome publicity, increased insurance premia, or exclusion from further opportunities (for example, the tender procedure for government building contracts will ask bidders whether they have been convicted of any health and safety offences).

Consequently, one can ask whether companies should be fined at a higher level than individuals (as is the case in Australia), or whether alternative sanctions should be imposed. One possibility has been adopted in the US, which provides for a form of corporate probation, allowing the court to monitor the ongoing conduct of a company. Indeed, one might go further and argue for a corporate death penalty, in other words the winding-up of companies found guilty of serious criminal offences. Alternatively, it has been suggested that regulation of companies should take place in a civil context and that civil law remedies will ease the burden of proof associated with corporate prosecutions. It should be remembered in this context that civil liability is much easier to establish than criminal liability, since in the civil law a company is generally vicariously liable for the acts of its employee acting in the course of his employment, regardless of the seniority or otherwise of the employee.

15.6 Irish approach

In *Superwood Holdings Plc v Sun Alliance Assurance Plc* (1995), the Supreme Court accepted the identification theory in the context of civil liability of corporations. However, there has been no express judicial consideration of corporate criminal liability in Irish law. The Law Reform Commission made a series of recommendations in 2003 in their *Consultation Paper on Corporate Killing*.

15.6.1 Law Reform Commission Proposals

The Commission was of the view that corporations should be subject to criminal liability for corporate killing. It was recommended that a statutory corporate killing offence, equivalent to gross negligence manslaughter, be established. It explained its rationale at p.166:

> "The establishment of a specific corporate killing offence would resolve the difficulties created by the residual uncertainty regarding whether corporations can be prosecuted for the common law offence of manslaughter ... A conviction of a corporation on indictment for an offence of corporate killing would be qualitatively different to a conviction under health and safety legislation ... It would mark the disapproval of the community and should have a greater deterrent effect than the offences under health and safety legislation. Moreover, its scope need not be limited to the workplace. It is envisaged that a prosecution for such an offence would take place when none of the other available sanctions were adequate to address the gravity of the matter."

The recommendations expand the definition of the scope of the identification doctrine in a number of ways: the offence would apply to all "undertakings", not just incorporated entities; the offence would apply to "high managerial agents" and not just top management; the recommendation embodies the concept of "reckless tolerance". For reckless tolerance to be proved, a high managerial agent of the undertaking must have been aware, or ought reasonably to have been aware, of a high degree of risk of serious personal injury to any person arising from the acts or omissions of another person and nonetheless have unreasonably disregarded that risk. The Commission recommended that an undertaking should not be found guilty of corporate killing where there is evidence showing that its highest level of management had done all that was reasonably practicable to prevent the commission of the offence.

Further reading:

Clarkson, "Kicking Corporate Bodies and Damning Their Souls" (1996) 59 M.L.R. 557; Conway, "The Criminal Character of a Company" (1999) 7 I.S.L.R. 23; McDermott, "Defences to Corporate Criminal Liability", Bar Review Vol. 5 Issue 4 Jan/Feb 2000, p.170; Wells, "Corporations: Culture, Risk and Criminal Liability" (1993) Crim.L.R. 551; Law Reform Commission Consultation Paper, *Corporate Killing* (L.R.C. 2003); Ahern, D., "Corporate Killing: The Way Forward?" (2003) 13 (3) I.C.L.J. 10; Brady, "Corporate Homicide: Some Alternative Legal Approaches" (2002) 12 (2) I.C.L.J. 12.

Index

theft—*contd.*
  depriving, 160
  dishonestly, 158–159
  statutory offence, 158
threat to damage property, 157
threat to kill or cause serious harm, 134
threatening, abusive or insulting behaviour, 187
traffic, endangering, 146
transferred malice, doctrine of, 69–70

trespass
  entering building with intent to commit crime, 190–191
  fear, causing, 191

violent disorder, 183–184

withholding information, offence of, 19–20